Walking through the Valley

Walking through the Valley

*Womanist Explorations
in the Spirit of Katie Geneva Cannon*

Emilie M. Townes,
Stacey M. Floyd-Thomas,
Alison P. Gise Johnson,
and Angela D. Sims,
Editors

WESTMINSTER
JOHN KNOX PRESS
LOUISVILLE · KENTUCKY

© 2022 Westminster John Knox Press

First edition
Published by Westminster John Knox Press
Louisville, Kentucky

22 23 24 25 26 27 28 29 30 31—10 9 8 7 6 5 4 3 2 1

Scripture quotations from the New Revised Standard Version of the Bible are copyright © 1989 by the Division of Christian Education of the National Council of the Churches of Christ in the U.S.A. and are used by permission.

Book design by Drew Stevens
Cover design by Lisa Buckley Design

Library of Congress Cataloging-in-Publication Data
Names: Townes, Emilie Maureen, 1955- editor.
Title: Walking through the valley : womanist explorations in the spirit of
  Katie Geneva Cannon / Emilie M. Townes, Stacey M. Floyd-Thomas, Alison
  P. Gise Johnson, and Angela D. Sims, editors.
Description: First edition. | Louisville, Kentucky : Westminster John Knox
  Press, [2022] | Includes index. | Summary: "In this volume, leading
  womanist ethicists and theologians come together to continue Katie
  Geneva Cannon's work in four critical areas: justice, leadership,
  embodied ethics, and sacred texts"-- Provided by publisher.
Identifiers: LCCN 2022036152 | ISBN 9780664267216 (paperback) | ISBN
  9781646982868 (ebook)
Subjects: LCSH: Womanist theology. | Cannon, Katie G.
Classification: LCC BT83.9 .W35 2022 | DDC 230.082--dc23/eng/20220906
LC record available at https://lccn.loc.gov/2022036152

For Katie Geneva Cannon,
Wise Guide, Pedagogue Extraordinaire,
Truth Teller, Friend, Woman of God

Contents

Part Three: Womanist Ways of Leading

Part Four: Embodied Ethics

Foreword

Katie Cannon of Kannapolis

NIKKY FINNEY

Kannapolis, North Carolina, a deeply segregated mill town, will forever have the privilege of being where Katie Geneva Cannon, smart and pluckish daughter of Esau and Corine Lytle Cannon, was born in 1950. Cannon's last name will also forever be imperfectly reflected in one of the most successful manufacturing histories of the twentieth century, Cannon Mills. Cannon is the surname of her people, those formerly enslaved at the Cannon Mills Plantation. Katie Cannon was the great-grandchild of those who had worked for several generations to build the business into a textile dynasty. The white Cannons and their perpetual wealth and upper-caste status never crossed over to Katie's side of the Kannapolis railroad tracks. As a great cracked mirror of human demarcation, it perhaps was Katie Cannon's first up-close blood portrait of the haves and the have-nots, a quizzical and intimate silhouette of American society. This early truth was Katie Cannon's permission, as a deeply reflective religious scholar, to ask and seek answers to monumental ethical questions for the next four decades.

Everything about Katie Cannon's youth revolved around the church. The Black Presbyterian Church where her blood elders were also the religious elders of the church. The Black church—where devout religious southern Black folk, only a stone's throw out of slavery, spent much of their time. There was nowhere else for a Black Christian family to matriculate. The Black church was the only world they owned. It was the only physical space where Black people held sway and say-so about who they were and who they dreamed to be. Katie Cannon of Kannapolis, daughter of a Black farmer and the first Black woman to ever run the machines at the Cannon Mills textile factory instead of cleaning the toilets, marched in perfect step with her family and tight-knit community: "We had to know the Bible as if it might not be there one day." She kept a deliberate and closed focus until other books and ideas made their way to her hungry mind and heart. Enter the Vietnam War, the Civil Rights and Black Power Movements, Brown versus Board of Education, the assassination of Martin Luther King

Jr., Black-gloved fists rising into the Olympic air, and more. There was nowhere else to turn but to her true self for seeking the answers to the deeper questions that began to visit. With her Bible still close, she walked smack-dab into the great social and political crosswinds and conversations of her day.

After reading and devouring Lerone Bennet's history-altering *Before the Mayflower*, Katie Cannon found the walls of her old world too small. "How could we Black people have such a rich culture, come from such a rich civilized people on the continent of Africa, and be told all our lives that we are a liability to civilization?" Black religious study was about to be Cannonized. The young woman from Kannapolis, with all her questions in tow, made up her mind not to follow the well-heeled road of deliberate lies and instead return to an old, trusted, albeit dusty truth now with a twist: Black people are the children of God, and Black women are their moral compass. Her founding of Black Womanist Theology built a new mountain on the old landscape of Christian ethics.

In an oral interview with the Presbyterian Historical Society in 1987, Katie Cannon of Kannapolis walks us through her brilliant unpaved life. She is asked why she took such an unusual path as a religious scholar. Cannon laughs, describing the attempts of others to make her someone she was not. "I'm just Black. Even the Black bourgeois tried to get me to pass as though white. 'She's not going to do it. She just can't pass.'" Katie Cannon goes on to explain her situation as if she is listening to one of her elders tell the story of one of her ancestors who kept running away from the plantation, no matter the level of punishment: "It's like having a dead man's genes. I'm mechanically Black."

I met the wondrous and mechanically Black leader, Katie Cannon of Kannapolis, in 2005. I was building a life as a poet, and my books were just starting to generate verve and energy. I didn't know she knew my work and therefore was surprised to hear from her. As president of the Society for the Study of Black Religion, she invited me to speak to a small group of Black biblical scholars. I thought she had invited the wrong poet. She assured me that she had not. Before I arrived, I worried that my stories and poems might not be religious enough. I combed through my stanzas to double check, looking for more linear Jesus moments. I didn't know Katie Cannon's connection to Zora Neale Hurston then or to Black culture or to Blackness. We were only just beginning our journey. I was a Black woman searching for my own flight path into the American literary tradition and was not finding a comfortable fit. Katie Cannon had found her own air current and was in full-throttle flight. That weekend I learned a precious thing. Katie Cannon never just invited anyone anywhere. When Katie Cannon called, you were being sent for, and a caravan of deep listeners, mighty thinkers, and joyful toe-tapping folks were always there, waiting.

There was nothing linear or one-dimensional about Katie Cannon. She was a human vessel of swirling circles and living color. She didn't entertain straight lines or absolutes, loved her African fabric, loved to laugh and tease. If she caught you off guard, she would hold her face in a serious gaze until she could no longer resist the laughter moving like a wave up from her belly and into her eyes. There are reliable ghosts from the Black Girl Etiquette class at Barber Scotia College in 1969 with stories of how Katie Cannon of Kannapolis sat with her arms folded in row 5. One day it finally hit her that etiquette was being taught to Black girls so that white people would not be afraid of the many colors and swirling circles that Black girls possessed, so that Black girls could move more easily into the white worlds that awaited them just beyond Scotia's door. Katie Cannon of Kannapolis was not having it.

All along the way of her life, there were those who saw Katie Geneva Cannon's job as a Christian social ethicist to simply be a believer like the rest of the church. They wanted her to just get on board and leave behind her edgy particulars, her Blackness, her woman-ness, her Southern-ness, all the natural and radical geographies of her life. They hoped she would learn to *transcend* her Black womanist leanings and tap down her chestnut skin to reach *higher ground*. But Katie Cannon of Kannapolis knew what the higher ground was, and she also knew why the Old Testament keepers wanted to avoid it at all costs. With this clear understanding of four hundred years of American culture and thousands of years of Christianity, she decided to spend the rest of her life teaching women and men to climb there with her, in order to tap *back* into themselves.

The last time I saw Katie Cannon of Kannapolis—the last time she sent for me—it was an invitation to attend the inaugural gathering of the Center for Womanist Leadership, in Richmond, Virginia, April 4–7, 2018. I arrived, and there she was, sitting at a circular table surrounded by her great and loving community—her church. "The poet is here," she said; "to do what she do," she added. She stood up and made a place for me because that's what Katie Cannon always did. Other womanist scholars and preaching women were already onstage and having church, one after the other testifying and blowing up the mic with their words, truth, sermons, and stories. When it was my time to go up on stage, she reached for the mic and my hand and looked up at me, whispering, "I am going to introduce you from the floor. I am not going up there onstage with you." I didn't understand. I needed her to go up there with me. I was in her house. "I will not go up there," she said. "When you stand up there and 'do what you do,' you make the whole room pregnant." She started to giggle softly up under her breath at having used the word *pregnant* in such a literary context. She giggled hard as if her old professor in Etiquette class, back at Barber Scotia in 1969, might possibly appear out of the ether and critique her Katie Cannon description of what happened when my words traveled through the microphone and landed out in the wide sea of the room. But the word was perfect and had been perfectly placed. Katie Cannon of Kannapolis had once again demonstrated what can happen when a woman of deep faith and clear understanding, freed from the confines of "what's proper," looks another free woman of faith in the eye, in the presence of hundreds of other free women of faith, robed in African cloth and swinging earrings, and decides that sweet Black freedom talk, spoken one heart to the other, is the most faithful language of all.

Acknowledgments

FROM STACEY M. FLOYD-THOMAS

I would like to acknowledge the labor of love that has allowed this project to flourish. The Black church worship tradition of call and response is akin to the womanist practice of mutuality and reciprocity. The writing of this text has been womanist worship, lending our life and labor to "where all the yeses line up," as Dr. Katie Cannon would often say. I thank Renita Weems and Melanie Jones for always saying "yes" to being the willing worker-warriors and wind beneath the wings of womanism, which is the soul that my work must have. I thank my kin, most especially Juan Floyd-Thomas (my soulmate), Lillian Floyd-Thomas (our star), and Janet Floyd (my sister beloved) as well as the legacy of love provided by the Floyd and Underwood family, both those living and those at rest, who have always been willing and able to provide the bandwidth and encouragement this work requires and to celebrate my every success. And to my village people who inhabit the fabulous spaces and give soul to the thriving of Black folk in a tradition that esteems the Cannon legacy and takes the forms of the Black Religious Scholars Group; Friendship West Baptist Church; Sabbath Sistahs Book Club of Nashville, Tennessee; The Womanist Salon Podcast Team; The Temple University cohort of Cannon mentees; Womanist Approaches to Religion and Society AAR Group; The Center for Womanist Leadership Design Team; The Katie Geneva Cannon Center for Womanist Leadership Staff; and the coeditors and contributing authors in this volume.

FROM ALISON P. GISE JOHNSON

I acknowledge my sister Debra Jennings, whose insights and critique as advocate, practitioner of social justice reform, and budding womanist scholar were invaluable. I also thank my daughter Anisa Johnson, who made herself available any time of day or night to listen to my work and editorially support this endeavor. I thank my Claflin University Department of Humanities colleagues for making my transition to this new space life-giving. Your extravagant welcome and impromptu collegial exchange made it easy to prioritize my writing, for the first time in my academic life. To my cowriters, Vanessa and Faith, I am extremely grateful for how our work together continues excavation of the nonnegotiable need for an applied womanism that destroys socially constructed differences between Black women; embodies collaboration as the image and likeness of God; and demands sacred strategic action to create holistically sustainable communities that honor Spirit, earth, and ancestors. And finally, to Dr. Emilie Townes, thank you for your unwavering commitment to seeing this work through. Thank you for your patience as I wrestled with the real soul work of writing; the painful limitations of writing with two fractured elbows; and the beautiful challenge, pressure, and hope of creating a usable resource that would make Dr. Katie G. proud.

FROM ANGELA D. SIMS

With appreciation for Black women who

— make a way out of no way,
— refuse to foreclose on their souls, and
— forge a path for others

FROM EMILIE M. TOWNES

To the generations of Black scholars who came before me and are following me—you are the reason I do what I do. To my spouse and rock, Laurel—you bring joy and serious talk all in one breath. To the faculty, staff, and students of Vanderbilt Divinity School—I cannot think of a better place to be to face the challenges of these days and celebrate the delights that are always peeking around the corner and keep us going and thriving.

Lesson Plan

God is my shepherd;
 I shall not want.
God makes me lie down in green pastures,
 and leads me beside still waters;
 God restores my soul.
God leads me in paths of righteousness
 for God's name's sake.
Even though I walk through the valley of the shadow of death,
 I fear no evil;
for you are with me;
 your rod and your staff,
 they comfort me.
You prepare a table before me
 in the presence of my enemies;
you anoint my head with oil;
 my cup overflows.
Surely goodness and mercy shall follow me
 all the days of my life;
and I shall dwell in the house of GOD forever.
    —Psalm 23, Inclusive Language Lectionary, Year B

Walking through the Valley echoes Psalm 23, which assures us that God will be with us through all things that we place in conversation with an extension of the work of the womanist Christian social ethicist Katie Geneva Cannon, who was the founding figure in exploring how the concept of womanism can be used in moral thought. Cannon argued that dominant (normative) ethics was designed, however unintentionally, to mark those of darker hues as morally deficient if not bankrupt because of the ethicists' understanding of what constitutes virtue, value, identity, and theological standpoint. Cannon's writings and lectures and classes ushered in other persistent voices that disputed this methodological and moral valley. This volume draws on the foundation that Cannon crafted for others to build from.

With some of the themes from Cannon's body of work as starting points, the coeditors of this text begin to explore the potential next steps for where her moral thought can lead contemporary womanist moral reflection and theological ethics broadly considered. The themes of justice, leadership, embodied ethics, and sacred texts come to the fore. In true participatory knowledge production, each editor has invited two womanist scholars to join them in a conversation about the theme in each part of the book. The writers prod and probe the possibilities and seek new moral insight as to how we might learn, yet again, that the world Cannon invited us to build, one of inclusivity and hope, is possible even in the dark valleys of discrimination, disenfranchisement, and systematic hatred. We invite our readers to join this conversation and engage the potentialities of taking on the task of this work.

UNEARTHING THE SACRED FROM OUR OWN TEXTS

Since its initial emergence in the 1980s, womanist theological ethics has sought to dismantle theological and sociopolitical constructs that disavow that Black women's full humanity is made in the image of God and endowed with the potential to enliven freedom and rightly divine the word of truth. Katie Cannon's training in both biblical studies and ethics has played an essential role in what she deemed the telos (ultimate end)—the "debunking, unmasking, and disentangling" of womanist norms for emancipatory practice.

A large part of this work involves women challenging ideas about their status that are derived from so-called sacred texts. While notions of biblical authority and *sola scriptura* make it difficult to unmask the power dynamics embedded and invested in traditional biblical interpretations, several generations of Black women scholars in the field of religion have nevertheless produced works deconstructing texts and their interpretations that for centuries have denied agency, worth, and legacy to Black women.

Although much has been accomplished, there remains much more to be done in terms of debunking textual myths, unmasking the truly sacred, and disentangling Black women's marginalization.

The authors in this part of the manuscript employ Cannon's ethical mandate by challenging the presumably unassailable, centuries-old notion of biblical authority that has silenced, shunned, and stunted Black women: their effort is to help Black women and others see the limitations and constraints that have been force-fed to society as the word and will of God. This intergenerational and interdisciplinary offering is designed to engage the enduring legacy of Katie Geneva Cannon for both the future of theological education and the edification of Black women who discern and drive the primary modes of inquiry that deal critically with tradition, structure, and praxis in all their fields of study.

STRUCTURAL POVERTY AND BLACK COMMUNAL SOVEREIGNTY

At the core of Womanist analyses of structural poverty are four axioms: (1) Poverty is essential to capitalist modes of production. (2) Capitalism hinges on control of land, labor, and relationships. (3) In racialized economies, distorted imaging of Black women's ecological and economic realities serve as essential commodities to be bought, sold, and leveraged for greater power. Finally, (4) poverty is an affront to the God of provisions, necessarily requiring, therefore, a response from Black women.

Guided by Katie Cannon's ethical analyses at the intersection of sexism, racism, and economics, with sights on freedom, and privileging the voices of activist womanist practitioners, this chapter posits a constructive approach to ecologically responsible Black communal sovereignty in the face of structural poverty. Of particular interest is praxeologically addressing issues related to spiritual apartheid, climate change, and external imaging of Black female bodies as sociopolitical production—how addressing these issues impacts ecological viability in general and Black women's eco-economic health more specifically.

WOMANIST WAYS OF LEADING

In this part, the authors employ an autobiographical/dialogical approach to illustrate expressions of womanist embodied leadership informed by commitments to and engagement in the academy and the Black church. With attention to ways in which Black women chart paths for themselves, nurture potential in others, and curate space for collaborative engagement, particular attention is given to identifying strategies advanced by women when "foreclosing on our souls" is not an option.

EMBODIED ETHICS

Eschewing the mind/body/spirit fractures that haunt moral discourse, this final part of the manuscript explores what happens in deep methodological and ethical ways when we bring our whole selves into moral discourse. Rather than subscribe to either/or dualistic thinking, the authors explore how the theo-ethical praxis of Katie Geneva Cannon continues to prompt new avenues of epistemological candor, to develop a moral praxis that is meant to release circles of liberation, hope, and sustenance in the work for justice and a healing world.

PART ONE

*Unearthing the Sacred
from Our Own Texts*

1

The Biblical Field's Loss Was Womanist Ethics' Gain

Katie Cannon and the Dilemma of the Womanist Intellectual

RENITA J. WEEMS

Some women deserve double honor. Katie Geneva Cannon (1950–2018) is one such woman. Katie Cannon occupies a unique place in the theological academy. She is the foremother of Christian womanist ethics, a once contested but now fixed part of the field of Christian ethics. She was a leading voice in the subjects of womanist ethics and theology and of women in religion and society. In her 1985 essay "The Emergence of Black Feminist Consciousness,"[1] Katie Cannon inspired a young generation of Black women scholars in theological studies—those like myself, a graduate student at the time—to use the word "womanist" as an alternative to "feminist" and thus to set our research on Black women's theological realities apart.[2] Katie's gifts as a womanist ethicist were shaped by humble beginnings in rural North Carolina. She arrived in her discipline by calling attention to its racist heteropatriarchal assumptions, which made it scoff at the notion that Black women possessed moral wisdom worthy of academic study. Katie, a Black girl from poor Southern working-class origins, would go on to pioneer a totally new field of inquiry in Christian ethics, known as womanist Christian ethics, centering Black women's epistemologies for thinking and talking about God.

Katie was the first Black woman to graduate with a PhD from Union Seminary in New York and the first Black to graduate from that institution with a degree in ethics (1983). But what is not so well known is that when Katie Cannon arrived on the campus of Union Theological

3

Seminary in New York City in 1974, she did not intend to study ethics. Katie's dream was to become an Old Testament scholar. Having just completed her Master of Divinity degree that spring from a historically Black theological school, The Interdenominational Theological Center (ITC), Katie came to New York with an acceptance letter to Union's PhD program in Old Testament studies.[3] She imagined earning a PhD in Old Testament and returning to ITC, where she envisioned a career as a Bible professor, teaching Black clergy and religious leaders. I am credited with being the first Black woman to graduate with a PhD in Old Testament (Princeton Theological Seminary, 1989). But Katie Cannon serves as a reminder to all that being the first at finishing doesn't mean you're the first at starting, dreaming, or trying. For years a quote by Alice Walker hung over my desk in my graduate school dorm room, a quote written ten years prior to Walker coining the term *womanist*. In the introduction to her second book of poems, *Revolutionary Petunias*, Walker wrote: "To acknowledge our ancestors means we are aware that we did not make ourselves, that the line stretches all the way back, perhaps to God; or to Gods. We remember them because it is an easy thing to forget: that we are not the first to suffer, rebel, fight, love and die. The grace with which we embrace life, in spite of the pain, the sorrow, is always a measure of what has gone before."[4]

I was familiar with this quote before I met Katie Cannon face-to-face. I clung to this quote to remind myself of the cost others had paid to make it possible for this specific Southern Black girl to dream big in the 1980s about earning a doctorate in biblical studies. I carried this quote around with me long before I discovered that I was not the first Black woman to enroll in a PhD program in Old Testament studies, long before finding out that a decade earlier Katie Cannon had enrolled in a PhD program in Old Testament and was ejected from the program after two years of study. It would be many years before I learned about Katie's ordeal in the Bible department at Union Seminary.[5] By the time I came across her story, I had completed my degree, and Katie had rebounded and was well on her way to becoming a preeminent scholar in Christian ethics.

This essay in memory of Katie Cannon is not another lament on how hard it is being a Black woman in the academy. I am a Black female intellectual who has survived for forty years, working both inside and outside of the academy. Along with Katie, I and other womanist colleagues can testify that it is possible to survive, even thrive, within and outside anti-Black, anti-woman, mysogynoiristic spaces. How? By learning how to rise above injury to do the work that you love. Cracking open spaces and blazing trails in work previously designed for whites and for men is difficult work. There is a guaranteed trail of tears awaiting Black women who pursue the life of the mind, as it does nearly all people of color who enter curricular halls not made with them in mind. But what I discovered, as did Katie and others of us who are part of that first generation of Black female scholars of religion, is that eventually it comes to you that the world is larger than the racist and sexist institutions that begrudgingly grant us degrees, promotion, and recognition for our work, and larger than the Eurocentric intellectual world, which threatens to devour us and spit us out. What makes a black woman intellectual keep going? The prospect of giving up and giving in to the anti-Black woman stereotypes and assumptions about you is a worse prospect.

"So, what does it mean and what has it meant to be a black female intellectual?" asks Black feminist critic Brittney Cooper in her book *Beyond Responsibility: The Intellectual Thought of Race Women*, in which she charts the far-reaching intellectual achievements of African American women as public intellectuals and the evolution of their thought from the end of the 1800s through the Black Power era of the 1970s.[6] To answer Cooper's question, to be a Black female intellectual in this country means, for one thing, to think, write, and teach under a cloud of suspicion that says you're not good enough, not serious enough, not smart enough. Forever the outsider, the interloper, the *other* in a world that centers whiteness and maleness as the abiding images of inquiry, Black women have rarely had the luxury to pursue a life of the mind; when they do, they are likely to wind up working in institutional spaces, where they are constantly put on to justify not just their production of knowledge, but also their very existence in the discipline. Katie Cannon's journey to becoming a preeminent scholar in womanist Christian ethics is the story of what it means to be a Black woman intellectual. Daring to seek a doctorate in the 1970s and daring to center that research on Black women's realities and moral voices, one had to be prepared to face obstacles. "Do the work your soul must have" was Katie's famously popular response to complaints about roadblocks to one's work. It sounds easier than it is. After all, patriarchy doesn't bend easily, and when it does bend, it seems impervious to actually breaking and focuses its energy on breaking anyone and everyone who threatens it. Katie would learn this firsthand.

In the 1970s Union Theological Seminary seemed to be a logical place for a student of color interested in doing Christian scholarship to enroll. By the twentieth century, the school had distinguished itself for its deep commitment to the broad paradigm of liberation theologies. The oldest independent seminary in the United States, Union Seminary had long been known as a bastion of progressive Christian scholarship, with a number of prominent thinkers among its faculty and alumni.[7] Black faculty at ITC had urged Katie to go for her doctorate at Union because of Union's bold hire in 1970 of a firebrand young scholar, James Cone, who would go on to become the main architect of a brand of theology that grew out of the Black power movement. Even though behind the scenes Union Seminary was experiencing serious financial troubles by the 1960s, the seminary remained the place to study in the 1970s for those committed to progressive religious ideas and liberation in any shape or form. In the 1970s the school boasted one of the largest enrollments of Black students at a predominantly white theological school.

Later Katie admitted that she had no idea what it meant as a Black woman to step into a predominantly white, male, elite insular theological institution and seek a seat at the table where its most prized discipline, Old Testament, was debated and decided. As the first Black to be admitted to Union's Bible department, Katie Cannon didn't know what she didn't know. In Katie's words, "I was the first black woman to try and get a PhD in the Old Testament, . . . and I did not know that brain power alone would not produce a PhD. . . . I did not know that it was 75 percent political—[that] someone had to take you on as [your] mentor."[8] Union Seminary was a vastly different intellectual environment from ITC, where Katie had been admittedly accepted as one of the boys. Like many students of color from working-class backgrounds who aspire to become professors but lack the vocational counseling to know what lay ahead, she found that graduate school can be tough, regardless of the discipline or the school one attends. Katie was clueless about the hierarchy in the guild of theological studies. She knew little to nothing about the hierarchy among the disciplines, with Old Testament studies having the reputation of being the most rigorous of the disciplines due to its language requirements. But Katie could do the work. Yet the confluence of sexism, racism, and classism that she experienced in the department would almost do her in. The arid, dispassionate debates, snubs from her classmates, the use of jargon, the foregrounding of the European canon, the centering of male subjectivity, the erasure of other voices—it was a world vastly different from the loud, heated, passionate, good-humored debates about God, African peoples, human suffering, divine judgment, rights, slavery and the Bible, and Black prayers she had known at ITC.

Katie admitted decades later of nearly cracking from the pressure of "the white trauma of Union" that she experienced as the only Black woman in the biblical studies department.[9] Ostracized, lonely, and frustrated, she nevertheless pushed forward, applied herself, and jumped all the hurdles necessary, she thought, to prove to her peers, her professors, and herself that she deserved to be in the program and could finish.[10] But two years into the program, after successfully completing her course work and preparing for her qualifying exams, Katie learned one of the harshest lessons for Black women aspiring to a life of the mind: despite what you think, intellect is not enough in the world of white supremacist capitalist patriarchy. Just as she began looking forward to drafting her dissertation proposal and digging into her research, her department adviser called her into his office with news that devastated her. He was not signing the application renewal form for her Ford Foundation Fellowship. What was the reason given for refusing to sign the fellowship renewal form? The department believed that Katie Cannon wasn't a serious enough student. "Based on what?" one asks. They had discovered that Katie was working as a supply pastor while a student in the doctoral program.[11] Holding down a job while a student in their program was allegedly proof to the department that Katie Cannon wasn't giving her studies her all. The precarity of Katie's financial situation as a Black female, first-generation student was well known in the department. But that didn't matter. Without funding, she couldn't afford to continue her studies. Refusing to sign off on her third-year Fellowship funding was a death knell to Katie's completing her doctorate in Old Testament, and her adviser knew it.[12] The department had found the excuse it needed to force the lone Black female student out of the program. That excuse was declared: Katie Cannon wasn't a serious-enough student. Translated: the nerve of this Black woman to think she can study for a Union Seminary PhD and have another life alongside. Never mind that Katie had completed her coursework. That wasn't the point. It was her temerity. A Black woman thinking she was equal enough to white men in intellect to study Hebrew Bible was already unthinkable, but assuming she could study and simultaneously hold down a job was a challenge to the Old Testament section's reputation as a first-class, rigorous program at Union Seminary.

Katie was crushed and humiliated. Word spread quickly throughout the small, tight-knit Union campus: Katie Cannon had been booted out of the PhD program. She learned a second important lesson from her days in Union's biblical studies department, one that she took with her the next forty years whenever she moved from one teaching post to the next: when and where a Black woman enters the halls of the white Eurocentric, cisgender, patriarchal academy, you can be assured there will always be those who will remind her: "*You don't belong.*"[13]

By the time I met Katie Cannon sometime around 1986, I was a graduate student at Princeton Seminary, questioning my vocational choice, wondering what convinced me to think that enrolling in a PhD program was something I wanted to do, that specializing in Old Testament studies was the way to go, that becoming a professor was possible, that being intellectual was something a Black woman should aspire to. We were both products of our generation of smart Black girls from the South who came of age in the middle of what one might think of as the bridge years of boomer unrest, just as the Civil Rights Movement was losing momentum and the women's rights movement was gaining momentum, in 1968–74. Katie was a few years older than myself, but we shared several things in common. We were smart, sassy, strong-willed young women desperate to escape the restrictions of our working-class Protestant homes, young Black girls who loved to read and learn and then at different times found our way to Northern elite institutions as radical Black nationalism and radical feminist consciousness were clashing and making headlines. Both movements, radical Black nationalism and radical feminism, proved crucial to us in helping to frame and explain the reactions and resistance we met as we sought a footing in our programs and in our journey into the academy.

In all the years that I knew Katie Cannon, she never told me about her dream of earning a doctorate in biblical studies nor did she admit that she had once enrolled in a doctoral biblical studies department. It was years before Katie talked openly about what she later described as "the white trauma of Union," which left her feeling awkward, clumsy, lonely, isolated, inferior, shabby, and unfit for a career in the biblical field. Even after I learned of her experience, I never queried her about it. I understood Katie's silence and empathized with the wound associated with the memory. Only now, thirty-five years after graduate school, have I begun to peel the layers back and take a look at my own memories of surviving a graduate program in biblical studies in the 1980s. Only in the last few years have I ventured to talk in public about what it was like to be the first and the only Black woman in the all-white biblical studies department of Princeton Seminary. I still wince when I hear myself introduced as the first Black woman to earn a PhD in Old Testament studies. I don't presume to understand all that Katie experienced at Union in the Bible department in the 1970s. Indeed, all graduate-school stories are unhappy. Each graduate student is unhappy in her own way. But I know from my own experiences of being Black and female in a predominantly white graduate department how it feels to be treated like an interloper. Let's face it. The world of academic biblical studies had a race and gender problem in the 1970s when Katie Cannon enrolled in the Bible department at Union Seminary, and it continued to have that same problem a decade later in the 1980s, when I was a doctoral student in the Bible department at PTS. The discipline has made significant improvements in the decades since then, with the influx of more scholars of color to the field, but the field still wrestles with its whiteness. The problem is not about this or that bigoted school, nor is it about this or that racist or sexist faculty member. The problem is intrinsic to the discipline itself. To be a Black woman scholar in the biblical field, one must first be willing to submit and receive training to be concerned with the questions of a white male biblical scholar.[14] After you finish the program, it's up to you to commence shedding the hegemonic baggage you have acquired from your field and teach yourself to think about your discipline and your role in it better than you have been trained.[15]

How Katie survived academic humiliation in one department and how she made her way into another department at Union Seminary is a longer story than can be told here. But one can be sure it's a tale of perseverance, grace, synchronicity, faith, prayer, and intervention (both divine and human). Kudos to Beverly Harrison, a white feminist faculty member in ethics who summoned Katie into her office after Harrison heard that her white male colleagues had booted Katie from her Old Testament program. She urged Katie to switch to the field of ethics, promising to help Katie achieve her dream of earning a PhD. It was risky. Harrison wasn't yet a tenured member of the faculty, but what she lacked in clout, Beverly Harrison had more than enough in grit and a determination to breaking with the "malestream ethicists" of the day by ushering more women's voices into the field.[16] Katie found a home in the ethics department at Union. Harrison's mentorship proved hugely important to Katie's successfully graduating in 1983 as both the first Black woman to earn a PhD in social ethics and the first

Black woman to graduate with a PhD from Union Seminary.[17] At the core of this story about Katie's experience in Union Seminary's Bible department, however, is not what happened to Katie Cannon. It is about who Katie Cannon was at heart, which allowed her to get up after a severe blow by the academy, brush herself off, and pivot. At heart, Katie was an intellectual, a Black female intellectual, to be more precise. Katie arrived at Union Seminary in 1974 *because* she was an intellectual, a thinker, a budding scholar, a woman bursting with questions, ideas, hunches, and suspicions that needed to be tested. What she sought was a home where her intellectual restlessness could be nurtured, directed, and sharpened. The racism, sexism, and classism she experienced in Union's Bible department couldn't quench Katie Cannon's appetite for thinking and learning. She just needed an intellectual home, a room of her own, in which to roll up her sleeves and proceed with proving that Black women's moral discourse was deserving of a place in the academy.

Finally, the story of Katie Cannon's journey to become a Black female intellectual is not just about the importance of finding the right disciplinary home, the right mentor, nor the right questions to send you off on a lifetime career project. Those things are important. But what is more truly critical to being able to do the work you must do is to be able to rise above the opinions of others and the obstacles they put in your way, to frame an identity for yourself and situate that identity within something larger than yourself. Katie's love for the Bible dated back to the time when she was a girl, sitting at her grandmother's knee and listening to homespun Bible stories. Katie loved studying the Bible, but the field of biblical studies did not love Katie back. Yet she did not give up her dream. She drew a lot on the Bible as a resource for ethical reflections and moral discernment. Her treatment of texts in her publications was always done with the highest level of skill and sensitivity, like someone with training in biblical criticism.[18] "It gave me another competence" is how Katie would come to rationalize her two traumatic years as a doctoral student in Bible: "Most people studying the Bible know very little about ethics, and most people doing ethics know very little about the Bible."

Katie Geneva Cannon triumphed in the end. She went on to become a pioneering figure in the field of social ethics. She has produced groundbreaking texts showing how the interlocking systems of oppressions faced by Black women have lots to do with shaping the moral and liberationist ethics Black women live by and showing that

Black women's moral discourse deserves a place in the Western moral canon. One of her legacies as a social ethicist is that she worked to bring the moral voices of the marginalized, especially Black women educated and uneducated, into the academy with the recognition that they deserve recognition as thinkers, themselves producers of knowledge and shapers of moral wisdom. Further, Katie became an exceptional teacher with students vying for the opportunity, even at her death, to pen testimonials to their prof's impact in the classroom, describing her classrooms as being like living laboratories, where she inspired and challenged students to think thoughts that debunked, unmasked, and disentangled the mythic lies telling the marginalized and those rendered invisible that they are not good enough, smart enough, qualified enough for this or that work. Katie Cannon proved that Black women are thinkers, intellectuals, field-defining producers of knowledge. The field of biblical studies that she sought to pursue at Union was not the field where she eventually landed. As Stacey Floyd Thomas, Katie Cannon's first doctoral student, observed, the gain for Christian ethics was the biblical field's loss.[19] Katie's eyes never lost focus of her subject matter: Black genius, Black women's moral wisdom, God's preferential option for the oppressed. Because she possessed an innate light that could not be extinguished by others, Katie managed to do for the theological academy, for the discipline of Christian social ethics, and for the field of womanist religious scholarship what her literary muse Zora Neale Hurston imagined for Nanny Janie's grandmother in *Their Eyes Were Watching God*: "Ah wanted to preach a great sermon about colored women sittin' on high."[20] We no longer are privileged to have Katie Geneva Cannon's luminous presence and her bold laughter, but we will always hear her from her perch on high. Katie left her work for us to continue.[21]

2

Unearthing the Ethical Treasures of Cannon Formation

STACEY M. FLOYD-THOMAS

> Womanism requires that we stress the urgency of Black women's move-
> ment from death to life. In order to do this, we recount in a logical
> manner the historical consequences of what precedes us. We investigate
> contestable issues according to official records. In other words, woman-
> ist religious scholars insist that individuals look back at race, sex, and
> class constructions before it is too late and put forth critical analysis in
> such a way that errors of the past will not be repeated.[1]
>
> —Katie Geneva Cannon

Katie Cannon largely defined her body of knowledge as "unearthing ethical treasures" formed and fashioned by Black women who have been historically discounted, discarded, and left for dead on the trash heaps of history. By necessity, the work of the womanist scholar exposes deep conflicts over "rightful" academic inheritance and "appropriate" scholarly representation, answering the call of historian Jill Lepore, who queries, "When Black History is unearthed, who gets to speak for the dead?"[2] Although Lepore is referring specifically to the rescu-ing of colonial-era African American burial grounds and attending to the recovery process of the remains, her sentiments can be expanded to overarching issues of inheritance and representation within academic discourse. The inheritance issue involves who controls and has the "right" to master and produce disciplinary bodies of knowledge as well as the necessary role and influence that representation and embodiment play in the formation of scholars and their scholarship.

In many regards, unearthing ethical treasures is an endeavor to which Cannon brought and utilized her skill as a trained biblicist; she eventually produced the framework for foregrounding Black women's real-lived experiences that shaped womanist ethics while simultane-ously informing the womanist thought of scholars in religious studies and theological education. "Katie Cannon became an enthusiastic and brave practitioner of human archaeology," attested her first biographer, Sarah Lawrence Lightfoot. Akin to philosopher Michel Foucault's theory of the "archaeology of knowledge,"[3] Lightfoot extoled Cannon's hallmark archaeology as "a deep examination of human relationships, development, and experience that seeks to uncover mask and persona and reveal the authentic core of a person's identity [through] sustained dialogue, whose success depends on extraordinary trust, empathy, symmetry, and synchrony."[4] Cannon excavated the history of womanist thought and pioneered the field of womanist ethics and its knowledge production. The primary concern of *Katie's Canon* is that discursive formations, or *epistemes*, are systemic regimes of thought and knowledge that have been governed by rules deeming Black women as intellectual impostors or disciplinary trespassers. More specifically, "Cannon formation," as I like to refer to it, *unmasks* schemas of privilege and *debunks* structures of power existing at subterranean scholarly levels, all in an effort to *disentangle* the implicit biases that operate subconsciously within intellectual production.

As a pioneer of womanist ethics, Cannon's work was no easy task, both at its inception and even now, some decades later. Much of the academy—including white men, white women, Black men, and even Black women feminists—received womanist thought as the furthest thing from an archaeology of knowledge and demeaned it as more along the lines of expository renderings of experience and simple storytelling. Like any trailblazer charting new territory, Cannon and generations of womanist inheritors have been routinely criticized for creating an approach within the academy and the church that privileges intersectional analysis and prioritizes Black women's ontology and epistemology as necessary resources for the work of Christian social ethics.

Keep in mind that Cannon did not set out to make the impact and impression she eventually left on the academy. To the contrary, it happened organically, as evidenced by the origins of her signature publication, *Katie's Canon*. It was in response to cultural anthropologist Bernice Johnson Reagon's prophetic idea in 1985 and the pragmatic urging and insistence of the 1994 cohort of us, her graduate students in 1994 in her "Proseminar in History of Christian Ethics" course; in response to those urgings, she came to publish this seminal collection of her essays.[5] However, like many pioneering agents of change—be they activists or academics—she utilized whatever tools and courses of action she had at her disposal to define her scholarly objectives, to form their concepts, and to build their undergirding theory. The incorporation of her social teachings as a Black woman alongside her academic training within the fields of Bible and ethics made Cannon's work virtual prophetic acts of brilliance. Cannon's ability to "hit a straight lick with a crooked stick," as a "noncanonical other," compelled scholarly skeptics to come to grips with the fact that womanist ethics was neither a trend nor a fad.[6] She led a movement of Black women—scholars, students, clergy, and thinking women of faith—by claiming that our history cannot imprison us when we recognize it for what it is. She regularly proclaimed, "That's why we need to read and write even when the lights are out because this is the work our souls must have." So daunting was the weight of this work that, on one occasion, it almost caused her to faint while delivering the keynote plenary address at the Society of Christian Ethics.

Cannon devoted much of her life's work to attacking the core precepts that undergird history, while also incessantly discarding the teleological efforts of traditional scholars complicit in the maintenance of the status quo. The corpus of Black women's stories and testimonies Cannon uncovered via her archaeology of knowledge revealed more than the makeshift musings of much maligned models of a melanin enhanced matriarchy historically victimized by the *misognynoir* prevalent in mainstream society. Instead, Cannon's critical approach offers an undeniable and compelling rejection of historical narratives that seek to create a unified, uninterrupted continuity between past and present knowledge production. Cannon formation sought to "undo what history had done," borrowing the language of her mentor, Beverly W. Harrison. Never tiring or deterred from her mission, Cannon did not merely start a womanist movement: she shifted the atmosphere of religious thought, Christian social ethics, and theological education. David Gushee states this so well:

> Katie Geneva Cannon occupies a unique place in the history of Christian ethics. It is exceedingly rare to create an entirely new and lasting methodology or subfield in any discipline. . . . Cannon not only blazed a methodological trail, she also opened access to our discipline . . . to recognize that white European-American Christian ethics is a tradition, or better, a set of traditions, all emerging from Europe and migrating to America with the colonizers. It has a particular lineage, or a set of lineages. White Euro-American Christian ethics does not constitute the truth, or define "Biblical Ethics," or orthodoxy, or the center of Christian ethics, or the canon of Christian ethics. In whatever version—Orthodox, Catholic, Protestant—it is a historically dominant strand of Christian ethics, but merely a strand. . . . Further, white European-American Christian

ethics is a flawed tradition. It is flawed because of its participation in sinful domination and oppression, which includes colonialism, conquest, murder, slavery, Jim Crow, and continued racism. This is especially true of the colonial powers of Western Europe and the United States, which [history] is, for most white Christian ethicists, our heritage. . . . I am now convinced by Cannon (and others) that [these] power dynamics fundamentally alter people's social location, so fundamentally that they do not face the same moral situations. We have not always been appreciative of such help.[7]

In her groundbreaking and debut text, *Black Womanist Ethics*, Cannon offers an analysis of Black women's moral situation in the United States, demonstrating how the dominant ethics assumption "that a moral agent is to a considerable [degree] free and self-directing" does not account for the realities of Black women.[8] In turn, Cannon names the ethical virtues embraced by Black women out of their experience of race-class-gender oppression in order to "'hold on to life' against major oppositions" instead of waiting with baited breath to be a part of a canon that merely sought to insert Black women as a footnote, sidenote, or afterthought of history, or blew them off and away altogether. Cannon formation avoided the minefields of white/male prooftexting and instead mined the motherlode of Black women's moral wisdom as sacred texts and corrective resources for rigorous engagement and intersectional analysis. This was at once a seismic shift and epistemological revolution. It characterized a new way of knowing, one that takes the experiences of Black women as normative. This revolution affirmed Black women to be viewed as knowledge bearers and scholarly producers on behalf of their own health and well-being.

Cannon's founding of womanist ethics excavates a series of interrelated yet relatively invisible concepts. By way of illustration, in "Womanist Perspectival Discourse and Canon Formation," she calls for the uncovering of historical archaeology via her own autobiographical contemplation of her "fascination with words" ("word" being defined herein in its purest and simplest form as the most singular and discrete unit of discourse).[9] Cannon's work of unearthing ethical treasures echoes Foucault's notion of archaeology, insofar as it also can be broadly understood as a tool for uncovering, disrupting, and analyzing alternative histories of knowledge systems. But rather than engage in the unearthing of ethical treasures as an interpretation and analysis deemed necessary to reveal an evaluation of "constraints and limitations . . . imposed on discourse," Cannon used her archaeological exploration of previously unseen cultural artifacts and wisdom as a liberating means of honoring the ancestors and empowering their descendants. To be certain, these issues of restoring a chain of memory and being to reclaim the humanity of an entire populace—in this case, Black women—was never at stake for Foucault's earlier efforts. In the long run, Cannon's intellectual project and process not only cast a bright light on the previously ignored contributions and undervalued contemplations of Black women in both historical and contemporary terms; she had also effectively helped to reframe and redeem the archaeological methodology for those oppressed and marginalized populations who need such critical scholarly tools the most.

Cannon's teaching was as stellar and groundbreaking as her research. Throughout her career, Cannon shaped the teaching-learning experience of countless scholars and students beyond the campuses where she taught, to such an extent that students and scholars alike had to take seriously her mantra that in the classroom, as in life, "there is no value-free space." Teaching religion for Cannon was not a career move but a calling: "The call to teach is like fire shut up in my bones. As a Christian womanist liberation theological ethicist, embodied, mediated knowledge is a fundamental component of my pedagogy. I bring my biotext and students bring their existential stories, rooted in remembering, to the common, centering point in each course of study. Working together as co-learners, we introduce into existence new forms of moral praxis."[10] Esteemed highly as an exemplary pedagogue by both her peers and students, Cannon was not only awarded the coveted American Academy of Religion's Excellence in Teaching Award in 2011, but the award itself was also posthumously named in her honor as a wholehearted recognition of her legendary teaching.[11]

Legions of students of diverse backgrounds and social locations were so influenced and enthralled by her teaching that they often pondered whether they could or must become a womanist in her image. Although most womanists maintain that only Black women can be the producers of knowledge specific to their subject position and experiences of social difference, there is also consensus that anyone can utilize womanist methodology. For as womanist biblicist Renita Weems explains, "If someone offers you a window into salvation, you take it."[12]

The Cannon formation of teaching and learning womanist ethics was salvific: it saved the soul of theological education while not requiring students to lose their minds by "numbing up and dumbing down," as she would often quip. Cannon's pedagogy took seriously the challenge that Black feminist theorist bell hooks stated in her text *Yearning*: "How do we create an oppositional worldview, a consciousness, an identity, a standpoint that exists not only as that struggle which also opposes dehumanization but as that movement which enables creative, expansive self-actualization?"[13] She routinely offered her "Dance of Redemption" as the metalogue and dialogue of teaching the womanist idea[14] as an ongoing praxis and spiritual discipline, which involved the seven essential moral acts of

> *Conscientization*: recognize and articulate the cognitive dissonance experienced when your reality does not fit what is considered to be normative;
>
> *Emancipatory historiography*: research the systems and theories that hold the structures of oppression in place that inform your dissonance;
>
> *Theological resources*: reflect on how theological disciplines and your spiritual community either uphold or liberate the structures of oppression;
>
> *Norm clarification*: reconcile how your values are clearer and to whom you are accountable in doing the work your soul must have;
>
> *Strategic options*: refuse to trim the contours of your suspicion as you strategize and brainstorm ways to put your knowledge to work and the implications for every action;
>
> *Annunciation and celebration*: remember that, to make a real-lived and lasting impact, this work can never be solo-driven or executed in silos but must be a collaborative endeavor with a collective function sustained by communal solidarity and celebration; and
>
> *Re-reflection/strategic action*: recall that with added perspectives and in every revolution, there will be further insights and strategies for action in anticipation of the next revolution.

Although her research opened the canon of Christian social ethics to include her own work and her teaching opened the minds of her students, it was her mentoring that opened up many doors for womanist scholars during a time when the standard number of Black female representation among Association of Theological Schools constituent institutions was routinely zero.

Cannon's mentoring provided life lessons for the formation of womanist scholars and clergy that fostered the fortitude necessary for their survival. Cannon urged Black female intellectuals to routinize the practice of disentangling oneself from what Hortense Spillers calls the terrible weight of being a marked Black woman: "always seen as a particular figuration of the split subject, . . . embedded in bizarre axiological ground, . . . so loaded with mythical prepossession that there is no easy way for the agents buried beneath them to come clean. . . . In order for me to speak a truer word concerning myself, I must strip down through layers of attenuated meanings, made an excess in time, over time, assigned by a particular historical order, and there await whatever marvels of my own inventiveness."[15]

To free herself from the myth-making wreckage that both the academy and church tried to make of her life and soul, Cannon had to cultivate a practice of self-reaffirmation, which in many instances necessitated that she publish the atrocities that had occurred in her own personal and professional lives. She knew that her experiences of misogynoir were no exception, but were rather universal for Black women; so she championed the cause of womanist scholars and clergy to save themselves from the madness of being theologized or theorized as being sinister or suspect. In her essay "Structure Academic Amnesia: As If This True Womanist Story Never Happened," Cannon recounts the harrowing details of being physically assaulted when she was a student at Union Theological Seminary in New York City. While en route to an event for women of color in the Presbyterian Church, she was verbally accosted and physically assaulted by a white man dressed as a hotel employee. According to Cannon, her assailant was shocked and enraged to see her, a Black woman, wearing an ecclesial collar. He viciously berated her with taunts such as "How dare you defy Jesus Christ!" This deranged white male hotel worker then "slammed [Cannon] into the wall." Although seriously rattled and dismayed by what she called "the body slam incident," she escaped and then proceeded to do the work that her soul must have. Some years later, Cannon eventually shared this story during an interview with a Black female *Wall Street Journal* reporter regarding the vocational plight of women in ministry. However, as she shared this previously undisclosed incident, she was confronted with a particularly ugly insult to injury: the journalist reported that she found little to no evidence corroborating her account of the attack, which she claimed rendered Cannon's entire story invalid.[16]

This is the cultural context in which Cannon and the countless womanists she has inspired find ourselves both within the academy and in society at large. According to Cannon, "to be a Black womanist ethicist places me in a most precarious predicament."[17]

> [Ours] are countless real-life dilemmas . . . for Black women in the theological academy who grapple with the fact that our existential situations are oftentimes classified as questionable, anecdotal evidence; our genuine perceptions and factual registration of cutting-edge issues end up encoded as sporadic wanderings, downloaded as rambling, make-believe, episodic soap operas flowing into the institutional sea of forgetfulness. It is as if this true Womanist story never happened.[18]
>
> Within learned institutions, structured academic amnesia is relentless. Intellectual rank and scholarly authority are assessed as unalterable, fixed, mechanical phenomena. By this I mean that when Womanists refuse to play the game of the illusive objectivity, a game that is incapable of tolerating ambiguity, ignores emotions, weeds out passion, resists spontaneity, maintains rigid predictability, and celebrates the isolated solo-self, then the prescriptive authorities impose theoretical frameworks categorizing our truth as a lie. Each and every time that we are not willing to dissect people, places, and things; that we stand over against the intellectual propensity to tear apart foundational experiences, meanings, and elements by way of supranational technical, abstract, referential facts, then we get demoted to the status of second-class thinkers.[19]

Our intellectual gifts, talents, and scholarship are deemed lacking value by virtue of simultaneously being embodied as Black and female in a white man's world wherein "all the women were white and all the Blacks were men, but some of us are brave."[20] Furthermore, in *Invisibility Blues*, Black feminist cultural critic Michelle Wallace contends: "Because Black women are perceived as marginal to the production of knowledge, their judgement cannot be trusted. . . . As a consequence, Black women are not allowed (by themselves as well as by others) to make definitive statements about the character of power, agency, and resistance within and beyond the Black community. If and when they persist in doing so, the discouragement is great."[21]

Cannon's revelatory mentoring bears witness to the ways in which ongoing scapegoating, gaslighting, whataboutism, and dog-whistle politics persistently marks and targets Black women while trying to convince us that what is happening at the moment actually is not. *What does it mean that academia is so structured that Black women are severely ostracized when we re-member and re-present in our authentic interest?* Cannon explores this metaethical query with pointed questions of her own in unmasking the perennial attempts to dismiss Black women's truths as lies: "What does it mean to structure academic amnesia? To whom, then, do we turn when we are told that our truth is a lie? How, it is asked, can Womanist realities be verified in institutions of higher learning where the dailiness of our authentic experiences cannot be proven by scientific methodology?"[22] Cannon, and countless other womanists of her generation and beyond, had to go "in search of their mothers' gardens," to paraphrase Alice Walker, in order to find the resources as well as the resiliency to survive in an otherwise vicious and barren land.

In an effort to move them from cognitive dissonance to conscientization, Cannon mined the previously ignored resources of Black women. She relied on literary, historical, sociological, and theological resources to remember Black women's real and lived experience not merely as a scholarly endeavor but also as the necessary coping mechanism for having a soul while doing scholarly work. With this turn, Cannon formation shows how Black women live out a moral wisdom in their real-lived context that does not appeal to the fixed rules or absolute principles of the white-oriented, male-structured society. Black women's analysis and appraisal of what is right or wrong and good or bad develops out of the various coping mechanisms related to the conditions of their own cultural circumstances. Consequently, Cannon formation reminds us that there is no possibility of full personhood without a grounded sense of place, both literally and figuratively. From the moment of our birth until our ultimate demise, we are all searching for a context to claim and call our own. Philosopher Martin Heidegger referred to this as *Dasein*: the human *being-there*, with the emphasis squarely indicating that a core part of the human condition depended on how we inhabit space as a physical, psychological, and phenomenological reality. Thus, when Black women in the academic realm are mistreated and disregarded on a dually systematic and systemic basis, that creates a "No (Black Wo)Man's Land," in which we were all supposed to wither and die.

Clearly I am adapting the term *no man's land*, a phrase that has been associated for centuries with unbearable and deadly terrain long before it was used to describe war-torn, ravaged battlefields.[23] I invoke this brutal imagery of war zones to discuss and describe the plight of

Black womanist scholars such as Cannon who are entering into the halls of academe to discover a veritable "No (Black Wo)Man's Land," an unfamiliar and unwelcoming space that seeks to leave us destroyed, dismembered, desiccated, and turned to dust in order to maintain the status quo. In a great many ways, this reflects Cannon's colleague and womanist theologian Delores S. Williams's notion of the "wilderness-experience," which she frames as "a symbolic term used to represent a near-destruction situation in which God gives personal direction to the believer and thereby helps her make a way out of what she thought was no way."[24] Whereas Williams was unapologetically reading the contemporary plight of Black women through a prism of sacred texts, biblical imagery, and theological premises, Cannon was largely insisting on tapping into the immediate, intimate real-lived conditions of Black women's experiences. The brutal austerity of the "No (Black Wo) Man's Land" that Cannon, much like Williams, illustrates has never been a metaphorical reference as much as it has been a metaphysical reality for so many Black women trying to find and make a home for themselves in the world, especially in this instance within the academy.

Womanist work is rigorous analysis that is real and relevant, with being and belief directly linked to acting and doing. As one writer contends, "When a Black woman in America reaches a high level of visibility, authority and success, you can always count on somebody in power undercutting her when given the chance."[25] The reification—or maybe even deification—of the academy as "No (Black Wo)Man's Land" strongly echoes what Koritha Mitchell calls "know-your-place aggression," in which Black women must withstand and overcome pejorative labels, dehumanizing stereotypes, subpar socioeconomic status, governmental policies steeped in misogynoir, and even deadly attacks on our intellects, citizenship, communities, livelihoods, and even our lives.[26] But the work of Cannon formation defies such death-dealing circumstances by insisting that we cannot and will not be dispossessed from a place that we have built brick by living brick and have made our home. Reflecting on her youthful travels across the African diaspora, Cannon recalled the following anecdote:

> The analogy that comes to mind takes me back to the summer of 1971, when I was a member of an Operation Crossroads Africa work camp of twelve young adults in the town of Pleebo, near Cape Palmas, Liberia. Our assignment was to build a library. None of us had ever done construction work before. Nevertheless, for approximately six hours every day for sixty days, we adorned our pith helmets,

brogans, and work gloves; shouldered pickaxes, shovels, and spades; and rode on the back of rickety, wobbly dump trucks hauling sand from the oceanside to our work site in our effort to dig and pour a foundation. This common undertaking in any construction project is of utmost importance, because the foundation is the portion of any structure that transfers the weight of the building to the ground. The foundation is the first part of the building, in some ways the hardest part, though the least accommodating and least elegant. It establishes the basic footing for future construction.[27]

Cannon further recalls:

Those of us who have been busy doing womanist work from the moment that we enrolled in seminary believe that we have built a solid womanist foundation. We officially began constructing this womanist house of wisdom in 1985, and as intellectual laborers we continue to work day in and day out so that our scholarly infrastructure is built on solid rock instead of shifting sand. Let us celebrate this analogous reality by acknowledging that the second generation of womanist scholars has completed the structure of the womanist house of wisdom.[28]

To borrow Cannon's metaphor, each person involved in the building process and the work at hand both transforms the environment and is transformed by it. As much as Cannon was engaged in archaeology of knowledge, she was also demonstrating an architecture of possibility with womanism at its core. As such, Cannon formation unearths the sacred texts and social contexts that prove Black women's moral adeptness not only at overcoming oppressive systems intended to potentially obstruct and obliterate them, but also to amass the immense wealth of moral wisdom that normative academic disciplines and theological discourse fail to engage. In the process of unearthing the ethical treasures she hoped to find, Cannon was unafraid to dig in the dirt to build a solid foundation for the good of all. Audre Lorde's words on the danger of losing hold of one's identity formation remain timely: "If I didn't define myself for myself, I would be crunched into other people's fantasies for me and eaten alive."[29]

As womanist theologian M. Shawn Copeland reminds us, to know the good does not always conclude with one choosing to do good. It is in this spirit that Cannon formation proves most vital. To wit, womanist critical cognitive praxis is committed to creating space that necessarily concludes in a commitment to decisive action—to transform both religion and society. Audre Lorde warned us that "the master's tools will never dismantle the master's house. They will allow us temporarily to beat him at his own game, but they will never enable us to bring about *genuine change*."[30] Tools for genuine change or transformation include nurture and interdependency; the acceptance, understanding, and appreciation of difference; and friendship. While the truth of Lorde's maxim rings loud and clear, the sum total of Cannon's scholarly contributions lends itself to the reconsideration that Lorde's wisdom is not incorrect but is incomplete, from a womanist perspective. Put another way, Cannon formation insists that, for Black women to reclaim their identity, they must tell their stories. This goal is best achieved via "biomythography," as Lorde calls it, which is a "deliberate amalgamation of autobiographical fact and mythically resonant form" that recognizes the effect of social oppression on Black women who retell their own stories as they struggle for moral agency and the rediscovery of a self-identity that has always been muted. Cannon describes this lifelong experience as being "repeatedly unheard but not unvoiced, unseen but not invisible."[31]

As both scholarship and praxis, womanists must professionally, personally, and politically "connect our cultural values, oral traditions, and social experiences to our spirit forces in the quest for meaning amid suffering."[32] Existing within structures that weren't made for our flourishing means establishing our own goodness, our own holiness, and our own story as worthy within and outside of these spaces. That is work we must first do internally, and then within communities, congregations, campuses, and classrooms, as the structures themselves—whether tangible or intangible—will neither necessarily nor readily offer it. This is not new work, but an ongoing endeavor for each generation, for as Ralph Ellison stated in his 1970 classic "What America Would Be Like without Blacks":

> Since the beginning of the nation, white Americans have suffered from a deep uncertainty as to who they really are. One of the ways that has been used to simplify the answer has been to seize upon the presence of Black Americans and use them as a marker, a symbol of limits, a metaphor for the "outsider." Many whites could look at the social position of blacks and feel that color formed an easy and reliable gauge for determining to what extent one was or was not American. Perhaps that is why one of the first epithets that many European immigrants learned when they got off the boat was the term "nigger"—it made them feel instantly American.[33]

Cannon formation wrested womanists from the weight of this

wreckage, a feat accomplished by unearthing ethical treasures through her scholarship, teaching, and mentoring. The absence of her body frees her from bearing the weight of this work as it makes her legacy and lessons loom even larger. I am reminded that, as every semester was coming to a close, Cannon was fond of saying, "The time we have now we will soon have no more"—as if to warn us to take heed to build on what we gleaned, urge us to search for what we yet needed to generate, and remind us of the sacred text and call that "therefore every scribe who has been trained for the kingdom of heaven is like the master of a household who brings out of his treasure what is new and what is old."[34]

When all is said and done, Katie Geneva Cannon was groundbreaking not simply because she was a giant in her time, but also because she equipped us with the instruments, insight, and insistence to continue unearthing the ethical treasures that would otherwise go missing. In a time and context where Black women still do not matter, the work left for us is to continue mining the motherlode of their wisdom, unearthing many who can become a glorious cloud of witnesses rather than a dusty valley of dry bones. As not only this essay but the entirety of this volume rightly attests, Cannon still calls out to us afresh as illustrated in these sermonic words captured at the beginning of her own career:

> So at any point those of you who are participating and feel like leadership has disappeared, there's a cloud of witnesses. . . . Make sure you say Katie Cannon was there, and then she disappeared, and then she was there because of the cloud of witnesses [who] were around. . . . Know that I stand within a tradition. . . . And so, when someone says, "Well, what did Katie Cannon do?" You can say, "She didn't make it up." Black religions and spirits are not a superfluous appendage in the Christian tradition, but . . . we have something very rich, very important; and when people are open to that tradition, there's so much that can be learned to enhance the whole of the story.[35]

3

The House That Cannon Built and "The Hinges upon Which the Future Swings"

MELANIE C. JONES

> By wisdom a house is built,
>   and by understanding it is established;
> by knowledge the rooms are filled
>   with all precious and pleasant riches.
>   —Proverbs 24:3–4

In her essay "Teaching Afrocentric Ethics: The Hinges upon Which the Future Swings," womanist ethicist Katie Geneva Cannon tells the story of her vocation becoming nurtured by the leadership and humanitarian activism of Presbyterian minister James Herman Robinson (1907–72), founder of Operation Crossroads Africa, Incorporated, known to many as a predecessor to the Peace Corps. Cannon identified Robinson as in the "vanguard of progressive, contemporary thinkers on Afrocentricity before it was fashionable."[1] From one conversation over tea, Robinson drafted Cannon for her first of many travels to the motherland to visit Ghana, Liberia, and Côte d'Ivoire and participate in a summer-long youth program.

The program was held during the summer of 1971, just after Cannon earned her degree from the historically Black institution Barber-Scotia College in North Carolina, where she excelled academically, rising to the top of her class, and was elected as Miss Barber-Scotia College. The key assignment of the summer program required the work collective of twelve bright-eyed young adults, all of whom held no prior training in construction, to build a library in the town of Pleebo, near Cape Palmas, Liberia. Cannon and her comrades were enlisted to dig and pour a foundation. According to Cannon, "this common undertaking in any construction project is of utmost importance because the foundation is the portion of any structure that transfers the weight of the building to the ground. The foundation is the first part of the building, in some ways the hardest part, though the least accommodating and least elegant. It establishes the basic footing for future construction."[2] It is no surprise that the first assignment Cannon receives, just as she enters adulthood with a college degree in tow, is to build a repository of resources, a collection of writings and worlds, a home for the learned and the curious, a living institution that would nurture the imagination of future generations.

The metaphor of building, constructing, and laying a foundation outlines Cannon's methodology from the beginning of her journey and culminates in founding the Center for Womanist Leadership. Like securing a strong foundation, the framing process of building represents a second act that requires detailed and careful precision to map new rooms, doorways, and windows, thus implementing the design layout. This essay traces the founding and framing of The Katie Geneva Cannon Center for Womanist Leadership (KGCCWL) as an institutionalizing agent that carries Cannon's legacy forward for today's living and future generations through six high-priority initiatives: womanist wellness, wisdom, witness, worship, wares, and works.

Womanism describes a growing methodological approach and social movement that takes the survival and liberation of Black women seriously while advocating for the wholeness and well-being of all humanity. Pulitzer Prize winning novelist Alice Walker defined the Black Southern colloquial term *womanist* in her classic 1983 collection of essays, *In Search of Our Mothers' Gardens: Womanist Prose*, doing so by naming the distinctive political aims of Black women beyond the white feminist scope.[3] Though Walker's definition is a point of departure for many, the womanist paradigm has taken shape since the 1980s in multiple academic disciplines, including literature, history, theater and film, communication and media, psychology, anthropology, social work, gender and sexuality, architecture and urban studies, Black studies, and most notably, religious studies.[4]

Among many firsts, Katie Geneva Cannon was the first within the theological academy to source the term *womanist* in her 1985 essay "The Emergence of a Black Feminist Consciousness." Cannon provides a historical backdrop of Black women's experiences from the antebellum period through the Civil Rights Movement to analyze the triple jeopardy of Black women's oppression in America; all this illustrates the interconnectedness and inseparability of racism, sexism, and classism in the lives of Black women. Cannon characterizes Black women's moral situation in the face of formidable oppression and under the threat of multiple death-dealing struggles: the struggle for human dignity, the struggle against white hypocrisy, the struggle for justice, and the struggle to survive "in two contradictory worlds simultaneously, one White, privileged, and oppressive, the other Black, exploited, and oppressed."[5] For Cannon, a Black womanist consciousness, as an interpretive approach, provides Black women with the critical space to "chip away at oppressive structures, bit by bit,"[6] while also employing the virtuous acts and "search the Scriptures to learn how to dispel the threat of death in order to seize the present life."[7] In later works, Cannon widens the scope of sacred texts to include the Black women's literary tradition as valuable resources for constructive ethics and a living repository of the moral life of Black women.

Cannon's scholarship extends more significant influence than simply introducing womanism to the theological academy. However, alongside Black women scholars Jacquelyn Grant, Delores Williams, Renita J. Weems, Clarice Martin, Cheryl Townsend Gilkes, and a great cloud of proto-womanist witnesses, her work blazed new methodological trails that constructed a Black womanist tradition for an unrecognized population of Black women in the guild. Reflecting on the formation of the womanist house of wisdom in theological studies, Cannon writes as a first-generation womanist trailblazer: "From 1985 until now, womanists have been most vocal despite intense opposition via white supremacy, male superiority, and class elitism concerning Black women's substantive contributions as full-fledged members within theological discourse. While this is not an easy task, womanists contend that we must name—and continue to name—the particularities of God's presence in our everyday realities, because such clarity enhances our ability to tap the sacred foundation of our common humanity."[8]

Womanism, for Cannon, is rooted in liberation ethics, which she describes as "debunking, unmasking, and disentangling the ideologies, theologies, and systems of value operative in a particular society."[9] The critical task of womanism is to debunk the lies designed to ensure that Black women were never meant to survive, unmask the truth by asking the hard questions of the power relations that enforce damaging values, and disentangle the exasperating problems facing marginalized peoples and communities. Womanism further requires a constructive agenda to move from death to life by mining the motherlode of cultural traditions and real-lived textures that Black women use to resist and rebel against oppressive situations through justice-making resources.

Cannon describes her subversive standpoint as scholar and activist: "The dilemma of the Black woman ethicist as the noncanonical other is defined as working in opposition to the academic establishment, yet building upon it. The liberation ethicist works both within and outside the guild."[10] Cannon envisioned the Center for Womanist Leadership as an institutional endeavor to realize both the critical and constructive aims of womanism and to build a Black womanist home of our own.

FROM THE GROUND UP:
THE KATIE GENEVA CANNON CENTER
FOR WOMANIST LEADERSHIP

In their efforts to confront the terrors of their time—such as lynching, unequal citizenship, and racial segregation—and cultivate possibilities for communal uplift through educational advancement and social reform, the nineteenth-century and early twentieth-century Black movement women such as Ida B. Wells-Barnett, Mary Church Terrell, Nannie Helen Burroughs, Mary McLeod Bethune, and countless ordinary women understood the need to organize social organizations, mutual benefit societies, auxiliary church groups, settlement houses, and schools to institutionalize their intellectual contributions and fortify their prophetic social witness for future generations to build on. Like these Black foremothers, the formation of the Center for Womanist Leadership reflects the visionary insight and skillful construction of Katie Geneva Cannon. No one could imagine, not even Cannon, that her thirty-year-old dream of a womanist center, spawned by a conversation in a room in New York City with Delores Williams and Alice Walker in the 1990s, would manifest in full glory just four months before her untimely passing in 2018. In 2013, 2015, and 2017 local projects and pilot iterations of the center, through gatherings and luncheons named "Squaring the Womanist Circle," were designed to translate Black women's religious scholarship, artisanship, and activism into community service. Yet Cannon founded and organized the Center for Womanist Leadership in 2018 as her last living testament.

Union Presbyterian Seminary President Brian Blount describes the moment Cannon's organizing wheels began turning like a visionary prophet to shift her dream of a center to reality.

Several years ago, the Rev. Dr. Katie Geneva Cannon and I sat in my office and dreamed a dream. Her vision of a Center that would focus on work that was a vital part of her academic mission, and now legacy, bloomed before us. She spoke passionately about her hope to connect her scholarly work to the communal initiatives of improving the circumstances for women of color in Richmond, VA, and beyond. Her hands gesturing with conviction, she explained how the idea of a Center for Womanist Leadership might begin. A programmatic initiative was a great way to start. She called it "Squaring the Womanist Circle." And she was certain that this was not a program that Union Presbyterian Seminary could pull off on its own. Right from the start she began thinking of the scholars and scholarship at the Samuel DeWitt Proctor School of Theology at Virginia Union University. She then envisioned an even broader alliance. She called to mind womanist scholars from around the U.S. and the world who would be wonderful conversation partners. *And she began to build [it], right there in front of my eyes* [my emphasis]. The academic, ecclesial, and community response to Professor Cannon's vision was affirmation and celebration. And it was immediate. So, immediately, we set to work putting the full focus of her passion and the full support of the UPSem administration into motion.[11]

Laying the foundation of an institution was a job that Cannon knew she could not do alone. In true womanist fashion, Cannon galvanized and recruited a center design team of womanist scholars, current and former students, community leaders, and pastors in collaboration with Union Presbyterian Seminary and The Samuel DeWitt Proctor School of Theology at Virginia Union University to connect head, heart, and hands to this womanist vision in its nascent stages. The Center Design Team included a diverse, multigenerational group of Black women: Rhonda Bond, Courtney Bryant, Cassandra Calin, Faith Harris, Alison Gise Johnson, Ayo M. Morton, Paula Owens Parker, and Angela Sims, who worked night and day collaboratively with Cannon at the proverbial realms of a construction site, pulling together tools and commissioning resources to concretize her vision.

The Center for Womanist Leadership opened by celebrating herstory in April 2018: it launched officially on the forty-fourth anniversary of Cannon's ordination as the first Black woman ordained in the United Presbyterian Church. It also commemorated the enduring struggle for Black freedom on the fiftieth anniversary of the assassination of Martin Luther King Jr. The center was funded by major sponsors like the E. Rhodes and Leona B. Carpenter Foundation and key donors, such as actor Nick Cannon (nephew of Katie Cannon), who responded to Cannon's vision. The 2018 Inaugural Conference titled "Bearing Witness to Womanism: What Was, What Is, What Shall Be" featured womanist progenitor Alice Walker as the keynote speaker at a monumental opening night of more than 1,500 attendees at the historic St. Paul's Baptist Church of Richmond, Virginia. Fourteen womanist thinkers and activists presented at a sold-out event filled with panels and interactive sessions on the following day.

The 2018 spring conference, now a signature program of KGC-CWL, modeled the design of a Cannon classroom as presenters and attendees emphasized their "embodied social selves" and created "collaborative dialectic space," which Cannon described as "a learning environment where we can sandpaper with each other's thesis, antithesis, and synthesis."[12] The conference sought to explore pressing questions, engage in rigorous inquiry, and open communication essential to the well-being of Black womankind through panel presentations, table talks, plenaries, and multifaceted, transgenerational, and innovative conversations across disciplines and among activists who embody the kinds of interconnections that womanist work makes possible. According to feminist theologian Mary E. Hunt, "From the opening address by world-renowned author Alice Walker to the closing ritual when participants rendered homage to the elders and received their blessing, the gathering marked a signal contribution to women's work in religion."[13] Cannon tilled the soil and laid the foundation for what was sure to become a towering institutional home for womanist leaders and collaborators for many generations to come.

In Black women's social clubs and Greek-lettered sororities of the nineteenth and twentieth centuries, the Founders established the institutions as the Guiding Spirit. Next, the Incorporators contributed by doing the work of protection, preservation, and perpetuity to carry the agenda forward. The sudden passing of Cannon in August 2018 shifted the ground, sending local and global shockwaves of whether the center's foundation was settled and ready for the next act of setting the frame with the nuts and bolts that Cannon left behind. In honor of Cannon's significant tenure as the esteemed Annie Scales Rogers Professor of Christian Ethics from 2001 to 2018, Union Presbyterian Seminary renamed the center after its master builder and visionary founder as The Katie Geneva Cannon Center for Womanist Leadership in April 2019. I accepted the call in July of 2019, less than a year after Cannon's passing, to lead KGCCWL as its inaugural director, with the extraordinary task of developing an institution that had a solid foundation constructed by

Cannon and the design team but needed infrastructure, a team of expert womanist builders to "stay on the wall" to advise and support its efforts, a renovated strategic plan, an enhanced digital profile to strengthen its pillars, and a path to sustainability for perpetuity.

I have pondered long and hard about Cannon's naming of the center under the contextual framework of womanist leadership, which encompasses womanism's intellectual, spiritual, ethical, and activist dimensions. The stories of Black women's leadership are often missing or ignored in leadership studies and the narratives of the leadership legacies and models that are passed down or carried forward from one generation to the next. Womanist psychologists Toni C. King and S. Alease Ferguson address this gap by tracing the motherline in their edited volume. Linking Black feminism, womanism, and Black female leadership, King and Ferguson suggest that Black womanist leadership is "undergirded by four basic pillars: (1) the legacy of struggle; (2) the search for voice and the refusal to be silenced; (3) the impossibility of separating intellectual inquiry from political activism; and (4) the direct application of empowerment to everyday life."[14] These pillars illuminate the core values of KGCCWL that are also rooted in the coming together of Black women against the isolating experiences of oppression; an unapologetic commitment to the wholeness, liberation, justice, and self-sustainability of marginalized communities; and an unwavering impetus to stay in tune with the Spirit and the folk.

African American Christian social ethicist Robert M. Franklin defines moral leaders as "people who live and lead with integrity, courage, and imagination as they serve the common good, while inviting others to join them."[15] First, integrity represents "the art of centering down with intense focus on our most deeply held values, which then radiate outward in our behavior and demeanor."[16] Second, courage reflects "the fearless activation of one's deepest convictions."[17] Third, imagination identifies "the art of dreaming up where and how we can transcend the status quo."[18] As a consummate moral leader, Cannon lived into the "art of centering down, stepping forward, and dreaming up," an art that inspired and influenced countless others to join her organizing endeavors.[19] Embodying unctuousness at every stage of her vocational journey, Katie Geneva Cannon was in the vanguard of Black womanist leadership before such a concept was intelligible.

Leaning into Cannon's vision, the mission of KGCCWL is to nurture the soul work of Black women as we cultivate pathways to whole communities. When Black women, who represent one of the greatest leadership assets of the Black community, are inspired and equipped, new pathways for social transformation emerge. KGCCWL functions as an institutionalizing agent for womanist theory and practice that facilitates consciousness-raising in Black women through spirituality, scholarship, activism, and art to unearth unique gifts for transforming communities, which is the crux of womanist leadership. KGCCWL aims to inspire, equip, connect, and support Black women divinely motivated to serve as changemakers in their community. The programmatic agenda of KGCCWL convenes Black women seminarians, graduate students of religion, clergy, theological faculty, aspiring womanists, allies, and collaborators who seek to demystify hidden manifestations of systemic oppression and address persistent and effective strategies of justice-making in the academy, church, and world.

The presence of KGCCWL at a historically white theological institution affiliated with a historically white Christian Reformed tradition that was established before the Civil War in the Deep South bears a prophetic demand to confront a racist and sinful past. Like most theological institutions in North America, Union has benefited demonstrably in its resourcing from gifts of finance and land that were directly tied to the enslaved work of African American women and men. In line with its strategic plan for the church and the world, Union Presbyterian Seminary sought to repair this breach by endowing KGCCWL in 2020. Within the 270 graduate school membership of the Association of Theological Schools in the United States and Canada (ATS), the premier accrediting body of North American theological institutions, KGCCWL is the only endowed center in theological schools committed to affirming and developing Black women, one of the fastest-growing populations in theological education.

SETTING THE FRAME: THE WOMANIST INITIATIVES

In my final year of junior high school just outside Chicago, my family decided to build a new house from the ground up. First, the builders laid the foundation; then, they set the frame. The frame of the home represents the hidden, underlying structure that holds its core elements together. The six high-priority initiatives of KGCCWL—wellness, witness, wisdom, worship, wares, and works—fully embody Cannon's legacy and commitment to the spiritual wholeness and collective well-being of Black women in the communities we lead. The initiatives further represent the holistic interconnections that nurture the flourishing of womanist leadership.

Womanist Wellness

The Womanist Wellness initiative fosters the health, healing, and holistic well-being arm of KGCCWL, which provides breathing spaces, healing circles, and rigorous, invigorating, and inspiring conversation through supportive and empowering offerings of compassionate hospitality. In her namesake text, *Katie's Canon*, Cannon opens the volume by tracing the moral wisdom of Black women through the healing memory of her grandmother. "My grandmother, Rosa Cornelia White Lytle, was the "gatekeeper in the land of counterpane." She was always available with salves, hot towels, and liniments to cure physical aches and spiritual ills. As a charismatic healer, Grandma Rosie's practice consisted of diagnosis, treatment, and prevention in the maintenance of overall wholeness. Many days my soul struggled with whether to go to school or stay home and be healed from the injuries of the world inflicted unknowingly. In 1983, womanism became the new gatekeeper in my land of counterpane."[20]

Cannon understood Walker's womanism as "philosophically medicinal," as a "confessional concept," and as a "critical methodological framework for challenging androcentric patriarchy as well as a catalyst in overcoming oppressive situations through revolutionary acts of rebellion."[21] In Walker's definition, she describes a womanist as "not a separatist, except periodically for health's sake."[22] Care of the self is a necessary act of rebellion and resistance against the vicious threats and evil forces inflicted to stifle Black women's survival and liberation. King and Ferguson define leadership as "the desire, ability, and efforts to influence the world around us, based upon an ethic of care of self and other and fueled by a vision that one sustains over time."[23] The commonsense wisdom of Black women explains it this way: "If you don't care for yourself, you ain't good for nobody else." Womanist leadership begins with the care of the self by attending to the liberationist question "Do you want to be made well?" while confronting the trauma and charting a perpetual practice of rest and renewal.

In the age of multiple pandemics, there is a persistent call to address the spiritual, psychological, and physical health of Black women. In efforts to protect and nurture the spiritual livelihood of Black women by inspiring, ministering to, and replenishing Black women for new possibilities to blossom, KGCCWL provides vital opportunities of spiritual, emotional, and communal restoration for Black women; they often bear the loads of their communities in work that puts them on the frontlines of eradicating oppression; places heavy burdens of responsibility on them, making them susceptible to burnout and justice fatigue; and isolates them as the saviors of their communities with few, if any, outlets of support for their own well-being in a multi-traumatic world. The priority of renewal and refreshment makes way for Black women to learn new ideas and thoughts; reflect and listen; energize their bodies; fulfill the soul's cravings with food, rest, silence, and play; and go deeper into the spiritual self.

Womanist Wisdom

The Womanist Wisdom initiative encourages and develops womanist writers and writings to organize and produce a tangible collection of womanist thought for the perpetuity and proliferation of the womanist idea for practitioners and academics, otherwise known as the "town and the gown." In her early teaching years, Cannon used novels, then added nonfiction, biographies, and essays to discern Black women's God-talk until the catalog grew wider, filled with numerous works across disciplines that broadened the womanist canon.

> When I first began teaching at New York Theological Seminary in 1977, there were no books by Black women theologians. However, the primary materials now being published by Black women in the American Academy of Religion and the Society of Biblical Literature allow me to ask, and begin to answer, new questions about the ideologies, theologies, and systems of value of African American people. This pivotal shift is occurring as more women of all races, creeds, and colors earn doctorates from theological seminaries and departments of religion in universities. By asking heretofore undreamed and unfamiliar questions of every aspect of the theological traditions to which we are heirs, womanist, feminist, and mujerista scholars play a significant role in authorizing God-talk.[24]

There is room in this house for all of us, with so many dimensions of Black faith and life that are waiting to be explored. Like Cannon in 1977, in 2002 I enter classrooms of students who have never read a book by an African-descended woman and encounter faculty in theological institutions who have never included womanist voices on their syllabi.

KGCCWL recognizes the significance of centering Black women's scholarship and wisdom as viable sources and resources for theological education and the global community. As a site of participatory learning for scholars, students, clergy, laity, activists, artists, entrepreneurs, allies, and community leaders, KGCCWL seeks to institutionalize womanist wisdom by building Black women's historical archives through the cultivation and preservation of Black women's oral, aural, visual, and written stories and intellectual contributions. Through womanist publications and resources for public access, KGCCWL builds an arsenal of translatable and transferable practices, pedagogies, and processes for thinkers and practitioners across the globe.

Womanist Witness

The Womanist Witness initiative demonstrates KGCCWL's commitment to inspiring, equipping, and supporting emerging leaders. Cannon chose the 2013 theme "What shall I tell my children who are Black?" for Squaring the Womanist Circle gathering on the 150th anniversary of the signing of the Emancipation Proclamation, making a call to expose the emancipation agenda as unfinished and to share lessons with coming generations on becoming moral agents in the face of oppressive situations that seek to thwart life. In keeping with the tradition of midwifery, KGCCWL offers consciousness-raising programming and vocational development training for the sake of awakening in Black women their sense of purpose and call to community engagement and social change. KGCCWL functions as a convener, connecting womanist leaders for networking, problem-solving, information sharing, and mobilization around common issues. KGCCWL supports mentorship opportunities for Black women thinkers, activists, and artists to expand their knowledge base, improve existing efforts, collaborate with other progressive efforts to support Black women leaders in their work, and help cultivate future generations of womanist leaders.

Womanist Worship

With a commitment to multifaith and interreligious engagement, the Womanist Worship initiative seeks to foster connections with churches, religious institutions, and faith communities while calling them into greater accountability and justice concerning Black women's religious leadership. Womanist systematic theologian Delores Williams argues, "Womanist worship happens when African American women's experience is obvious in the leadership, liturgy, and god-talk of the church."[25] Womanists have long argued that Black women in the United States make up the majority population within Black religious traditions while continuing to bear the burden of unequal access to religious leadership. KGCCWL honors and affirms the justice-seeking, truth-telling, and wisdom-bearing gifts Black women bring and embody in preaching, music, dance, drama, liturgical curation, ritual, and diverse worship practices. Cannon paid particular attention to the Black rhetorical tradition and formulated a womanist preaching methodology for justice-making ministry. Now KGCCWL fully supports and encourages womanist proclamation in the pulpit and the public square because Black women finding their voice is an ultimate response to the call of the divine.

Womanist Wares

The Womanist Wares initiative of KGCCWL embraces the virtue of self-sustainability and self-sufficiency by establishing a womanist marketplace, thus generating a stream of revenue to support its programming through the sale of womanist products, developing sustainable models for raising funds, and nurturing a community of Black women entrepreneurs launching and growing businesses. In Walker's *The Color Purple*, the protagonist Celie lived into thriving by opening a pants-making business that helped her build her income, employ her community, and exercise her unique gifts of sewing. From literature to life, the cooperative economic building of Black movement women like Maggie Lena Walker, the first Black woman to own a bank in connection to the Independent Order of Saint Luke, illuminate entrepreneurship as a path for Black women to cultivate the world we want to see and sustain ourselves and our communities.

Womanist Works

The Womanist Works initiative values the arts and the divinely inspired creative productions of Black women in music, dance, theater, film, literature, fashion, crafts, photography, visual artistry, and more while also interrogating possibilities for cultivating whole communities. In addition to teaching and writing, Cannon valued art as a source of creative expression and spiritual devotion. Cannon's visual artistry in the form of doodles illustrates the movement work of KGCCWL. When Cannon sat down to create her doodles, she never knew the intricacies of their design at the start, but the patterns of lines, colors, shapes bending, curving, twisting, and weaving soon evolved into an artistic masterpiece. The arts represent an integral component of Black women's meaning-making, imagination, and creativity. KGCCWL commissions artists to tell the womanist story by developing alternate visions of freedom and curating new worlds for imagination.

HER LEGACY LIVES

Apostle Paul writes to the community of believers at Corinth in 1 Corinthians 3:10 (NRSV), "According to the grace of God given to me, like a skilled master builder I laid a foundation, and someone else is building on it. Each builder must choose with care how to build on it." As a millennial womanist who belongs to a generational cohort that is highly suspicious of the value of institutions for Black women in a contemporary era because of the gaping historical wounds at the hand of multidimensional oppression inflicted by theological schools, churches, and religious traditions, I often return to the basic building blocks of Cannon's methodology to debunk, unmask, and disentangle such oppression as counter-hegemonic strategies for imagining womanist futures. Cannon recognized her students as the "hinges upon which the 21st century swings."[26] I argue that the "future is womanist" because the transformative possibilities for the academy, church, and the world hinge on Black women. Likewise, KGCCWL is an institutional force equipped with six initiatives to guide Black women to wholeness as we transform communities.

No one can deny that Katie Geneva Cannon did the work of empowering, equipping, and setting people free. Cannon articulated a liberationist methodology and embodied a womanist consciousness that will be useful in print for the theo-ethical formation of religious thinkers and scholars beyond her lifespan and in practice for the cultivation of justice-seeking leaders and moral agents who will further her legacy. Cannon did the work her soul must have. She understood her assignment to lay the foundation and ground her work for future generations. Cannon's clarion call to us is to build on it.

PART TWO

Structural Poverty and Black Communal Sovereignty

4

Redeeming Black Survival

A Womanist Reading of Poverty as a Means of Re-Membering Black Sovereignty

ALISON P. GISE JOHNSON

The capitalist mode of political economy is the essential structural problem of contemporary society. As the most powerful and dynamic form of social organization ever created, the capitalist political economy generates political order that is ostensibly democratic but leaves economic power unchecked. . . . The "miraculousness" of capital culture . . . rests in its seeming capacity to create wealth from nothing. In such a culture, existence comes more and more to be based purely on the acquisitive instinct.

—*Katie's Canon*[1]

Across the United States, spaces that Black women have nurtured and sustained via politically powerful institutionalized understandings of survival are in the final stages of a fifty-year process of long-standing forced removal. Using as framework the ethical mapping of capitalism set forth by Katie Cannon in her chapter "Racism and Economics," my aims are threefold: (1) Define poverty as a commodity essential to the generation of wealth within political economies. (2) Characterize the complexities of *land-circumscribed poverty* as means of values supplantation essential to assimilation into capitalist culture. (3) Suggest a conceptual framework for sovereignty-based survival, entreating Black women invested in the survival of the whole community to devise ways of institutionalizing loving-kindness as a means of protection against efforts of the political economy to propagate poverty-induced soul murder.

INTRODUCTION

While preparing for the opening scene of the Broadway production of *The Color Purple* musical, I sat staring at the curtain, purple in color, if I recall correctly. Projected onto this improvised screen were the words "Dear God, I am a 14-year-old girl . . . " I reflect on that moment and consider the plight of Black women and girls to love and be loved, regardless, central in *The Color Purple* and in life. That love is enhanced when there is a stable physical place serving as shelter for that love. In this volume, as we consider the realities of Black women and the valleys we navigate, I am especially interested in the creation of poverty and housing insecurity that impacts the ability to love and to survive. Deconstructively, my concern is about the weaponization of poverty as a means of forced participation in capitalist political economies, overtly observed in the destabilization of Black communities through public housing legislation and policies touted as solution to "slums" and "pockets of poverty." Constructively, I offer this analysis as a cautionary tale to those enlisted to speak for and act "charitably" on behalf of communities continually experiencing *forced serial displacement* and as a blueprint through conceptualization of *sovereignty-based survival.*[2]

POVERTY AS COMMODITY

Poverty is big business, especially big real estate business. In its construction and maintenance, poverty generates wealth for private industries, real estate investors and developers, well-resourced universities, charities, political parties, and politicians. Under the guise of renewal, infrastructure improvements, data-driven research, and social programs, *constructed poverty* is a means of transferring public dollars into privatized wealth, all serving to maintain social stratification and, if managed well, resourcing political will.[3] When racialized through media (engendering paternalistic response or enraged indifference), poverty becomes a primary means for racial differentiation and distrust, shifting the illusory concept of poverty from political fodder to moral issue. Cast as questions of virtue or globally peddled through "*the poor shall always be with you*" religious ideology, poverty as gatekeeper remains primary in the inability to extricate or even imagine exodus from debt-based economies that scourge nature and threaten life. Subsequently, efforts toward social justice reform are confined to advancement within the social order and inclusion in political processes, in hopes of escaping poverty but making no real dent in dismantling it. Therefore poverty itself is an indispensable commodity to be bought, sold, and leveraged for power in political economies and is a sustaining driver of capitalism. At the intersection of these phenomena, I enter this work as a womanist scholar invested in the lives of Black women and the survival of the whole community.[4]

To a large degree, poverty is imaged in the bodies of women and children of color, globally, and Black women more specifically in the United States.[5] Cast as composites of prevailing immoral stereotypic images of Jezebel, sapphire, and welfare queen, poor Black women (and by extension Black women in general) are confined descriptively as incompetent, aggressive, promiscuous, and conniving no matter profession nor socio-economic status. Informing legislation, public policy, and individual treatment (personally, professionally, and medically), and serving as bookend to criminality imaged in the bodies of Black men, poverty as caricatured in the bodies of Black women and girls, makes vulnerable the health and wellbeing of Black communities and the human family as a whole. More specifically, in major cities many systemically financially crippled Black and Brown people are being "relocated" to less culturally and environmentally desirable and often resource-deprived suburban municipalities; moved to scattered mixed-income neighborhoods as means of diluting political will; and incarcerated in small rural towns, where their bodies will be counted for political representation, while being disenfranchised from voting. For purposes of social reform, it is essential to disaggregate the operative functions of poverty, including (1) masking systemic disenfranchisement for the purpose of generating unchecked wealth; and (2) reifying caste designations through constructing sacrificial zones,[6] wherein masses of working poor ethnic populations are isolated and placed under undue socioeconomic stress.

SURVIVAL AS THREAT TO CAPITALISM

Central to the success of capitalism is its ability to generate institutional order and morally tutor full participation in the "stay in your place" hierarchically constructed transactional social relationships fundamental to the political prowess needed to control land, labor, and relationships. According to Cannon, "Capitalism creates a political economic order in which the totality of relationships among groups and individuals is drawn into interdependence. Such a society comes to have enormous capacity for cultural assimilation because social interrelations are increasingly conditioned and mediated through national, political, and economic order. The people in the society depend significantly on this unified system to teach them fundamental behavioral patterns and thought processes."[7]

Historically, when there existed systems to protect Black people from forced acceptance of assigned social and economic positions as civil slaves *in perpetuity*,[8] communities would experience a modicum of freedom. Here freedom is defined as the ability of a people to construct primary sociopolitical institutions governing their world, based on chosen systems of values.[9] For nearly fifty years—from Black Reconstruction through the Progressive Era up until the 1960s, and in the face of continual battles to subjugate the lives of Black people—institutionalized survival endured as a rampart against requisite demands of capitalism. Underwritten by Black faith infrastructures,[10] Black communities, though continually under attack sociopolitically and economically, built and maintained the requirements for survival.

From the 1960s until the present, in retaliation for Black survival that stood in the way of necessary assimilation and values supplantation, domestic wars waged against "poverty" and "drugs" caused fissures that are eroding into gaping holes in the foundation of institutionalized survival. These major subversive and destabilizing attacks have come in the form of Civil Rights and Tough on Crime legislation. Superficially offering social inclusion and community safety, respectively, these laws compromised intracommunal well-being and subsistence for the masses of Black people and radically changed the nature of survival.

POVERTY IMAGED AS BLACK, FEMALE, AND PLAGUE

In the 1960s, with Civil Rights legislation and assimilation-focused integration, capitalism became embedded in Black communities by using the rhetoric of poverty as a tool for dismantling Black survival. On January 8, 1964, during the State of the Union address, Lyndon B. Johnson declared an "unconditional war on poverty."[11] Johnson stated, "Our aim is not only to relieve the symptom of poverty but [also to] cure it and above all prevent it."

Under pressure from local jurisdictions, instead of fully funding the equity investment strategies of the Community Action Program (CAP) established under the 1964 Economic Opportunity Act, public housing became primary in addressing issues of poverty. CAP funding, designed to develop locally sustainable economic infrastructures in forms of community development corporations, devolved into public housing authorities that resulted in dependence on government, destabilization of families and communities, and destruction of thriving community-based education and economies.[12]

Though most federal housing subsidies supported nonpoor households (representing over 60 percent of budget expenditures),[13] public housing became synonymous with poverty. Since public housing was primarily built in African American neighborhoods, poverty equated to Blackness. Further, poverty was imaged as Black single female with children, which equated to promiscuousness based on gender-specific policing-of-bodies policies and practices. Under Aid to Families with Dependent Children programs that employed "man-in-the-house" rules and "able-body" arguments,[14] Black women with children became not only the face of poverty, but also the embodiment of an unholy matrimony of immorality and criminality, especially as Black intimacy was constantly surveilled. Rahim Kurwa tracked the impact of housing-regulation policies that turn interpersonal relationships into liabilities, thus exemplifying a destructive triumvirate of poverty, criminality, and immorality:

> Before we moved into Pruitt-Igor, the welfare department came to our home; they talked with my mother about moving into the housing project, but the stipulation was that my father could not be with us. They would put us into the housing project only if he left the state. Mother and father discussed it, and they decided that it was best for the twelve children for the father to leave the home, and that's how we got into the projects.
>
> There was even a night staff of men who worked for the welfare department whose job was to go to the home of welfare recipients, and they searched to find if there was a man in the home. Sometimes men came back at night to be with their families. Some were found in closets, hiding.[15]

Poverty became inextricably attached to immorality and criminal behavior, located in Black female bodies, and a social and political plague to be avoided, destroyed, and, for some Black families of means, to be escaped. This rhetoric of poverty as plague, captured in Johnson's State of the Union speech's use of cure/prevention medical terminology, finds its roots in English memory. Edwin Black, in *War against the Weak*, notes the thoughts of nineteenth-century English philosopher Herbert Spencer (popularizer of the term *survival of the fittest*, predating its use by Charles Darwin):

> Man and society were evolving according to their inherited nature. Through evolution, the "fittest" would naturally continue to perfect

society. And the "unfit" would naturally become more impoverished, less educated and ultimately die off, as well they should. Indeed, Spencer saw misery and starvation of the pauper class as an evitable decree of a "far-seeing benevolence," that is, the laws of nature. . . . "The whole effort of nature is to get rid of such, and to make room for better. . . . If they are not sufficiently complete to live, they die, and it is best they should." Spencer left no room for doubt, declaring, "All imperfection must disappear." As such, he completely denounced charity and instead extolled the purifying elimination of the "unfit."[16]

In deliberately personifying poverty in the bodies of Black women/girls and creating technological solutions in the form of building projects, housing served as an effective tool in creating land-circumscribed poverty for Black residents and generating wealth through distribution of public resources inclusive of tax incentives, contracts, research grants, and social programming to private individuals and entities. More devastating, this weaponization of housing began the slow destruction of Black survival by instigating intragroup social stratification in the form of constructing social and geographic distance from the housing projects as motivation for participation in a capitalist economy.

LAND-CIRCUMSCRIBED POVERTY AND THE DESTRUCTION OF SURVIVAL INFRASTRUCTURES

"The 'miraculousness' of capitalist culture . . . rests in its seeming capacity to create wealth from nothing. In such a culture, existence comes more and more to be based purely on the acquisitive instinct."[17]

In 1962, the 4,321 apartments of the Robert Taylor Homes projects opened to low-income families. These twenty-eight high-rise buildings (equaling 4,321 apartments) populated the skyline on the northern border of the Southside of Chicago. On the southern border, surrounded by unregulated industrial waste sites and landfills, the Altgeld Gardens housing project was built in 1945. In Chicago, like other cities and rural towns, these symbols of *land-circumscribed poverty* at the intersection of economic deprivation and environmental exploitation signaled the success of capitalist modes of production. *Land-circumscribed poverty* relates to the symbiotic relationship between structural and cultural poverty, characterized by population confinement, inequitable control of resource distribution, and depopulation/removal as means of morally tutoring capitalist values.

In this arrangement, structural poverty is built into economic systems as a function of government: public funds in the form of researched-based studies, contracts, corporate tax-increment financing incentives,[18] and grants are distributed to either stimulate economic growth or stall it through divestment. In capitalist modes of political economies, these patterns of distribution are discernable and essential to maintaining power.

On the other hand, cultural poverty—theorized as consequential to individual choices and artificially defined ethnic/cultural behavioral proclivities including teen pregnancy, crime, health disparities, gun violence, incarceration, and divorce rates—functions in more covert ways as cultural production.[19] This cultural poverty serves in two primary capacities requisite to capitalism: cultural poverty (1) constructs the *oppositional other* (in the form of weak-minded, immoral, civil slave) needing to be "saved" or requiring punitive backlash; and (2) justifies financial resourcing for research and (typically superficial) interventions, over-policing, and charity. Symbiotically related, structural poverty is tasked with providing solutions to cultural poverty.

Utilizing segregation as means of wealth/poverty generation and of morally tutoring ideologies of difference as deficit, the symbiosis between structural poverty and cultural poverty is effectively galvanized. As exemplified in the research of Mindy Thompson-Fullilove and Rodrick Wallace,[20] processes of redlining, highway construction (through ethnic, indigenous, and Black communities), urban renewal, planned shrinkage, catastrophic disinvestment, deindustrialization, foreclosure, and gentrification cause *forced serial displacement* on the structural level, precipitating psychosocial fallout at the cultural level termed "rootshock." This process of removal, confinement, and divestment structurally impacts access to resources for maintaining social and physiological survival. According to Thompson-Fullilove,

> a persistent policy of serial forced displacement of African Americans has created a persistent *de facto* internal refugee population that expresses characteristic behavioral and health patterns. These include raised levels of violence, family disintegration, substance abuse, sexually transmitted diseases. . . . [Observably] social organization declined, and disease increased. Violent behavior emerged as a new behavioral language. . . . African American death rates of obesity-related disorders such as diabetes and hypertension range from a quarter to half [higher when compared] against the rate for White Americans, a circumstance attributable to the policy-driven

concentration and persistence of psychosocial stress in that population associated with serial displacement.[21]

Cultural poverty sets into motion continual cycles of generating wealth for those well-resourced, deepening land-circumscribed paternalistic dependence, exacerbating disparities for those caught in poverty, and destabilizing infrastructures of Black survival. Mass incarceration (building of prison industrial complexes) and "fair-market mixed-income" housing (using public funds to financially underwrite gentrification while simultaneously diluting the Black political power base and causing homelessness)[22] contemporarily leverage the next well-designed iteration of structural poverty to increase wealth for invisible investors/developers and lubricate the capitalist machine through contracts and research dollars to study the oppositional other.

VALUES SUPPLANTATION AND THE MAKING OF POVERTY

While the symbiotic relationship between structural poverty and cultural poverty is observable and well-documented by using race-based segregation as an analytical matrix, axiology more than race is the primary facilitator of capitalism. Cannon suggests that the existence of capitalist culture is based primarily on the *acquisitive instinct*. The term *inquisitive instinct* is historically defined in the work of R. H. Tawney in response to British practices grounded in Adam Smith's "invisible-hand" theory,[23] and in the indefeasibility of private rights as presented in the philosophy of John Locke.[24] The *acquisitive instinct* is conceptualized as natural impulse, wherein self-love equates to means (private ownership of land)[25] and ends (individual generation of wealth). Pursuant to self-love, according to the *acquisitive instinct*, "is emphasis upon the sanctity of rights and upon the infallibility of the alchemy by which the pursuit of private ends is transmuted into the attainment of public good."[26]

Endemic in a worldview grounded in self-preservation and institutionalized through a *member-object* axiology wherein the highest value lies in acquisition and maintenance of objects,[27] the *acquisitive instinct* is primitive in orientation, pointing to the cultural practice of a people who have grown up in an oppressive and violent environment.[28] Primary ends of this group center on safety and control, with requisite means of profit, property, territory, and security. Paired with the creation of rhetorical rules of rightness designed to politically and morally mediate exploitative relationships, the *acquisitive instinct* exhibits little to no reflective capacity in that every social and political institution is forged by these values and exists to ensure its survival through emotionless control. According to Brian Hall, the main orientation of this phase is to "look out for number one," characterized as having no investment in the emotional life, viewing the environment as alien and oppressive, and being driven by potential for uncontrolled fantasy and delight.[29]

Although this value analysis assists in understanding the origins of the American expression of capitalism, what is essential to comprehend is that capitalism seeks to morally tutor these values globally, nationally, and locally in every neighborhood, school, religious institution, home, and relationship. Beyond wealth creation, *land-circumscribed poverty* functions as a means of placing communities under so much stress that ancestral values grounded in relationality may become dismembered and hybridized by those systems of values incapable of valuing life, instead feeding on soul murder.[30]

Soul murder is employed by psychologist Leonard Shengold to explain the effects of child abuse and deprivation. This term is used by historian Nell Irvin Painter to describe the psychological trauma that the first iteration of land-circumscribed poverty, slavery, had on the psyche of children. Of this she writes:

> Sexual abuse, emotional deprivation, physical and mental torture can lead to soul murder, and soul-murdered children's identities are compromised; they cannot register what it is they want and what it is that they feel. They often identify with the person who has abused them and are angry and hostile toward themselves and others. Victims of soul murder do not inevitably turn into abusers—there is no direct or predictable line of cause and effect—but people who have been abused or deprived as children grow up at risk psychologically.[31]

Poverty feeds off deprivation. Mindy Thompson-Fulilove makes clear that for any efforts to destroy the grip of poverty-induced soul murder, "it is not enough to reduce stress on a pregnant mother. It is necessary to have reduced stress on her mother, and her grandmothers before her, as effects may persist across three generations."[32] In other words, the trauma (whether consciously identified or subconsciously operative) of land-circumscribed poverty has epigenetic impact across at least three generations. Whether confined in government-assisted housing or isolated in gated communities, the vestiges of poverty-induced trauma interface with capitalist values that lead to acceptance of what Marimba Ani terms a "rhetorical ethic . . . designed to create an image that will prevent . . . successfully anticipating European [acquisitional and emotionless] behavior, and its objective, . . . to encourage nonstrategic (i.e., naive, rather than successful) political behavior."[33]

When Martin Luther King Jr. realized that legislated integration made no concessions for real social transformation and simply institutionalized a *rhetorical ethic*, he confided to Harry Belafonte:

> I'm afraid that America has lost the moral vision she may have had, and I'm afraid that even as we integrate, we are walking into a place that does not understand that this nation needs to be deeply concerned with the plight of the poor and disenfranchised. Until we commit ourselves to ensuring that the underclass is given justice and opportunity, we will continue to perpetuate the anger and violence that tears the soul of this nation. I fear I am integrating my people into a burning house.[34]

SOVEREIGNTY-BASED SURVIVAL AS RAMPART

Though calculated as a threat to systemic American capitalism, sovereignty-based survival necessarily stands as a rampart against trauma-informed poverty. With no interest in integrating into a moral house on fire, sovereignty-based survival relates with communal moral imperatives to sustain life. By institutionalizing, in every sociopolitical arrangement, means to stem the tide of systemic unmetabolized trauma,[35] sovereignty-based survival embodies an alternative to social practices that generate poverty, that seduce groups/individuals to participate in objectifying transactional relationships, and that destroy human-included ecosystems. Replacing *object-member* axiology focused on the acquisition and maintenance of objects, *member-member* axiology relates to a strategic communal effort that at this moment in history must be given consideration. As groups of Black and Brown people are being forcibly relocated to new geographic spaces, and as poor people of European descent are reduced to political fodder, there is great need to intentionally develop holistically sustainable communities.

Beyond sustained biological existence and practice of cultural rituals as performance, strategic consideration ought to be given to developing networks of complex sociopolitical economies grounded in diverse axiologies of peoples. Our society needs to pivot on capacities to consistently institutionalize cultural ways of being and values in such a way that, in every aspect of concrete social practice, values reflective of ideological foundations are tutored. Beyond charity and mere existence, sovereignty-based survival is a strategic investment in systemic resilience and well-being.

Therefore, survival has never been, nor will it ever be, an individual endeavor. It is a communal task. As such, according to Jerome C. Ross, survival is established and maintained as seven requirements are fulfilled:[36]

Administrative structure	Sociopolitical arrangement designed for operation
Economic independence	Generation, acquisition, and management of community supplies and demands
Ideological standardization	Determination and establishment of rules with means to enforce and protect
Common language	Spoken tongue of group
Selective appropriation	Balance of extra-communal influences and intra-communal accommodation
People or population	Defined by shared values
Land or place	Physical and virtual and fortified

Practically constructed through an aggregation of Community Action Programming, *member-member* axiology, and Ross's "Requirements of Survival" can serve as a conceptual framework for how to *re-member* sovereignty-based survival. This is reminiscent of times after the Black Reconstruction, the Progressive Era in the North and Southwest, and the Freedom Movement strategizing when the ability to live with dignity became tenuous.[37] Such efforts toward self-sufficiency in the face of legislated segregation took the form of sovereignty-based survival. Threatened continually by the capitalistic need to eclipse systems of value and destroy economic independence, Black survival would thrive in many urban centers and rural locales. Beyond mere creation of Black communities (defined geographically as designated spaces), with values intact, people of African descent generated infrastructures of survival that would weather storms of racialized capitalism. Community-sustained micro-economies, sociopolitical might, limited assimilation into exploitative larger culture, and capacity to teach relationship-based values (primarily through cultural productions, schools, political organizations, and religious institutions)—these generated a "we-were- poor-but-we-didn't-know-we-were-poor" mindset and an ideology of resilience founded in core beliefs of sufficiency, requisite to building institutionalized loving-kindness.

With attention given to the seven tasks of survival, informed by *member-member axiology* sustained across three generations and structured based on Community Action Programming, sovereignty-based survival is the alternative giving rise to the reality that the opposite of poverty is not wealth, capitalistically defined; the opposite of poverty is survival, holistically constructed.

5

Excavating Darkness

Unearthing Memories as Spiritual Practice in the Service of Social Transformation

ALISON P. GISE JOHNSON AND VANESSA MONROE

> For each of us as women, there is a dark place within, where hidden
> and growing our true spirit rises, "beautiful / and tough as chestnut /
> stanchions against (y)our nightmare of weakness"[1] and of impotence.
>
> These places of possibility within ourselves are dark because they
> are ancient and hidden; they have survived and grown strong through
> darkness. Within deep places each of us holds an incredible reserve of
> creativity and power, of unexamined and unrecorded emotion and feel-
> ing. The woman's place of power within each of us is neither white nor
> surface; it is dark, it is ancient, and it is deep.[2]
>
> —Audre Lorde

Stories are darkness no longer hidden that expose true spirits as authentic sources of power to holistically transform spaces, emotions, and
communities. This excavated dark richness in the form of narrative is
sacred. The sacredness lies in its ability to complicate the definition of
life and love, pull us toward justice, redefine righteousness, and usher
us toward a sovereignty of the soul—if told without editing through
lenses of respectability or the source silencing invalidation of shame.
Composites of epigenetically lived complexities—some with details
too painful to fully remember; some with joys indescribable by words;
some ancestral, hovering above the level of consciousness; some rich
with strategic know-how—these unearthed parts of our darkness help
us to "remember what we never knew"[3] and morally tutor us toward
a good not yet fully realized. Like the gravitational pull of dark matter, there is an unilluminated force, an intrinsic longing for restorative
intimacy transcending superficially prescribed and often divisive sociocultural and religious interaction.

This longing, this sense of Spirit-led reunifying love, though at times
interrupted, silenced, or forced into dormancy by natural disaster,
trauma, or social othering, never dies. It simply awaits human archaeologists[4] who with great care expose pieces of varied pasts, weave them
together in the form of memories, and present them as thresholds that
bridge the human soul and ancestral spirits; archaeologists who host

divine encounters, convene redeeming dances with Spirit to undo the power of social and political othering,[5] and usher us into transformative wholeness.

This archaeological work is the work of soul friends[6] (whether artists, writers, academics, ministers, nurturers) that create pathways of remembrance and give permission to cross thresholds into authentic darkness, believing that, as Howard Thurman writes: "There is in every person an inward sea, and in that sea there is an island, and on that island there is an altar, and standing guard before the altar is the angel with a flaming sword. This is your crucial link with the Eternal. Nothing can get by that angel to be placed upon that altar unless it has the mark of your inner authority. What passes over the threshold is simonpure [completely genuine]."[7]

In this contemporary moment, when it seems love is lost and irrational divisive anger triumphs, there is still hope for soul sovereignty if given practices and pathways wherein we remember: "It is still possible to speak with our heart directly. Most ancient cultures know this. We can actually converse with our heart as if it were a good friend. In modern life we have become so busy with our daily affairs and thoughts that we have lost this essential art of taking time to converse with our heart."[8]

THRESHOLDS INTO DARKNESS: A METHOD

As soul friends who demystify, debunk, and disentangle socially constructed valleys, inherent is a sacred call to do the work of human archaeology. That involves unearthing intergenerational sacred memories and remnants of fractured experiences buried deep within each woman and inviting divine encounters. Of specific interest, as womanists, is constructing a methodological means of accessing memory as resource for spiritual practice that ushers us through the valleys of life. This spiritual practice is created for Black women experiencing unarticulated deep hunger to be free from internalized othering; free to explore our love for Spirit; free to love self, regardless; free to experience sovereignty of the soul.

Based on Katie Cannon's "dance of redemption,"[9] we married historical methods, biblical exegesis, storytelling, and womanist theology to create a womanist matrix[10] as resource for generating representations of the past that are invested in holding space for Spirit. Constituent to its use in general are two elements. The first dimension is a *conscientization narrative* developed by using divergent memories and myths, social histories, biographies, and archival sources to generate historical perspectives useful for ethical analysis, especially relating to constructive, culturally informed social and spiritual formation. Designed for consciousness-raising, not necessarily "historical accuracy," these stories are unapologetically subjective, passionate, and relational. The stories written impenitently depart from normative historical method, often written in dispassionate tones. That is, the subjective interpretations that accompany all representations of the past are not masked by claims of objectivity. In fact, impetus for creating the narrative arises out of real-lived experiences that do not align with expectations of how life ought to be; or are instigated in moments when wisdom is needed. These narratives are like the egg held by the Sankofa bird in that we are reaching into the past in order to move forward.

The second constituent element, *comprehensive analysis*, is characterized by (1) an overt investment in restoring didactic functions of histories/stories beyond purposes of apologetic or respectability, leaning more toward personal and communal constructive rebellion and rebuilding as sacred act; and (2) an analytical hope for expansion in the ways Spirit is viewed for the purpose of efficacy in nurturing womanist spiritual practice. The analysis looks to African cosmological considerations of Spirit for interpreting sacred texts and guidance toward constructing a restorative ethic of communal darkness,[11] where community "is a sacred phenomenon created by the Supreme God, protected by the divinities, and governed by the ancestral spirits."[12] For Black women, it is the space that invites us to release our darkness, giving rise to women's spirituality that leans into advocacy powered by a stripping away of social constructions of self and thus getting closer to reality, where the natural, the spiritual, and the divine assess the places where we walk. In this space, the commitment is to propagate the possibility of being a soul friend to someone else by releasing ourselves into availability.

RELEASING OUR DARKNESS

In African traditions, spiritual practice destroys distance between heaven and earth, between past and present, between temporal and eternal. As exemplification of the womanist matrix, it is a conscientization narrative, "Learning to Release." We unearth the life of Jochebed (mother of Moses),[13] found in the Hebrew narrative of Exodus. In this story a Levite woman gives birth during a time of legislated genocide. To save her child, she creates a basket, places him in it, and sets him afloat. The basket attracts the attention of Pharaoh's daughter; she sends her servants to retrieve the basket and, through a miraculous moment set in motion by an adolescent girl (the infant's sister), a contract is made for a Hebrew woman (Pharaoh's daughter does not know she is the child's mother) where the child will be breastfed, weaned, and returned to Pharoah's daughter to be raised.

In the creation of the narrative, the Hebrew story is paired with the parallel story remembered in Islamic tradition in the Qur'an. The sacred text begins with Firaun (the Islamic word for the Pharoah), who as leader has exalted himself and divided the people. In response, a "We" god convenes conversation with the mother of the baby, giving her insights as to what is required of her, understanding that in response she will feel overwhelmed, and offering her comfort with the promise that this well-thought-out plan will be beneficial in restoring balance.

Written as prose, details of the mythic memory are interpreted through the lens of lived experiences of Black women—some infertile, some forced to give up children and dreams conceived in inhospitable sociopolitical environments. More generally, in alignment with Cannon's *Dance of Redemption*, the origin of the idea for this conscientization narrative erupts from deep desires for ancient paradigms of liberation; longing for definitions of worship yielding possibilities for hosting Spirit; convinced that the practice will release the incredible reserve of one's own darkness for the survival of the whole community.

"LEARNING TO RELEASE": A WOMANIST MATRIX SAMPLE

She's coming for him soon.[14] His warm beautiful brown face snuggled against my fast-beating heart. I hold him close and long. She will come for him. Was it supposed to be easy for me because she paid me to do what every mother was created to do? Was I supposed to be eternally grateful because she drew him from the waters?

She's coming for him soon. I can't hate her. She could have left him to drown. She could have surrendered him to be killed. But no, she saved him. I can't hate her, but I surely despise systems that would put each of us in these god-awful positions: Her, charitably trying to save one baby; Me, having no chance nor resources to raise my own. I can't hate her, but my soul mourns his loss, though he still lives.

It's kind of strange. Seems so long ago when those of us who were pregnant were all excited. We stood in the court, touching one another's bellies, comparing sizes and shapes, guessing whether boy or girl. We compared notes on the changes in our bodies: stretch marks, tender breasts, and the inability to sleep. In the evenings, we compared bellies: some were just starting to show; some sat high and some low; some were humongous. We laughed.

"Come feel this!" one of us would shout when the mass began to move. What a miracle! Each of us knew it was a miracle when a baby reached full term. Well aware of the realities that not all women can conceive, not all women have conceived out of love, not all babies make it into this world alive or healthy. So as we laughed and dreamed and imagined, we also prayed. Prayed for our sisters whose wombs had not conceived such joy. Thankful for the possibility, thankful for the hope, thankful for each day that work did not cause irreparable harm to that which we carried within.

Knowing that we could never raise these babies without the help of other women, men, community, and ancestors. These weren't just our babies: they belonged to us all, to be nurtured by us all, and cared for and protected by us all. Despite enslavement, we knew that these beautiful gifts were being sent to help us fulfill our divine communal call.

Then came the day when all of our secret joy and empathetic prayers shifted into manipulative desperate subconscious calls to a seemingly silent irresponsive heaven, *Please God, not a boy, please God. Please give us girls. Yes, a girl that would not have to be hunted and killed because of an insecure pharaoh. Please, God, make it a girl.*

Labor began; and with every push, desperate insecurity gave way to profound gratefulness. There was no concern about sex or gender. There was only hope in what was happening. Life was pushing forth. Through pain and agony, new life crowned and was delivered.

And there he was, my boy, a beautiful boy. Looking deeply past his eyes, my heart leapt when seeing the rich darkness of his soul. "He is *good*," my own soul disclosed. *Good!* I knew what that meant. *Good*, meaning God has not made a mistake. Not perfect, but *good*. *Good*, meaning he has potential that is to be nurtured in the sacred circle of community. *Good*, meaning that I had to do everything in my power, by whatever means necessary, to reveal and fulfill his potential. He was *good!*

Without prayer or effort, Wisdom erupted, "Give him suck; then when you fear for him, cast him into the river and fear not, nor grieve; surely We shall bring him back to you and make him one of our messengers." As revelation gave way to vision, my heart saw Noah, building an ark. Without blueprint, without full understanding of what was to come, by faith he constructed a vessel designed to preserve a promise. Trusting revelation more than ridicule, plank by plank, nail by nail, he worked day and night in compliant confidence. And I knew I had to do the same.

It sounded crazy, and perhaps it seemed desperate, but I too started to build an ark to save the promise lying in my lap.

Wanting to escape having to explain the spirit voices that directed this mission, evening by evening, I created, in secret. Lit only by the light of the moon, I walked the water's edge and gathered reeds; and while they were yet pliable, I wove. Designing the basket to accommodate his length; fitting it snuggly to his swaddled frame; ensuring that his movement would not unintentionally cause the craft to capsize.

Over the course of many weeks, nightly, gazing at the sky as any priest could, I read the sacred text interpreted by the positions of every star, moon, and planet to know the patterns of water currents, to estimate the tides and the depths of water at particular points along the riverbank. I looked for the sign helping me to know when it was time to launch. In my mind, I charted the course of his voyage. In my secret moments, I reviewed the design details, reexamined the ark and rehearsed the launch, over and over. The day, I imagined, would be clear and the waters calm. On some level, not knowing exactly what would become of him, still, I practiced trusting. Trusting the "*We*" that promised his return.

Then occasionally, unexpectedly, out of nowhere, sadness loomed large like a storm rolling across the horizon. My focused master-building, interrupted. Memories of tears and screams of women suffering the trauma of legislated death of their babies rushed over my heart. Emotionally overwhelmed, deafened by the cacophony of life-destroying edicts looping in my head: "Kill the baby boys, kill all the baby boys!" Momentarily, experiencing paralysis, unable to move or hope or dream.

Depressed perhaps. Angry for sure. Unable to imagine what would be perceived as irresponsible, casting my own baby into the waters, feeling deep emptiness when considering the loss, I ceased weaving.

And then just as quickly, without warning, a warm undetectable wind whispered to my soul, "Give him suck; then when you fear for him, cast him into the river and fear not, nor grieve; surely. We shall bring him back to you and make him one of our messengers."[15] Peace arose, saving me from debilitating depression. Peace arose, silencing my own screams directed toward heaven. Peace, not denial of the atrocities. Peace, not loss of compassion for those around me. No, it was a peace that translated my anger into constructive action. With tears in my eyes, I returned to weaving. I wove the roots of a believed past with promises for a continued future. Faster and faster, I wove and planned and prepared, refusing to be paralyzed by fear of being found out. I wove without permission. I wove without the ordination of a committee. I wove motivated only by my gut instinct and rehearsed revelation.

I sealed it with rich black bitumen and pitch, created in sacred places. It was finished.

Looking toward the sky, I knew that the day had come when all preparation was complete. The only thing left to do was to release my hope into the arms of the waters. Kneeling. Swaddling him in his heritage-identifying blanket. Kissing him one more time, covering his ark of safety, I released him. Trusting that he would return. And he did.

But now, the day has come to release him, again. Never anticipated having to let him go twice. Never knew I could feel heaviness and hope at the same time.

She's coming for him soon. I'm trying not to hate her. She could have left him to drown or surrendered him to be killed, but just for a few moments he was given back to me, to nurse him, to nurture him.

But she's coming for him soon. I hold him. His warm beautiful brown face snuggled against my fast-beating heart. I hold him close and long. Finished nursing. Finished nurturing. Trusting that "*They*" will fulfill the promise. Fervently praying for his return—for *Good*, next time.

MINING THE DARKNESS

The power of the story is not just in the writing and the ability to weave a unified narrative together out of disparate sources. The conscientization narrative is designed to bring to the level of consciousness the reality of one's own darkness and the voice of the always-speaking Spirit(s) to be mined for resources that give guidance and transform valley experiences. Historian Nell Irving Painter, when trying to decide what her next book would be, had an encounter with a then-unknown spirit. She knew she wanted to write a biography, but she did not know about whom. She expressed the incident in this way:

Dr. Painter says that she had just finished her book on Hosea Hudson and was stretched out on a couch one day with her cats, trying to recoup while reading Arnold Rampersad's biography of Langston Hughes.

"I found it inspiring," she says.

"Then this voice came to me and said, 'Do me!'"

I said, "Who the hell are you?" It was Sojourner Truth.

That was in the mid-1980s. Asked how she felt when, after several years of research, she discovered that at least three other scholars were also working on biographies of Truth.

Dr. Painter says with a hint of a smile, "I like to think of the spirit of Sojourner Truth going about to likely biographers."[16]

In this process of writing soul narratives, we set out to provide a spiritual resource for Black women. As we entered the process fully, it was apparent that we encountered ancient Spirit(s) inviting the mining of our own darkness, which would connect us to one another and a Divine presence. The encounters offered three insights found in our darkness to be shared communally with those excavating darkness and soul friends supporting the effort: (1) There is need to redeem "*Let us/ We*" God, both male and female, to fully access darkness. (2) When serving as soul friend to Black women, collaboration is reclaimed as spiritual practice. (3) Spiritual practice is a tool inviting availability to hold space for deepening the darkness.

REDEEMING THE "LET US" GOD

When reading the Qur'an, we are introduced to a spiritual "*We*" that sees what is going on in society and directs Jochebed to act. This Divine Multiplicity would be disturbing to many if not already familiar with the "*Let us*" God in Genesis (1:26) who creates all facets of life in relationship for the sake of a sustainable environment. This "*Let us*" God seems to be the same as the "*We*" presence in the Qur'an. A plural God who becomes unified through the oneness of purpose to create with balance and be in intimate relationship with all of life, both male and female, animals and plants, earth and cosmos.

Other indigenous sacred memories retain understandings of the multiple unity of God, embracing gender and species differentiation. "God, you've been my mother and my father, my sister and my brother," the traditional prayer of historical African Americans proclaims. Great

Mother and Father Spirits found in all of nature are central to the faiths of indigenous peoples, globally. When we are courageous enough to wrestle the faith from man-only-ness and secure enough to suspend the need to focus energy on justifying or abhorring the presence of women in ministry, we invite re-membering the Divine "*We*" of "*Let us*" create humankind in our image and likeness, both male and female. Though the image embodying both male and female is important, beyond apologetic, the richness is an invitation to collaboration.

RECLAIMING COLLABORATION AS SPIRITUAL PRACTICE

Black people, yet more specifically Black women, are thought to be deeply religious. What is not as easily assessed is the ability of Black women to access authentic spirituality, primarily because many spiritual practices considered normative are not the ways in which Black women mine their darkness or commune with divine presence(s). Alone, silent, and praying can be embraced by Black women, but to some degree it may be a hard sell. Black women can engage those practices; but we wonder, Are there other ways that the authentic may be accessed? In Africana traditions, it is the call and response of a relational God found in "the stillness at the core of the shout, the pause in the middle of the 'amen,' as first steps toward restoration."[17]

In 2020, I (Vanessa) convened what I called Lenten Rhythms for my multiracial church. I designed it as a space to journey through the Lenten season in some rather typical ways: fasting, prayer, and so on. Only Black women came, some of whom had no idea about spiritual practices of Lent. But for those who did, there was resistance. Lent was equated with sacrifice. As people who rarely get to hold on to anything, as a group they had no interest in "giving up" anything when everyday life represented a litany of invitations to sacrifice; or they just didn't feel as if they had anything left to give up. The first night, on the spot, I was forced to go back to the drawing board to rethink Lent for this group (artist, corporate executives, new college graduates): in a split second I remembered the unexpected outcome of "Learning to Release," an invitation to collaboration. Without preparation, instead of discussing fasting or any other practice, the assignment for the week became this: "As soon as you awaken, say, 'Good morning, God. Thank you for inviting me into this day to collaborate with You, and You with me.'"

One week later, when the women reported back, their lives had shifted how they walked into jobs, and relationships changed. No longer focused on partnering with people who were not sure about the value of these Lenten Rhythms participants, no longer feeling unsure about divine presence, these women experienced shifts in what it meant to be persons of faith(s) and what that looked like in daily life. Overwhelmingly, they accepted a resource to quench their longing for divine closeness and real presence.

As Black women forged in a *member-member* axiology, spirituality is grounded in a relationship with a God who invites collaboration, welcomes us into each day, and journeys with us toward wholeness and healing. We easily accept that the God of the universe is near to us. We've seen Spirit in the stories of our mothers and grandmothers, those who lived while making a way out of no way; we come to understand that ours is a rich tradition of relationship with the Spirit who collaborates with us. Organically the spiritual practice of collaboration aligned with the four-element womanist methodology articulated by Delores Williams in reflection of the four-part definition of womanism created by Alice Walker. Constituent to the Williams method are the following: (1) a multidialogical intent, (2) a liturgical intent, (3) a didactic intent, and (4) a commitment both to reason and to the validity of female imagery and metaphorical language in the construction of theological statements.[18] To be sure, we wanted that to be the outcome for women who would happen upon "Learning to Release," but the analytical surprise was that the darkness provided space for both God-talk and for God to talk. Spirit did not only show up to help: in fact, Spirit voiced a need for help. In the narrative and in the lives of Black women, Spirit(s) shows up and issues an invitation to collaborate with a "Let us/We" God typically overlooked in biblical reading and spiritual formation. This therefore suggests a deepening of the darkness that extends the idea of restoring relationships beyond normative forgiveness motifs or evincing of Spirit limited to a manifestation of force, a unifying presence of a small marginalized group, or an unexpected power devoid of commitments to social transformation.

DEEPENING THE DARKNESS

Deepening the darkness is an unanticipated outcome of spiritual direction. Extending the expectations of spiritual practices for relieving stress, ushering in a sense of contentment, or changing the way one looks at the world simply to be able to navigate, this idea of deepening darkness holds space for Spirit to deepen capacities of relationality. Humans access needed resources to unearth their darkness, finding wisdom and peace; and Spirit enlists those who become available to collaborate in the institutionalization of peace. There is therefore a transition from *sensus numinous* (God manifesting divine character in perceivable ways to humankind) to *sensus communis* (invitation/expectation to multiply the experience systemically through divinely inspired strategies in spaces devoid of the nature of the divine, which is clearly revealed in darkness). As unearthed in the conscientization narrative "Learning to Release" and in the lives of the women who gathered to participate in Lenten Rhythms, evinced is an observable schemata: This *"Let us/ We"* Spirit(s) intentionally disrupts patterns of exploitation grounded in division that compromises collaborative social relationships.

In the work of spiritual direction, the one called to watch over the journey of another is considered Soul Friend. In Black women's spiritual practices informed by collaboration, soul friendship is multiplied. It is extended to those open to excavating darkness, with the unexpected invitation to become soul friend to the Divine.

6

Rooted Woman or Root Woman

One Black Woman's Story at the Intersection of Earth, Faith, and Action

FAITH B. HARRIS

UPROOTED

> It began with theft; we must never forget that the land was being taken and the animals captured and killed at monstrous rates and the plants and landscapes were being altered irreversibly over decade after decade, and century after century. Peoples in the colonized world were being forced to think of themselves in disorienting ways, away from the land, away from the animals, and into racial encasements, forced to isolate their bodies from the land now turned to private property. Christians forced them to do this and imagined this was the right thing to do because this is how we saw things—isolated bodies and privatized land.
>
> —William James Jennings[1]

The question for our time and people of the African diaspora located in the United States and elsewhere is this: Just what does climate change have to do with us?

The above statement is a critical ethical question especially for African peoples and generally for the two-thirds world. It is crucial because it has everything to do with how the people of the African diaspora (and the two-thirds world) will fare economically, politically, socially, environmentally, and spiritually in the face of the climate crisis. I have heard this question from my Black and Brown community more times than I can remember. It is both an interrogation of climate change and a challenge for justice. They interrogate not the reality of climate change but how in the mainstream it is disconnected and disoriented from their lives. They challenge the efficacy of asking Black and Brown folks to offer solutions or sacrifice their upward mobility to stave off the inevitable. They know it is inevitable because they suffer from the craven greed and demonarchy that brought the climate crisis on us. They recognize that they are latecomers to the table of greed that fostered environmental exploitation and devastation. They know that neither they nor their ancestors were the benefactors of this exploitation. They know that their grandparents and great-grandparents were also exploited as commodities, raw resources, beasts of burden, and labor. They also know that during the late nineteenth century, the engines of industry revved forward, sucking up natural resources, reconfiguring them, and spewing them out as new products for consumption in mass quantities; yet their families were, for the most part, excluded from the benefits.

At the start of the industrial age, most of our grandparents were still in the fields of the South, producing cotton and tobacco, as sharecroppers earning barely enough for subsistence. Their challenge to me suggests, "We can't be held accountable for the way this capitalist machine has made all life a commodity." After all, as Charles Long argues, Black bodies were among the first mass commodities of capitalism.[2] These Black bodies, both women and men, had their own cultures, languages, religions, and practices until the introduction of European traders. So they were taken to stone fortifications or factories on the coast of West Africa, to be manufactured into slaves and packaged in the hulls of ships and sent to the new world for purchase as raw material, tools, a natural resource from the so-called dark continent. The English, French, Spanish, Portuguese, Italians, and Dutch under the authority of kings and popes brought those Black bodies to this hemisphere for the project of structuring a new world economy for and by the new disorder:

> The new imperial disorder rises arrogantly over the bones of the bodies of conquered children, women, and men. The bodies of the indigenous peoples were the first to be sacrificed, eliminated, and contained; then the body of the earth was raped and mastered; finally, the bodies of yellow, brown, poor white, and Black children, women, and men were squeezed through the winepress of "new" empire-building. Globalization, the dominative process of empire, now cannibalizes the bodies, the labor, and creativity . . . of global Others. In sacrilegious anti-liturgy, the agents of empire hand over red, yellow, brown, white, Black, and poor bodies to the tyranny of neoliberal capitalism, to the consuming forces of the market.[3]

Surely, I am told, we have no part in a discussion of the way our climate is warming after nearly 600 years of colonial expansion and 150 years of intense carbon output. The extractive, exploitive economy of the empire mindlessly drums on, sucking up more and more of the earth's resources to be consumed in its insatiable quest for wealth: that is the problem. After all, Black, Brown, and indigenous folk are still working through the social, psychological, and cultural trauma

resulting from these previous historical exploits of empire on our ancestors and continued even to this generation.

We are entangled in the reality of faster climate change from the
very beginning of early modern colonialism. Those colonial forces initi-
ated the acceleration of temperature rise with the deforestation, introduction of alien species from other regions into the conquered places,
genocide, burning of fossil fuels, killing off species, polluting water,
farming with monocultural practices, and extracting industries. These
practices, which brought us to our current crisis, involve us and impact
us. We will never forget New Orleanians' experience with Hurricane
Katrina, who are still, more than fifteen years later, in recovery. Katrina
was a watershed moment for many, like me, now dedicated to environmental justice. We know that becoming a refugee in our land could
happen at any moment due to severe weather and systemic racism.

Black and Brown children experience much higher rates of asthma
than any other group. Richmond ranks as the third asthma capital among
U.S. capitals. In Flint, Michigan, at least two generations of children will
suffer brain damage from the city's water fiasco. Although not directly
a result of climate change, it a clear example of environmental injustice
and the capitalistic exploitive impulse described by the Copeland quote
above. In the state where I live, Virginia, are ten thousand miles of coast-
line threatened by rising sea level, and the vast majority of the people
living in low-lying areas are Black and Brown or of low wealth. They are
only a storm surge away from ruin and refugee status.

Copeland characterizes the present capitalist economies, which con-
sume all to feed its insatiable greed for power and trinkets. We are
entangled because what is at stake is more than our homes, livelihood,
and communities. What is at stake is life as we know it. At stake is the
survival and thriving of future generations. At stake is the very mandate embedded in the fabric of life to be free and flourish. If we are to
embrace the fullness of life, we must flesh out a sustaining theology and
ethic that puts us in the right relationship with Earth and our neighbor.
A womanist vision of wholeness, radical freedom, and active participation in the beloved community or "kin-dom" is a viable response.
This term is employed by Ada Maria Isasi-Díaz: "Kin-dom became the
language she used to describe God's *libertad*, the liberation of God at
work among people, the good news for those who suffer at the hands
of kings."[4] Such a response will require embracing a fully actualized
liberation that acknowledges the rightful inclusion of the whole of life:
human, animal, plant, air, water, and soil as a constituent to kin-dom.

EARTH

Genesis 1 and 2 offer two distinct narratives or storied metaphors for creation. Both reports place human beginnings in a garden. In these stories,
we find that the garden is the locus for divine-human interaction. Humans
first meet the Deity in the garden setting. The garden is also a metaphor
for Earth, the ideal locus for a social system designated for flourishing. The
garden is not merely the human home but also a holy ground for human
and divine fellowship. It is in the garden where humans first connect to
the world of spirit. In the garden, humans receive divine guidance for life.
They learn what to eat and what is not good to eat. It is in the garden where
humans learn about vocation. The vocational mandate given is to be care-
takers and stewards of the earth. This first vocational mandate sets the tone
and lens for sustainability and liberation. We are not all called to be farm-
ers. Still, the vocation for everyone—even in today's overpopulated, highly
technical, and digital information-driven society—is that even the most
technologically based work should be approached with care for Earth, our
garden, as an ultimate good. Our inventions, by-products, use of natural
resources, as well as how much waste, what kinds of waste, and the means
we use to dispose of waste—these should all be viewed through the lens of
their impact on the health of all living.

The "garden" (Gen. 2) was also the sacred setting where humans were
introduced to their spiritual source: relationships and interrelationships
of human to creatures, human to earth, human to human, and human to
the divine: all these began in the context of the garden. In this second creation narrative, all the creatures were brought to the human for naming
and determining whether they were suitable partners or helpmates. This
story is not suggesting that a bear, tiger, or lion might be the right partner
for the human. But instead, it is a lesson for the reader. It demonstrates
how valued the animals were and how interrelated and interconnected
human and animal life should be. The garden narratives suggest that the
Creator had in view a political, social, and economic system designed for
human flourishing. It was intended to be a system based on relationship,
care, interconnectedness, and responsibility.

SOCIAL ECONOMICS

Walter Brueggemann, in his book *Sabbath as Resistance: Saying No to
the Culture of Now,* makes the case that the fourth commandment is
the interpretive link for the first three commandments prescribing

relationship to the Deity and the last six prescribing relationships toward neighbor (Exod. 20).[5] Sabbath-keeping, as mandated in the fourth commandment, was never an arbitrary rule for religious piety or to demonstrate fealty but instead was the intended basis for economic, political, social, cultural, and spiritual life. The commandment to keep the seventh day as a Sabbath, a day of rest, is a covenantal imperative that, among other things, reveals the biblical socioeconomic system, according to Brueggemann.

The law of the Sabbath is an economic system for the sake of the whole Earth. This Sabbath economic system was in stark contrast to the system operating in Egypt, where there had been no end to the taskmasters' coercion to provide cheap labor. There were ever-increasing quotas to fulfill the demands of the Pharaoh's greed. The children of Israel were tools in a system of acquisitiveness where the Pharaoh and a very few elites amassed material wealth.[6] The man Moses came bearing an invitation to kin-dom and a new socioeconomic system and faith. The God of Moses promised liberation from the tyranny of endless work and misery. The God of Moses pledged to give them a land teeming with milk and honey. The God of Moses pledged to guarantee a collective sense of identity and a sense of belonging for them. The God of Moses promised relationship and ritual to provide meaning and healing for all.

In contrast to the endless labor they had experienced in Egypt under Pharaoh, the people of faith were to rest on the seventh day to acknowledge the goodness of God's provision, to reconnect, to put into sync and balance the communal relationships among servants and householders, as well as the environment. This day of rest was also for their servants and their animals, and a Sabbath year was stipulated for the land (Lev. 25). All living things, all parts of creation, were owed a time of rest and restoration because, in the Sabbath's political and social economy, there was to be equity. Survival was contingent on relationships and cooperation. All were interrelated, having come from the same source. Although the benefits of rest are clear, there is far more to the fourth commandment than a day of relaxation. The fourth commandment flattens hierarchies and makes equal the status of all life and land together. The Sabbath was designated as a time to celebrate and acknowledge life as a valued gift, to be respected and cherished.

An additional lesson from Sabbath economics is that prosperity derived from the land without reverence for the ground leads to the belief that a person is autonomous and communal relationships are unneeded. It leads to the arrogance of "I built this" and "I made this" rather than an acknowledgment that wealth is a communal effort based on an original gift and Giver. The day of the Sabbath rest acknowledges that all life is of the earth and dependent on the same earth. It is a reminder that people, nature, and animals are not raw commodities, exploited for the endless production of wealth. Sabbath is rather a weekly reminder that security is based on the right relationships to the divine, nature, and neighbor. Sabbath is an opportunity to realign and to balance human life with all other life. Whenever persons are out of sync with their environment, they become anxious and try to purchase security for themselves through amassing things and wealth. These attempts lead to the exploitation of creation and neighbor. The fourth commandment aligns reverence for the Creator with the value and intrinsic worth of all life. The Sabbath law was designed to make clear that humans, the environment, and animals are all our neighbors and deserving of the fullness of life. The Sabbath law is a metaphorical lens for organizing politics, economics, and religious life.

Today's economic systems, like those of Egypt, are impossibly coercive and antithetical to a Sabbath economy. This coercive economic system fosters anxiety to acquire more and more. There is no limit to the greed, covetousness, and competition in such economic systems. In summary, Brueggemann argues that systems based solely on the acquisition of material goods will eventually turn neighbors into competitors because life, when based on production, will need to structure the relationships into either producers or consumers. This structure destroys the fabric of mutuality and devalues the environment, the land, the earth. Land and its resources in such an economic system are simply property to be possessed, bought, sold, and endlessly exploited for wealth. Life on the land, understood as a birthright, inheritance, and gift, is opposed to this sort of exploitation.

ROOTED: MY ECOWOMANIST STORY

According to bell hooks, "The wild spirit of unspoiled nature worked its way into the folk of the backwoods, an ancestral legacy, handed down from generation to generation. And its fundamental gift was the cherishing of that which is most precious, freedom. And to be fully free, one had to embrace the organic rights of earth."[7]

Our current climate crisis is a result of an anti-Sabbath economy and social structure. A Sabbath economy values mutuality, care, interconnectedness, and interdependence with all life. A Sabbath social structure reverences the wild spirit of unspoiled nature and the organic rights of earth. These are ecowomanist values as well. Melanie Harris, in *Ecowomanism: African American Women and Earth-Honoring Faiths*, employs Kimberly Ruffin's coined term *beauty to burden* as a paradigm for expressing African Americans' historical relationship with the earth.[8] "Beauty" is named because the earth, especially the earth where one is born, represents home and a place of deeply held spiritual connection. For many African Americans, the South is that special place of connection to the earth, thus as home. The "burden" in the paradigm stems from the reality that in the same place where one might feel the sense of home and spirit, there was slavery, Jim Crow terror and oppression, the violence of lynching, and being driven off the land.

This notion of *beauty to burden* has a particular resonance for me. Only recently did I learn of my deep connections to Virginia and North Carolina. Curiously, by way of a DNA test, I discovered information about my patrilineal line previously unknown to me. Deep familial connections were broken for my family with my father's generation. My patrilineal great-grandparents with their eight children left North Carolina for Pittsburgh, Pennsylvania, in the first wave of the *great migration*, arriving around 1915.[9] The same is true for my matrilineal line. My great-grandparents left Amherst County, Virginia, for Pittsburgh, arriving about the same time.

My matrilineal grandparents maintained loose connections with their Virginia family while, as far as I know, my father's grandparents did not. My father made his career choice with the U.S. Army, enlisting, like so many, during World War II. We never lived in Pennsylvania, North Carolina, or Amherst County, Virginia, near family as I was growing up. We rarely visited family. I have a vague memory of a trip to Virginia to see my mother's distant relatives, but it was very brief, I was very young, and no lasting connections were made for me. I can count the times I was in the company of my father's father. My father's biological mother passed away shortly after he was born. I knew only one of the three women my grandfather married after her death. She was the woman who raised my father and his sister. I never met my mother's father; he had left or died long before I was born. My mother's mother was the closest of all my grandparents to us. She moved to New Jersey when diabetes forced her to stop working as a live-in housekeeper and cook for a wealthy Pittsburgh family.

My research into my genealogy opened a new understanding of the *beauty-to-burden paradigm.* As an African American with a graduate-level education in practical theology and Christian social ethics, I knew that my story in some way tied to slavery, the South, and the land. But the only experiential knowledge I had of that story came from a conversation among my grandmother's brothers, my mother, and aunts during the repast after my grandmother's funeral. They argued about who would pay the taxes on land in Virginia now that my grandmother was no longer living to do so. I didn't know, at that time, how vital their decision to "let it go" would be for me. That decision cut me and my siblings and the generations after me off from the opportunity to go home as so many are doing in the *new great migration* southward. Their fateful decision and the disruptive nature of army life combined to leave me with a profound sense of rootlessness. I often felt that I was spontaneously generated. I had very few connections to my extended family. I rarely saw or heard about my mother's siblings. I remember meeting only three out of her ten brothers and sisters. My father had one sister, who had a son. The family narrative of them was "they had disappeared." Through genealogy research, I learned that she, Pauline, had also joined the Women's Army Corps during World War II. She was married after discharge and moved to Ohio with her new family. I didn't know I had seven great-uncles and great-aunts on my father's side living in Pittsburgh until the DNA test and genealogical research results. I suspect the disorientation of the entire family migration to the North, breaking ties with the earth-home family identity, wreaked its havoc.

According to Melanie L. Harris, "Ecowomanists base their theology and ethics with ecomemory, which is the collective or individual memory of the earth and relationship to and with the earth. It can be a collective set of values that guide the earth commitments of an entire community or a singular story that reflects themes or values about the environment and one's connection to the earth. In many cases, ecomemory is passed down through different generations and considered a part of family and communal legacy and intellectual heritage."[10]

Rootedness is established from the experiences, stories, and tales of the parents and grandparents or possibly from memories of working in the garden with a parent on family land. I am a second-generation urbanite. My mother and father did not have a memory of the South and living on family-owned land since they were both born in the North, in Pittsburgh. My sketchy ecomemory is rooted in the stories: my mother often talked about her mother's *victory garden.* Victory gardens were planted in urban areas at the government's encourage-ment during World War II, when the nation's production and dis-tribution efforts were harnessed for the war and troops. I suspect my grandmother had a garden pre-war and post-war as well. My mother's story always described how beautiful and delicious the fruits and veg-etables were from her mother's garden. Nostalgically and wistfully, she would tell that story of days when everyone around them was poor but always had fresh and good food to eat from their gardens. She would tell the story with a twinkle in her eyes and her head held high. I could almost taste a blackberry or smell the soil on her hands. Her stories passed down to me are my ecomemories. They were so embedded in my psyche that, the first year I bought my home, I planted a garden, with absolutely no know-how but with intuition and those ecomemo-ries as my guide.

I don't know the specific reasons my two-family lines picked up everything and moved to Pittsburgh around the same time and from different states. I can speculate that it had everything to do with Jim Crow laws and the resurgence of the KKK. I found my patrilineal great-grandfather listed on the 1900 U.S. Census as a farmer in Hen-derson, North Carolina; twenty years later he was listed as living in Pittsburgh, working as a laborer. I knew there had to be a critical rea-son for him to uproot his wife and seven children (some already mar-ried) and bring them to Pittsburgh. He left the beauty of the land and his spiritual home to become a mere laborer in Pittsburgh's racist and oppressive city. My research continues to learn those reasons and the story of their life in North Carolina. On my mother's side, it seems that siblings migrated, but parents remained in Virginia. Maybe their move was based on leaving the farm for what they hoped would be more opportunity than being driven off their land. But they, too, lost their rootedness and connections to the ground. My mother pieced together earth connections by tending her mother's *victory garden* and looking for hickory nuts and poke salad [sallet] greens whenever we were near wooded areas during the rest of her life.

In her book *Belonging: A Culture of Place*, bell hooks tells of growing up in the backwoods of Kentucky with her grandparents. "*To tend the earth is always then to tend our destiny, our freedom, and our hope.*"[11] The freedom she writes about is the profound sense of rootedness to earth and spiritual strength from the earth I have experienced in my garden or while camping outdoors in the woods. Besides my daily excursions into the wooded area behind the army base where I lived as a child, my

first wilderness camping trip was when I experienced both wild freedom and belonging simultaneously. Wilderness camping taught me
about purifying water to drink, keeping gear safe from bears, fishing
and scavenging for berries, and cooking outdoors. The lessons learned
(mostly about myself) prepared me for travel to Israel and Africa, where
amenities like clean bathrooms were rarely available. It also taught me
about interdependence; everyone on our trip had a critically vital role
in keeping us safe, fed, and hydrated. At night, after eating and securing the camp gear high in trees and lying on my back, looking up
at the star-filled sky, I knew I was part of a grand system of life. I
knew survival on this planet was challenging but satisfying when in
harmony with the community. I knew, as Melanie Harris suggests, that
I was "*bound connected to the earth in divine relationship with the sacred
earth*";[12] or, as bell hooks expressed it, was "*cherishing, . . . embracing
the organic rights of the earth.*"[13]

The valuing of the earth and cherishing my connection to the earth
through ecomemory does not allow me to gloss over discovering the
exploitation of my ancestors when slavery for African bodies was the
law. I was stunned to find one James Wyche, listed as my fourth great-
grandfather in my ancestry search. James Wyche, a white plantation
owner's estate, included my third great-grandfather, Albert Wyche
(a mulatto), and thirty-two other individuals willed to James's white
children after his 1845 death. Stunning is the incredible perversion of
willing your children from an unknown slave to your white children.
The perversion is the way Black women's bodies were sources for the
extractive economy, whether through violent rape, coercion, or simply
exploitation of the privileges of white male supremacy. The children
sired by this white plantation owner and born to this unknown slave
were mere commodity, possessions passed down along with furniture,
horses, and farm tools. Who was she? What is her story? Her designa-
tion is the hint, "unknown slave," but she had a name. She had an
origin. She had roots somewhere.

The United Church of Christ declares, "Advocacy is an action taken
by individuals, groups, or organizations to defend, support, or protect
others. Generally, advocacy is standing with or standing for a person or
group that is disadvantaged or denied justice in society. In the effort to
bring about justice, advocacy may include education, affecting public
policy, joining coalitions, and participating in nonviolent direct actions.
Effective advocacy enables and supports individuals and groups working
to correct the injustices or abuses to which they are subjected."[14]

My story is rooted in the *burden* of the paradigm of *beauty and burden.* The burden of carrying within my lineage the terrors of this unnamed African woman also drives my advocacy for the earth, climate, and environmental justice. I used to view my story as an extension of the Black church's work during the 1960s Civil Rights Movement and, more generally, including liberation, feminist, and womanist theology. However, that movement was to remove the vestiges of slavery and Jim and Jane Crow from our Black life in America. The African American church has been given much credit as a model for human rights and liberation worldwide. Yet we seem to remain in a perpetual state of threat to our free existence as a people in this country and world. In addition, the Black church has yet to embrace fully that Black women are full partners in the co-creation of the community. The Black church has remained anchored to the white supremacist theology and reading of the biblical texts of its white fundamentalist peers. My friend William Lamar describes the many (not all) Black churches "as white fundamentalist evangelicals in Black Face." It has not meaningfully engaged the movement to stave off the coming climate crisis. It has not made rectifying environmental injustice a priority, although both issues are about the survival and thriving of its constituents.

Wati Longchar, a South Asian theologian, defines liberation theology in his essay "Liberation Theology and Indigenous Peoples": "*Liberation is the struggle against the systems and structures that disrupt the purposes of God for humanity and the whole of creation.*"[15] We know that some Black preachers have provided this assurance of God's ultimate liberation as early as the brush arbor meetings. When the enslaved Africans would sneak away to worship and practice their religion out of the vision of the overseer and landowners, they knew liberation. Ecowomanism calls for us to expand and deepen that commitment to freedom, reclaiming the land as an integral part of the community.

Longchar makes two critical points for our consideration. First, he suggests that "the Bible is a book about the community and its stories of struggle against oppression and domination. . . . The exodus event is a collective experience of liberation for the people of Israel. . . . God's liberating activities—God's interventions and immediate, intimate encounters—take place in the community of persons"[16] and not simply with and for individuals. They also include stories of Jesus in the New Testament, a liberator in the time of Roman rule, and accounts of the Sadducees' and the Pharisees' corrupt religious domination of the poor, widowed, blind, and sick among the children of Israel. He suggests that these narratives are not messages about individual or personal salvation or about a list of dos and don'ts. "Let my people go" implies that God "is interested in community salvation from oppression and devastation and not individualized personal salvation." Therefore, our liberation work is to save communities, not merely individuals. We are responsible for collective action to relieve the oppression caused by a system and structure that exploits, dominates, coerces competition and individualism, and destroys the people's land.

Longchar continues his definition of complete liberation theology by examining indigenous peoples who are not only communal but also are intimately connected to space and land. "Despite the cultural and ethnic diversity, indigenous communities all over the world share striking similarities . . . of cosmology, religion, customs, ideology, and worldviews, . . . and most importantly, they share a special relationship with the land. The land is the basis for the social organization, economic system, and cultural identification." The land is sacred because it is understood as a cocreator with God, as suggested in Genesis 1:24, where the text reads, "And God said, 'Let the earth bring forth living creatures of every kind.'" It was the earth that partnered with God in creation. The land also provides an identity for the people. The people belong to the land as much as the land belongs to them. The land is the temple where people become one with sacred power, ancestors, spirits, and other living creatures. The garden narratives echo this truth.[17] Longchar makes a critical point for liberation theology, connecting it with land and indigenous people. He declares that indigenous people only understand land ownership in the broader communal sense. While they know that the land ultimately belongs to the divinity, they believe that all have equal rights and freedom to live on and benefit from the land. This view is strikingly different from our contemporary understanding of the land. Many who are liberationists have not thought of land or factored an ethic of the land into their theology. As acknowledged earlier, quoting Brueggemann, land in the culture of now is owned, bought, sold, and exploited by individuals. Land in the capitalist system is used for the wealth it provides individuals, but this is not so with indigenous peoples. Longchar cites a tribe of the Naga people of India, where they call their supreme being *Lijaba*. Li means land or soil, and *jaba* means real, so for the Naga people, Lijaba implies that the supreme being is "the real soil." They believe that the supreme being enters the soil or indwells in the soil with the seeds planted and rises again with the crops as they mature for harvest. There is much to be mined from this metaphor; one thought is how this idea of the supreme being echoes the sentiment of Isaiah 6:3 that "the whole earth" is a manifestation of the Creator's glory. Being connected to the land/soil is being connected to the source of all life: the Creator. In the Naga people's worldview, the soil, the earth, the environment is the dwelling place of god and humans and animal life. How curious that in our Western Christian theology, we place God outside and above the earth to remain unsullied by the created life teeming in the soil. We sterilize God to the point of extinction from our relationship to the world.

I am convinced that justice for the earth is the key to liberation and human dignity and fullness of life for Black people. In my view, harmony with the land is the starting point for theology and the search for liberation. Therefore, the first act of liberation is the identification of a physical place as the spiritual, cultural grounding of faith. A green gospel includes the land. It recognizes the importance of green spaces, where fruit trees and vegetable gardens may be planted and where landmarks may mark places for performing rituals and instilling identity and tradition. The faith community that expresses rootedness, identity, mutuality, and connectedness with the environment and to the people where it is positioned will be a liberating presence for the entire community.

As an ecowomanist, I eschew economics that exploits human, animal, and environment, which fosters an ever-increasing desire for more material goods and wealth. Ecowomanists recognize that God's vocational call, even for our times, is to care for the earth. Ecowomanists call for radical communion with the earth, where the earth is understood as the locus for our rootedness, political and cultural identity, social and religious practices, and the place where the divine dwells. Viewing theology through an ecowomanist lens calls for reviving the original principles of the Genesis garden narratives. *First,* this view rejects the only centuries-old Protestant evangelical doctrine of personal and individual salvation in favor of the biblical communal salvation of entire peoples found in the book of Exodus. *Second,* the doctrine of dominion that commodifies every aspect of our lives is replaced by the biblical and radical inclusive interdependence of all life as witnessed in the garden narrative and in the mandate of the fourth commandment for a Sabbath economy and politics. *Finally,* the excessive emphasis on praise and worship needs to be refocused to embrace the prescription for full proactive prophetic participation in the public square for justice. Amos cries, "*Let justice roll down like waters, and righteousness like an ever-flowing stream*" (5:24, emphasis added).

We need a shift of our theological perception from somewhere in the heavens to the earth, where we live, work, play, and love. We recognize and embrace the vision of the first humans in the garden, walking and talking with the divine. However, we cannot graft an earth-centered concept onto otherworldly doctrine. In our theological constructs, divinity must move from outside of the universe to incarnate the world. If our beliefs suggest a god above, away from the everyday life we live, we will struggle with environmental injustice because we will not see this world as sacred. If the divine is not here with us, we will never see here as holy.

PART THREE

Womanist Ways of Leading

7

Walking through the Valley

A Leadership Exemplar

PAULA OWENS PARKER

A colleague who has a successful career in leadership development once shared with me that "direction, protection, and purpose are key ingredients of a great leader." When asked to say more, she explained that a great leader inspires and energizes people to achieve success through reaching common goals in a connected and cohesive way, thus giving direction. They put in place measures to protect themselves, their people, and their organization; they promote ethical interactions among team members, thus providing protection. The core component of a great leader's role is in creating, defining, and implementing clear structures and processes that enable everyone around them to know what to do next, thus giving order. In this way, a leader can set up the team for success, encouraging freedom for workers to move on their own volition, with agility in their thinking, with everyone connected to one another's work and contribution. A leader can delegate tasks to the team, thus creating depth in knowledge and personal growth. Effective leaders provide clarity and ensure that the team is equipped with resources needed to maximize the team's potential and is informed by an understanding of deliverables and project deadlines. During our conversation, I thought of Dr. Katie Geneva Cannon and how she modeled these essential leadership concepts in her classroom.

Prompted by this conversation, I was inspired to learn more about the adaptive leadership model to which my colleague referred. In their chapter "The Theory behind the Practice," Ronald Heifetz, Alexander

Grashow, and Marty Linsky suggest that adaptive leadership (1) offers change that enables the capacity to thrive, (2) builds on the past, (3) occurs through experimentation, (4) values diversity, and (5) takes time.[1] Dr. Cannon, the ultimate academic and organic scholar, exemplified all these skills and more. She bequeaths insights and valuable lessons on leadership to us; from which we can continue to learn.

CHARTING PATHS: REMEMBERING WHAT WE NEVER KNEW

The Womanist Theology Primer: Remembering What We Never Knew; The Epistemology of Womanist Theology, written by Cannon in 2001, invites readers to consider conditions required to recall what is not necessarily obvious or a part of one's conscious awareness. She acknowledged that some people would wonder aloud whether what she poses is a semantic paradox, an oxymoron, or just a mixed-up verbal quibble. Nevertheless, she chose the title to illustrate the point that womanist theology is a composite picture of history and pedagogy, with the multilayered experiences of Black women who want to make their religious truth claims and theo-ethical praxis intelligible to the world by explaining the connection between our doing, knowing, and being.[2]

To remember what I never knew compels me to think about being in situations with which I felt familiar but with which I had no memory, having instant connections with persons whom I had never encountered, or reading something and wondering how the author knew my exact thoughts. What comes to mind is a sense of awareness of the larger dimensions of existence. It is time-twisting, mind-twisting consciousness, a synchronicity of the past, present, and future. Some would call it a kairos moment, an inbreaking into another dimension.

Although the history of enslaved Black women in the United States reveals abuse, exploitation, separation, and suffering, many used their resources of biblical imagery, spirituals, African traditions, and mother wit to survive, develop self-esteem, protect themselves, and speak truth. These enslaved Black women developed survival strategies, despite oppression and marginalization, to protect and empower themselves, their families, and their people. The insular character of enslaved life fostered a sense of community among many persons of African descent. Enslaved women created a support network to share life responsibilities, such as childcare, healthcare, and religious ceremonies. This mutual association with each other created a strong network among Black women. Drawing on combined resources of tradition, instinct, and necessity, Black women rose to the challenge of creating institutions desperately needed within their communities.[3] They joined together—especially after the withdrawal of Union troops from former Confederate States—forming clubs, societies, and associations to face their newfound freedom and navigate life in a white male-dominated world.[4] Together these women fought quietly for reform as they combated stereotypes and sought to uplift one another. The overarching aim of Black women's clubs was to elevate the social standing of their race through personal betterment. The character of these clubs was formed around interests and skills of women and community needs. Missions included kindergartens, day nurseries, mothers' clubs, health care, literary societies, education, and social justice.[5]

Scholars mark the National Association of Colored Women's Clubs' (NACWC) emergence in 1896 as the beginning of the movement. The NACWC predated the formation of the National Association of Colored People (NAACP) by fifteen years. The early establishment of the NACWC illustrates a deep conviction of Black women to serve their community. The significance of the NACWC should not be underestimated: it afforded a rallying cry and a network of support for Black women across the country. In 1897, Mary Church Terrell, the first president of the organization, stated the following in her address:

> We have become National, because from the Atlantic to the Pacific, from Maine to the Gulf, we wish to set in motion influences that shall stop the ravages made by practices that sap our strength, and preclude the possibility of advancement. . . . We call ourselves an Association to signify that we have joined hands one with the other, to work together in a common cause. We proclaim to the world that the women of our race have become partners in the great firm of progress and reform. . . . We refer to the fact that this is an association of colored women, because our peculiar status in this country . . . seems to demand that we stand by ourselves. . . . Our association is composed of women . . . because the work which we hope to accomplish can be done better . . . by the mothers, wives, daughters, and sisters of the race.[6]

During the nineteenth and twentieth centuries, Black clubwomen financially and emotionally supported their families and, through extension, the entire African American community. To add to their burden, these women were battling the significant societal ills of racism, sexism, and classism that placed them in a highly vulnerable position. Nevertheless, despite the enormity of the task, Black women forged ahead, creating a better world for African Americans in their wake.

The legacy of fierce determination in the face of racism, sexism, and class elitism is what greeted Cannon when she entered the doctor of philosophy program at Union Theological Seminary in New York City in the fall of 1974. This faith-fueled justice-seeking resolute boldness of Black club women is the tradition that bolstered her when she and her colleagues confronted the racism, sexism, and class elitism in the academy. Groundbreaking books by two scholars had begun to disrupt the theological and religious environment that greeted Cannon and her peers in the academy. While riots raged in New York City, Black theologian James Cone's *A Black Theology of Liberation* was published in 1970.[7] In this book, Cone challenges the traditional white patriarchal interpretation of biblical texts and asserts that the theology of Black people, informed by a distinctive lived reality in the United States, is markedly different. In 1973, Mary Daly, an Irish Catholic theologian, published *Beyond God the Father*.[8] She challenges the way white men interpret Scripture and posits that women's (albeit white women's) interpretation of Scripture should be taken seriously. The young Black women PhD students found themselves at a crossroads, realizing the need for a theological viewpoint that reflected their lived experience as Black women.

One aspect of leadership is charting unknown paths, creating novel approaches as one considers what has been done, appropriating what can be incorporated, and determining what to discard in order to move forward. Refusing to deny who they were and believing they had something to say, Cannon and her Union colleagues—Jacquelyn Grant, Delores Williams, Linda Thomas (at the time a master's student)— charted their own path. Then, in the spirit of their ancestors, they developed survival strategies for themselves.[9]

Cannon was the first, in 1985, to propose womanism as an approach to consider intellectual and communal possibilities. The term *womanist* owes its origins to Pulitzer Prize-winning author Alice Walker. A womanist is a Black woman who, despite systemic oppression, develops survival strategies to build community, resilience, and interdependence for her family and her people. She takes seriously the interlocking and intersectional experiences premised on multiple forms of social stratification.

Womanist theology gives voice to a God who cares for those who want, need, and desire love and compassion. It declares and affirms a God who cares for those lost in the quagmire of bureaucracy, downsizing, prisons, and poverty. Womanist theology brings to light a God who cares for those who become just another number in an overworked, underpaid caseload. It confesses a God who cares for those who have become weary and disheartened and sometimes engage in self-destructive behavior. Womanist theology attests to a God who cares for those who watch their jobs move overseas, who become drug and firearms runners to help their family pay bills. It seeks to discover, analyze, and honor the lives and gifts of those who are forgotten and dismissed. Womanist theology embraces a message of hope and transformation and honors the *imago dei*, the image of God, in all persons.

NURTURING POTENTIAL: "I AM GOING TO GIVE YOU THE BEST I HAVE SO YOU CAN DO BETTER"

Dr. Cannon was a member of both the Feminist Studies in Religion and the *Journal of Feminist Studies in Religion* boards from their inception. In memory of Dr. Cannon, the organization published select quotes from her "Across Generations" interview conducted by Dr. Alison P. Gise Johnson, who asked, "Why do you nurture the way that you do?" Dr. Cannon replied: "Every Black teacher I had told me, 'I'm going to give you the best that I have; and I want you to be better.'" It is from that perspective that I approach nurturing and mentoring my students. . . . Though much of my life has been formed in that academic world, my sense of mentoring was not deformed by it. Nurturing is my ministry. And I have to do it in a way that offers to every student an experience of school as sanctuary."[10]

Dr. Cannon names this philosophy of teaching "Black women's liberation pedagogy." It carries the spirit of the Black women's club movement. It is an approach to learning in which Dr. Cannon strove to teach in a way that was neither offensive nor insulting to her students. Her motivation was to master techniques, strategies, and processes so that her father, who never learned to read or write, could comprehend everything she said.

A significant influence in the development of Dr. Cannon's courses was Reverend Dr. James Herman Robinson, an African American Presbyterian clergyman and humanitarian, best known as the founder of Operation Crossroads Africa, a cross-cultural exchange program considered a forerunner of the Peace Corps. He was in the vanguard of progressive, contemporary thinkers on Afrocentricity before it was fashionable. In her pedagogical essay "The Hinges upon Which the Future Swings,"[11] Dr. Cannon elaborates Robinson's people-to-people diplomacy, the hinges upon which the future swings, which she employed in theological education. In his foreword to *Africa at the Crossroads*, Gayraud S. Wilmore offers two roughly equal and succinct summary statements that address the most engaging concerns and operating principles governing Robinson's Afrocentric ethics: (1) to help us think theologically about some of the exasperatingly complex problems of society and (2) to provide the means by which we can develop methods of applying new knowledge to break the economic, political, social, cultural, and even religious boundaries by which we are circumscribed.[12] These two objectives are the fundamental principles in Cannon's signature course, "Resources for a Constructive Ethic: The Black Women's Literary Tradition."[13]

Dr. Cannon's pedagogy was thickly layered and complex. As a scholar, Dr. Cannon was prophetic. The branch of inquiry for developing womanist theology and ethics did not exist before Dr. Cannon laid its foundation. Dr. Cannon recognized that, both in the academy and in the sanctuary, the voices of Black women were often mocked or seen as insignificant. In her landmark book, *Katie's Canon: Womanism and the Soul of the Black Community*, she writes passionately about the task of the womanist interpreter. Dr. Cannon is clear that

> womanism requires that we stress with urgency the African American women's movement from death to life. . . . We investigate contestable issues according to the official records, which seldom offer any indication why things have gone wrong nor why benefactors of oppression strive to maintain certain principles, values, and taboos as the center of social reality. In other words, womanist religious scholars insist that individuals look back at race, sex, and class constructions before it is too late and put forth critical analysis in such a way that the errors of the past will not be repeated.[14]

Cannon's groundbreaking approach has enabled subsequent scholars and practitioners to look at the experiences of Black women across the African diaspora. In addition, she influenced other methodologies through her work and life, including *Mujerista*, LGBTQ, and postcolonial theologies.[15] Introducing Black women's literature as primary texts, she mined nuggets of wisdom, persistence, and experiences of Black women in an environment where Black women's voices were often ignored.

As a teacher, Dr. Cannon created space in her classroom for transformation, for hearts to be changed, veils to be lifted, and perceptions to be revised. She created an environment for students to be able to *step into* their questions and reconsider their assumptions. Dr. Cannon named the obvious but unspoken. She was keenly aware of what people did not know they did not know. Second, Dr. Cannon set high expectations for students' work and walked with them through the problematic spaces that often emerged in ethical-theological reflection when one dares to ask challenging questions. Third, she sought to cultivate the classroom as community, such that students were not just learning content or getting to know a field but were also getting to know people, beginning with themselves. Learning alongside people who became friends is a different experience than simply sitting next to someone in a lecture. Fourth, she encouraged various approaches to learning, including creative expression, as sources of theological ethics. Finally, Dr. Cannon expected students and colleagues to give body, mind, heart, and soul to the task of embodied engaged knowledge—no less than what she gave to prepare students for liberation work in the church, academy, and community.

As a mentor/adviser, Dr. Cannon often told her advisees that her default presupposition was that every human is born with a purpose. Her operative presupposition was premised on a belief that God wrote everyone's purpose on their hearts in the process of creation, and one's ultimate allegiance is to do the specific work to which God calls one. She encouraged anyone who had the privilege of being her student, advisee, mentee, friend, or acquaintance to follow their dreams and visions by responding affirmatively to God's call and inner conviction. Dr. Cannon made people feel that they were intelligent, worthy, and belonged in the world of academia. She always encouraged her students to write their own stories.

As a friend, Dr. Cannon was a coach and confidante. Her empathy extended to everyone, and her generosity was legendary. She was brilliant yet down to earth and could hold her own with the most rigorous scholars, disarm you with her sharp wit, and give hope to the most depressed person.

As a leader, as in all areas of her life and ministry, Dr. Cannon's leadership style was exceptional. It was experienced in one-on-one settings and in the classroom. Her mere presence created a social/spiritual moment. For Cannon, self-awareness was vital. In a July 2013 interview, she discussed how important it is to know who you are. She was unwavering in these beliefs: "Identity is essential for agency: we have to know who we are: 'To thine own self be true' [Shakespeare, *Hamlet*, 1.3]. If you don't know who self is, how can you be true? If you can't love self, you can't love [your] neighbor."[16]

Doctor Cannon's leadership style permits people to define their own reality. She embodied a leadership style that allowed for thoughts to be shared and not suffocated, intellect to be nurtured, and tools provided to name and embrace one's preferred approach to leadership. She discerned gifts in others and fostered their development by instruction, by example, by providing opportunities, and by advocacy on another's behalf. She expected everyone to do their best and assisted in making that a reality.

Doctor Cannon was a visionary. She saw potential on a personal and societal scale. Indeed, Dr. Katie Geneva Cannon knew how to lead those in her care into those possibilities with her guiding principles: recognize gifts and graces, identify the soul work, affirm creativity and improvisation, nurture spiritual discernment, and advocate for and provide opportunities for exposure to share those gifts.

CURATING SPACE: THE HINGES UPON WHICH THE FUTURE SWINGS

In a November 21, 2015, plenary session at the American Academy of Religion, Dr. Cannon was asked what advice she would give to graduate students. Her initial response was this: "Go through the door. Women go overboard trying to prove we are as smart as we are. We know what we want to write about, we know in our heart of hearts what we have been called to write about, but somewhere we have come to believe that that's not academic excellence. So instead of following our heart and going through the door, we keep bumping up against the concrete wall and give up. Go through the door."[17]

In 1998, I started The Daughters of Zelophehad (DOZ; cf. Num. 27; 36; Josh. 7) with a mission to provide transitional housing for mothers and children in crisis for two years. The organization's strategic initiatives were to provide counseling, case management, and a curriculum that would create new paths, nourish clients' potential, and curate space for a better lifestyle. The staff, all Black women, were from

different churches and denominations; 98 percent of the population
served were Black women and their children. Finding a church of their
choice and encouraging spiritual growth was an essential feature of the
program. If mothers did not have a faith community of their own, our
team introduced them to the community's diversity and styles of worship. In retrospect, I wonder how my awareness of the Black women's
club movement might have been instructive when I started DOZ. I
question what I might have done differently had I known that in April
1896 my great-grandmother and her four sisters established a chapter
of the United Order of Tents, the oldest Black women's club in the
country. It was organized in 1867 by two emancipated women and
traces its origin to Black women's participation in the Underground
Railroad in Norfolk, Virginia, before the Civil War. This statement in a
1991 program bulletin honoring the United Order of Tents notes that:

> [The] organization . . . felt the call to the elevation of Negro wom-
> anhood, to cast off the spell of slavery, and urged Negro women
> to unite in liberating themselves physically, morally, and mentally
> from the abasement of Negro womanhood. Women from all walks
> of life [were] working together to serve the community, to serve [hu]
> mankind, and most of all to seek and attain the many rights and
> privileges which had been denied them for so long.[18]

Had I known I was part of history, with a family legacy that began
with enslaved and free women before the Civil War, maybe the future
for DOZ would have been different. Maybe knowing my cultural and
family history, knowing more of my true self, would have fortified a
now dormant agency and kept its door open.

Dr. Cannon's leadership style lays the foundation for us to walk
through doors. A presenting question for ongoing consideration is how
her approach to ethics, theology, and pedagogy will enhance body and
soul work. Cannon's soul work was to equip, empower, and set people
free to do the work their soul must have. Guided by a mission to identify gifts and graces, Cannon's ability to make space for others' gifts to
grow and flourish—as she guided, affirmed, and encouraged unique-
ness and commonality—demands that we take seriously how her contributions can be expanded, enhanced, adapted, and integrated into
one's divine call.

A critical concept foundational to Cannon's mission is *sawubona*,
a common greeting among the Zulu tribe of South Africa. *Sawubona*
means, "I see you, you are important to me, and I value you." It is a

way to make each of the other persons visible and accept them as they are, with their virtues, nuances, and flaws. It means all attention is on you. I see you, and I allow myself to discover your needs, see your fears, identify your mistakes, and accept them. I take you for who you are, and you are part of me.

Sawubona conscientizes us to the importance of directing our attention to another person. It reminds us to understand others without prejudice and to leave grudges behind. It prompts us to be aware of other people's needs and to give importance to individuals within a group. Thinking this way can be instrumental in our ability to see each other's needs, forgive mistakes, and promote cohesion in our communities. When we truly see another person, we see their divine essence, a spiritual light that is energizing and empowering.

Dr. Cannon's pedagogy and leadership style equipped, empowered, and set me free to walk through doors. I go through doors to curate space for intellectual and spiritual healing of individuals, families, and communities. I bring my soul work of contemplative intercessory and healing prayer to sharing stories, unique cultural histories, generational trauma and resilience, and spirituality in an environment of accountability and mutuality. The Zulu greeting *sawubona*, "I see you," is an essential concept in creating a community committed to justice-oriented praxis.

Womanism is a social-change perspective rooted in Black women's lived experiences and problem-solving methods that emerge from familiar spaces with hope-filled expectations to eradicate all forms of oppression for all peoples, restore balance between people and the environment/nature, and reconcile human life with the spiritual dimension.[19]

Contemplative intercessory prayer, designed to investigate the impact of the trauma of racism, sexism, and class elitism on one's faith, families, and communities, offers different modalities of healing opportunities to alleviate moral and ethical injury and create pathways to resilience and resistance. As I worked in the nonprofit world, a critique that consistently surfaced was the difficulty of engaging with Black churches. After learning about the Black women's club movement, I realized that there was a historical explanation. The community work was and still is embedded in the lives and the work of women who may not necessarily worship in the same church or denomination. However, they had and have a shared ethic of responsibility that was informed by and responsive to Black life generally and the conditions of Black women specifically. Mary Church Terrell expresses this ethic beautifully: "We are daughters, sisters, mothers, and wives. We must care for ourselves and rear our families, like all women. But we have more to do than other women. Those of us fortunate enough to have education must share it with the less fortunate of our race. We must go into our communities and improve them; we must go out into the nation and change it. Above all, we must organize ourselves as Negro women and work together."[20]

Women are carriers of the culture. We carry what we learn from family members, especially the women in our families. We must be more intentional about telling our stories so that our narratives will be sources of knowledge for future generations. Following in pathways carved out by Rev. Dr. Katie Geneva Cannon, we branch out into areas that are yet to be explored, mindful always of a responsibility to perhaps open a door through which we and others will walk.

8

Even When One's Face Is on Fire

A Womanist Approach to Leadership

ANGELA D. SIMS

To effect change in higher education requires leaders, faculty, trustees, donors, students, and other stakeholders to take inventory of an institution's history and to examine defining moments in that school's life. I reflect on a childhood experience shared by Katie Geneva Cannon, about an incident that occurred while she was assisting an aunt employed as a domestic; I do not recall the specific date or class in which these words were spoken. The reality of working through physical pain caused by hot grease splashing on the face speaks to various ways in which Black women identify and navigate systems designed to thwart our ability to survive. This account of coping with life even when one's face is on fire can function as a leadership metaphor as Black women "courageously uncover the pain, make it articulate, reckon with it, and enter it into the public/private discourse."[1]

Cannon's description is an example of her ability to use not only the Black woman's literary tradition but also Black women's lived reality as a source to "interpret and explain the community's sociocultural patterns from which ethical values can be gleaned."[2] Cannon's approach to conscientization demands that we accurately name what impedes our ability to lead with integrity and to thrive. Or, as she said, "How many times do you have to say, 'My face is on fire,' before someone listens?"[3]

A womanist approach to leadership is informed by both an intersectional analysis and a contextual assessment of interlocking cycles of

95

oppression. As such, Black women question institutional commitments to equity when unaccompanied by a call for accountability and responsibility. When the promise of equity, justice, and fairness is met with reluctance to dismantle systemic oppression, especially at institutions of higher learning that for centuries have privileged constructions of whiteness often reflected, for example, in admissions criteria, syllabi, and program-learning outcomes, Black women leaders forge alliances as they strive to make a difference. As states pass legislation to limit the teaching of critical race theory within public colleges and universities,[4] leaders in higher education must (1) reimagine the ways in which our collective efforts signal that we have an opportunity to assess the relevance of our institution's mission and core values; (2) evaluate methods by which we collaborate and engage with organizations and persons with whom we have shared values; (3) invest in our school's greatest assets, our students and employees; (4) be mindful of our hiring practices; and (5) be clear that change and cultural shifts can be and are often painful and met with resistance. To name and address a need for training to deal with anti-Black, anti-Asian, anti-racist, and anti-trans[gender] attitudes and action may be antithetical to stated outcomes of conscientization and cultural awareness. Let me be clear: I am not saying that these initiatives are not needed. I am, however, concerned when this form of "anti" training is not done in tandem with a decentering of whiteness as an unspoken yet assumed normative point of reference. We look for any measures that can result in sustained positive change.[5]

Even as (or perhaps exactly because) some persons wield power with threats to withhold funding from institutions whose curriculum includes critical race theory, leaders in higher education who do not waver in commitments to peace and justice do so mindful of costs associated with decisions to dismantle systems of racism embedded (sometimes so subtly that it might go unnoticed and thus unaddressed) in the institutions at which we serve. Yet, change is possible in higher education, and it can begin with chief executive officers who decide that a process of dismantling white supremacist systems operative in our institutions will begin with us. Presidents and deans who want to impact positive institutional change must attend to matters of miseducation, beginning with an ongoing process of Board development. Dismantling systems built and sustained on a lie is no easy undertaking. When institutions align budget priorities with a commitment to equity, CEOs do so mindful that change begins but does not end nor should be borne exclusively by us.

OVERLAPPING EXPERIENCES

While the term *intersectionality* is not a word that most people use in everyday conversations, we can use Alice Walker's nonfictional works to examine how a concept has a profound impact on persons for whom justice is often elusive and an illusion. During the second decade of the twenty-first century, reversals in human and civil rights in the United States of America correlate with one's core values.[6] For example, a critical ethical analysis of the rising illiteracy rate, the resegregation of public schools, the complexities of class and race that are foundational to an exploitative prison industrial complex, national gentrification, and the merging of church and state under the guise of faith-based funding— such analysis might suggest that freedom is little more than an illusion. In her essay "Choosing to Stay Home: Ten Years after the March on Washington," Walker's assertion regarding freedom can serve as a historical point of reference for individuals who want to understand costs incurred by people who committed their lives to confront injustice, so that justice might indeed one day be realized by persons relegated to the margins of life. If then, "in the end," as Walker asserts, "freedom is a personal and lonely battle, and one faces down fears of today so that those of tomorrow might be engaged,"[7] gratitude and respect is owed to nationally recognized and unnamed Black women across centuries and generations who are exemplars of leadership in the church, the academy, and society.[8]

Coined more than thirty years ago by legal scholar Kimberlé Crenshaw, a professor of law at Columbia University and the University of California at Los Angeles, to describe the unique way Black women experience the law, the term *intersectionality* refers to the notion that a person's identify is often shaped by multiple constructs—race, gender, sexual orientation, socioeconomic status, and so forth—yet rarely does life or the law account for the complexities of these overlapping experiences.[9] "Black women," Crenshaw argues, "often experience intersecting patterns of racism and sexism in ways that cannot be wholly captured by looking at race and gender separately."[10] Yet, even in 2020, Crenshaw aptly notes that "our legal regime, along with our antiracist and feminist discourse, seems incapable of recognizing how multiple forms of discrimination can combine to impact people, further marginalizing persons already on the margins"[11] and, in some cases, pushed over artificially constructed discriminatory boundaries.

Jason A. Gillmer, the Hemmingson Chair in Civil Liberties and

Professor of Law at Gonzaga University School of Law and Director of the Center for Civil and Human Rights (at Spokane, WA), acknowledges that "Crenshaw's theory of intersectionality has only grown in salience since she first gave it a name." "People are," he says, "coming to understand more and more that invisible intersections often compound bias and discrimination." He further notes that Crenshaw's clear intersectionality "is not just about Black women. Sexual orientation, class, religion, immigration status, disability—in addition to race and gender—all shape individual experience." For Crenshaw, it is "important that we use intersectionality theory to see where power comes and collides, where it interlocks and intersects." When we, as Crenshaw asserts, "shine a light onto these intersections, we can better address instances of injustice and inequality for traditionally marginalized and underrepresented people."[12]

With voter suppression in full force across the United States as names are being purged from records, an insurgence of white nationalism jeopardizes the safety of many in this country. An anti-intellectual sentiment is present in all sectors of society. Ella Baker's words, in response to the 1964 murder of three civil rights workers by a Ku Klux Klan lynch mob near Meridian, Mississippi, remain a call to action: "We who believe in freedom cannot rest; we cannot rest until it comes."

WOMANIST PROCLIVITIES

I am a product of the church and, more specifically, the Black church. From my maternal grandmother and other mothers of the church, the mantra "Knowledge is the one thing no one can take from me" was an almost constant guide as I acquired knowledge, skills, and abilities necessary to navigate life. I discovered that sometimes wanting to know more and in greater depth than was considered "good" for me had its own consequences. This "womanish" behavior, a term with which persons born in the 1980s and later may not be familiar, was both a curse and a blessing.

As a young girl growing up in a hamlet in northeast Louisiana, I can recall several occasions where "womanish" behavior resulted in punishment in some form or another. Since the established practice was that "children were seen and not heard," I learned very early how to use quiet to my advantage. Some may describe my behavior as "nosey," but

I prefer to consider it an expression of inquisitiveness. After all, there were no rigid guidelines governing where I could or could not read. To this day I am amazed at the information I cataloged by simply sitting quietly under an opened window.

I commuted with my mother to school from the first through the eighth grades. We carpooled, with three other teachers, twenty plus miles to a rural community until we relocated to the East Bay region of California in 1970, the year that the courts mandated the desegregation of Louisiana public schools. In retrospect, I realize that my mother and her colleagues saw themselves as much more than educators. They were an integral part of this community that they served and went to what I consider great lengths to make a positive difference in the lives of the students and families with whom they interacted. Many of my mother's students remained in touch with her, and perhaps in some small way she helped them to see life beyond the cotton fields.

As a nine-year-old know-it-all, though, I was convinced that picking cotton was not difficult and that, given the chance to prove my hypothesis, I could fill a sack as quickly as the most experienced picker. Of course, no one with whom I shared this insight refuted me. But I soon discovered just how difficult and tiring a day in the cotton fields was on the body, especially a girl-child's body. My career as a cotton picker lasted less than thirty minutes; if not for the kindness of my classmate's father, in whose field I was hired out, I would not have earned enough to participate in the Saturday excursion to town. Technology has replaced the human pickers, but many residents in this small northeast Louisiana parish continue to live below the poverty level in a town where the cotton gin keeps on working.

When I conducted oral histories in 2009–10, I was reminded of the devastating effects of brain drain on a community. Most of the persons in my parents' generation have died, and few in my generation returned after college. To love one's self, regardless, may sometimes translate to not being able to contribute to the renewal of one's place of origin. With few friendship ties remaining in the parish seat that was my home for fourteen of my formative years, I strive to lead in a manner that honors the educators, religious lay leaders, and community leaders who invested in my development. This translates into establishing and communicating expectations, fostering a climate in which persons can take risks, providing professional development opportunities, and facilitating connections with external mentors.

CONTEXT MATTERS

When I think of my own journey from a one-room kindergarten, to a segregated elementary school surrounded by cotton fields, to a segregated junior high school that sparked an interest in the sciences, to desegregated junior and senior high schools in California that exposed me to languages and expanded my literary lens, to college at Tulane University in New Orleans, Louisiana, where interruptions from pursuing my dream resulted in an almost fourteen-year hiatus in my studies, I do so mindful of a responsibility to curate space where others can imagine possibilities that emerge when one is intentional about developing nurturing relationships. During this interruption of my own intellectual pursuits, I sought to nurture my children's giftedness and brilliance that I believe are inherent in each child, with parents, guardians, and other caring adults challenged and encouraged to recognize and cultivate that which makes each child unique and special.

I resumed my undergraduate studies at Trinity University, a Catholic woman's school in Washington, DC, and graduated summa cum laude while working full-time in mid-level management. With stellar LSAT (Law School Admission Test) scores, I did not consider geographical relocation an option and limited my applications to universities in the District of Columbia and Virginia. Upon receipt of invitations from law schools in other states declaring that they would accept my application beyond their stated deadline, I was devastated when I was not admitted to any of the local schools of my choice, nor was I wait-listed. Before a public talk in 2016, the only person with whom I shared this disappointment was a classmate. When I spoke with her, she listened quietly. After I finished my self-pity rant, she asked me, "From what are you running that God wants you to do?" In that moment, I realized that my attempt to bargain with God was futile. It did not matter that what God asked contradicted my own religious tradition's understanding of what women could and could not do in the church. At that moment, all that mattered was obedience to God.

Given my stance that preparation is a response to the Divine's call, in 1995 I entered a Master of Divinity degree program at Howard University. This was by far a defining life experience. I completed my studies second in my class and spent the 1998–99 academic year working closely with three of my professors as I engaged in extensive interdisciplinary reading, research, and writing on the life and theology of Ida B. Wells Barnett, Dietrich Bonhoeffer, and Martin Luther King Jr. The following year my family affiliated with a historic Black Baptist church in Prince William County, Virginia, whose pastor was a seminary graduate. The almost four years of practical experience and exposure I received from my pastor and our church's leadership, coupled with a year of clinical pastoral education at Children's National Medical Center in Washington, DC, continues to inform my teaching. Though both my parents and godparents were educators, I never envisioned this as my vocation of choice.

In 2003, I embarked on an educational and formation journey that has forever changed my life. As I reflect on wisdom gleaned from Katie Geneva Cannon, distinguishing characteristics of my postgraduate experience can be viewed as a gateway, with indicators that denote changes required in the way one engages in intellectual discourse and professional development. For certainly, if academic deportment cannot be distinguished from practices of shaming and hazing that are often associated with group conformity, one ought to question the value of the experience. Perhaps my time with Dr. Cannon, at what is now Union Presbyterian Seminary, was simply a privileged glance at what can occur when a scholar embraces her understanding of vocation and exercises the moral courage to encourage a student to read deeply and to cling to freedom, while ever conscious of compromises inevitably required and alert not to *foreclose on one's own soul.*

With all but the dissertation completed to satisfy requirements for a doctor of philosophy in Christian social ethics, I accepted an invitation in 2007 to join the faculty of Saint Paul School of Theology in Kansas City, Missouri. My twelve years at this seminary of the United Methodist Church was, in some respects, a living laboratory where I gained a greater appreciation for using my corporate accounting and management experience in support of a school's mission. Fourteen years after the conferral of my PhD degree, I find myself serving as the first woman president of a more than two-hundred-year-old institution whose current campus is in a commercial business park parallel to a railroad track. Some of you may not be aware of the ways in which transportation systems have served as lines of demarcation to determine types and quality of services provided to families on either side of tracks, highways, or major streets.[13] The railroad tracks that serve as a boundary for the Neighborhood of the Arts and the Beechwood Neighborhood are a constant reminder to me that to realize a vision to become a seminary of and for the community—committed to practices of peace, service, and justice—demands a dismantling of biases, misconceptions, lies, myths, and racism. This is the hard yet necessary work of leadership. It requires a willingness and ability to meet seminary constituents where they are and together become active listeners as we engage in the work of internal transformation.

INTENTIONAL TRANSFORMATION

At the time of writing, I am in my fourth year of service as president of a 203-year-old seminary, a merger of schools that counts among its graduates Walter Rauschenbusch, Howard Thurman, Samuel DeWitt Proctor, and Martin Luther King Jr. In 2014, Ted A. Smith, professor of preaching and ethics at Candler School of Theology at Emory University, launched Theology between the Times (TEBT), a multiyear project "in recognition of seismic social, cultural, and demographic shifts that demand a reassessment of how we approach theological education."[14] Though an early participant in this program, when I attended the October 2021 Justo and Catherine González Lecture Series sponsored by TEBT, a notion of theological education at an intersection, at a crossroads, raised questions initially about funding, accreditation, and the myriad hours and resources allocated to assessment. At the same time, theological education as fluid is an invitation to adopt an asset-based approach, to identify *loose ends*, a practice that is also community centric. Ultimately, though I concur with Elizabeth Conde-Frazier's description of this moment in theological education that "the times are ripe for reform,"[15] I question how receptive key stakeholders—donors, trustees, administrators, faculty, students—will be to engaging in a process of reformation that requires a deep interrogation of the way things are as a preliminary step to imagining ourselves as co-laborers with and on behalf of others. Latinx contributions to theological education suggest that much is to be gleaned from *collaborative models of theological education* that are contextual and relevant and that value, affirm, and curate space where mutual learning can occur.

While Conde-Frazier addresses a specific multidimensional context and provides examples of the ways in which the Association for Hispanic Theological Education (AETH) networks with a variety of entities, her chapter 4 prompted me to consider how AETH might also serve as a model for the Society for the Study of Black Religion (SSBR). Founded in 1970, SSBR is a by-invitation-only member society dedicated to scholarly research and discussion about the religious experiences of Blacks. We see a concerted assault against a wide range of efforts and ideas that raise awareness about the history of racial injustice in the United States, its embeddedness in our society, and the resulting inequities observed today. As I read *Atando Cabos: Latinx Contributions to Theological Education*, and especially chapters 4 and 5, I could not help but wonder what SSBR might be if the organization were not so wedded to perpetuating a model reflective of the typical academic guild structure such that members miss opportunities to truly shape theological education. To be clear, there is value in these intellectual exchanges. At the same time, if these dialogues are limited to a small audience, what is the greater good to which SSBR may be called?

Here Conde-Frazier's adaptability in engaging curriculum caused me to pause as I considered, what about SSBR's current membership process may reinforce notions of exceptionalism that are not held in tension with anti-racism and other justice commitments. Also, since SSBR is not a Christian-based organization, though most of our members identify as such, should this be grounds for not considering ways in which the organization could be a leader in reforming theological education? How might the work of Black religious scholars—such as E. Franklin Frazier, Tracey E. Hucks, C. Eric Lincoln, Henry Mitchell, Albert J. Raboteau, Dianne M. Stewart, and Love Henry Whelchel—inform a social-historical analysis of Black religious life? What questions would AETH consultants ask that will require honest answers about organizational and individual identity? Will members who are theological educators be required to name some of the ways in which we are vested and invested in a model of theological education that is increasingly disconnected from peoples and communities our students say they are called to serve? What if SSBR took seriously AETH's community-centric approach to theological education and cultivated relationships with Black churches—home churches, store fronts, and megachurches; historical Black denominations, mainline affiliated, and nondenominational; rural, suburban, and urban churches—as an expression of God's kin-dom here on earth?

As multiple pandemics continue to disproportionately and badly affect poor, Black, indigenous peoples, and persons of color, the mission of the institution at which I serve—to form students in theological and multireligious studies to serve, care, and advocate for all peoples and the earth—is a core tenet of womanism. Just as persons are not formed in isolation, neither are higher-educational institutions. For such a time as now, AETH's collaborative model of theological education is an adaptable framework by which to develop a contextually relevant curriculum and thus address the lived realities with which Blacks in the United States contend.

COLLECTIVE AGENCY

In a 1974 letter to *Ms.* magazine, Alice Walker discusses her experience as a first-time attendee at the National Black Feminist Organization Conference. In this concise editorial, Walker provides examples that, almost fifty years later, continue to demand the attention of anyone who is concerned about the treatment of women, and thus of any people who have been conditioned to deny their sense of personhood. Yet, suffice it to say that Walker does more than allude to issues related to fear, paralysis, solidarity, self-awareness, and revolution.

In her correspondence to *Ms.* magazine, Walker identifies a corrective avenue: purpose every day "to save the life that is your own." To begin this process, she asks any who are "committed to survival and wholeness of entire people" to consider "how simple a thing it seems to me that to know ourselves as we are, we must know our mothers' names. Yet we do not know them. Or if we do, it is only the names we know and not the lives."[16] This observation is supported, in part, by the lack of materials that attest to our mothers' struggles. For, as Walker implies, a survey might reveal, "when we look back over our history, it is clear that we have neglected to save just those people who could help us most."[17]

If we are to consider the significance of engaging in a process to reclaim hidden treasures, what tools, other than perseverance, are required to go beyond a surface or cursory inquiry? How does one prepare to intentionally confront the mothers whose lives have not been preserved on paper? When interpreting retrieved insights from the complexity ascribed to *living a life unaware*, the courage to tell the story of a collective existence emerges from women who "gather together to assure understanding among Black women so that understanding among women"[18] becomes a catalyst to live so that others might also live.

SOUL WORK

While serving in senior executive leadership in the academy can be extremely rewarding, it is often a lonely experience. Cultivating relationships with colleagues and creating space in which to cry, laugh, vent, and process requires time to establish trust. To think or envision loneliness as a gift may require one to acknowledge a call to a solitary work that dictates an ability to hear what others cannot hear or refuse to position themselves to understand. This concept of separation as a "radical vision of society"[19] is often counter to a normative construct, so often depicted in the media as social interaction or in the academy as shared governance.

To accept this gift of loneliness—a time with one's self, with one's God, with one's ancestors—is an opportunity to articulate in multiple expressions an alternative representation of reality "that has not previously been taken into account."[20] This process of coming to terms with one's self and the gift extended may require a turning away from what is familiar. Yet this is often a challenge for persons who are in relationship with others—partner, significant other, children, parents, siblings, friends—and can be construed as an impossible task. Here I caution us to be attentive to how distractions, life-work rhythms, and sleep hygiene may be antithetical to a womanist approach to leadership. With a little creative imagination, coupled with a commitment to love yourself regardless, purposely schedule moments and spaces to which you can retreat to embrace the work that your soul must have in order to survive and thrive.

9

"Not Meant to Survive"

Black Mothers Leading beyond the Criminal Line

NIKIA SMITH ROBERT

When fifteen years old, my mother conceived her firstborn in abject poverty, and by early adulthood she gave birth to me. By the age of twelve, I received the first parcel my brother sent me while he was in prison. Hellbent on disrupting intergenerational struggle, my mother would go to any length, including bending rules and breaking laws, to desperately ensure that the encroaching economic destitution and looming darkness of a nefarious criminal system did not eclipse the future possibilities for her children's survival and social thriving. She developed what ethicist Katie Geneva Cannon called "living an ethics under oppression." My mother drew from a value system that inverted dominant societal standards so that her agentic survival practices were not dictated by negative social perceptions of deviance and an unjust legal system. Rather, her community and children appraised her self-directed actions as sources of salvation and moral integrity.

As I reflect on experiences of indigent Black mothers—like my own, who break laws to provide for their families—I consider the ways in which their unlawful survival strategies demonstrate a subversive style of leadership that is instructive for connecting unwavering faith in a liberating God with moral agency to overcome death-dealing circumstances fraught by social inequities, a pervasive carceral state, and the dismal reality that "we were never meant to survive."[1]

This essay captures interior struggles of Black mothers and their families who were not meant to survive the pervasive threat of the prison system and calamitous conditions of multiple oppressions. The primary argument avers that poor Black mothers' agentic survival practices, especially when contravening the law to provide for their families, provide a model of leadership that is wholly womanist and instructive for negotiating and navigating oppressive systems. This generative womanist way of leadership emerges from the practical wisdom of poor Black mothers who balance the vicissitudes of life to provide for their children against social inequities and a depraved system of criminality and incarceration. Black women's embodied representation of leadership teaches us the value of assigning moral worth to self-directed practices that push the boundaries of dominant standards. We learn that when survival is at stake, breaking the law and transgressing normative boundaries is sometimes necessary, right, and should compel us to dismantle oppressive power structures that lead to desperate choices of survival in the first place. This truth also reveals the salvific qualities of lawbreaking as a necessary survival strategy as we work for a more just and equitable society beyond punishment, criminality, and incarceration.

Organized in four parts, I begin by using statistical data to center Black women's unique experience with criminality and economic hardship within the womanist canon and larger criminal studies discourses. Second, I use vignettes to introduce the moral failings of a *criminal line*, a term I create to capture the twenty-first century's problem of mass punishment and the ways in which perceptions, laws, policies, and regulations disproportionately target Black women as deviant, criminal, and unworthy of moral concern. Third, I expand Katie G. Cannon's virtue ethics by applying her notion of "living ethics under oppression" as a counter construct to the punitive orientations of a criminal line. Finally, I present a three-pronged womanist theo-ethical approach to public policy and transformative advocacy as a liberative intervention to help religious leaders and laity to advocate for Black mothers and undermine the carceral state.

CENTERING BLACK MOTHERS' EXPERIENCES IN THE U.S. CARCERAL STATE

In 1985, Katie Geneva Cannon borrowed from Alice Walker's four-part definition to conceptualize the emergence of womanist ethics in her article titled "The Emergence of Black Feminist Consciousness."[2] In the same year, women were the fastest growing population in prisons.

An ACLU report about the over-incarceration of women in the United States indicates that, "with more than one million women behind bars or under the control of the criminal justice system, women are the fastest growing segment of the incarcerated population, increasing at nearly double the rate of men since 1985."[3] As womanist scholarship developed through study, consultation, and publication, the foundational works used sociohistorical and theo-ethical analyses to center Black women's experiences with interlocking systems of oppression, while engaging in ideological critique against Eurocentric epistemologies and challenging regressive theological teachings and practices in churches. Later womanist thinkers pushed beyond the categories of theology and ethics into varied disciplines, topics, and religions. However, as womanist scholarship expanded and mass incarceration became more pervasive, Black women's experience with imprisonment did not figure prominently into womanist discourses.

Unconscionably, the United States is a world leader in mass punishment.[4] Black women make up 30 percent of women who are incarcerated but only 13 percent of all the women in the United States.[5] As a significant but largely unobserved population, nearly 80 percent of incarcerated women are mothers.[6] A ripple effect ensues when children lose a mother, families lose a breadwinner, communities lose stabilization, churches lose a pillar, and the economy loses resources because of the exorbitant spending that incarceration requires. The allocation of government spending for prison construction, policing, and imprisonment essentially take away funding from job creation, education, affordable housing, and other social services essential for poor Black mothers' survival. As a result of economic investment in the carceral state and divestment in communities, poor Black mothers often go underemployed, underpaid, undervalued, and treated as a perpetual underclass. Consequently, impoverished Black mothers are not only disadvantaged by racial, gender, and economic inequalities but also are often criminalized for trying to survive and secure quality of life for themselves and their families.

Mothers who commit crimes for survival are a smaller and obscured population in the criminal system. The common profile of incarcerated women is typically drug offenders in relationship with an intimate partner and women who have endured physical and/or sexual trauma. However, paramount to this analysis is uncovering moral struggles of impoverished Black motherhood and the unique burdens of imprisonment when mothers are acting as sole caregivers and providers amid racial, gender, and economic inequities.

In a discussion about women offenders and economic barriers that impede survival, political activist and Black feminist philosopher Angela Y. Davis argues that Black women become "perfect candidates for prison" due to a scarcity of "surviving social services" such as employment, economic resources, and education. Davis posits, "Huge numbers of people lose jobs and prospects for future jobs. Because the economic base of these communities is destroyed, education and other surviving social services are profoundly affected. This process turns the men, women, and children who live in these damaged communities into perfect candidates for prison."[7] Many women who are economically destitute resort to moral decision-making that, out of desperation, can lead into the criminal system.[8] Thus, economy and survival go hand in hand when unpacking Black mothers' unique burdens in coping with criminality.

For example, my mother sometimes forged doctor's notes to get a day off work during inconvenient school holidays when she could not afford backup childcare. She manufactured a higher tax refund to secure disposable income to pay bills, including tuition for an after-school program that kept me safe from the drugs and violence that were common in our Harlem neighborhood. She also falsified lease renewal agreements to mitigate astronomical rent increases and the threat of displacement because of privatization and gentrification. Ostensibly, at each turn of navigating the deleterious conditions of poverty and the intersecting oppressions of racial and gender inequities, my mother could have easily become a perfect candidate for prison due to a scarcity of social safety nets and infrastructure to ensure human flourishing.

Importantly, punishing mothers who break laws to subsist can far outweigh their acts of survival because of the cumulative harms caused to individuals, families, and communities. At the 2016 Criminal Justice System Convening conference, U.S. Attorney General Loretta Lynch aptly remarked, "Put simply, we know that when we incarcerate a woman, we often are truly incarcerating a family, in terms of the far-reaching effect on her children, her community, and her entire family network."[9] Incarcerating mothers often causes grievous harms. These collateral consequences incentivize the need for alternatives to mass punishment, options that do not decimate an entire ecosystem but provide access to resources so that individuals, families, and communities can, at a minimum, acquire basic services needed to exist. As mothers, providers, and caregivers who bear a unique responsibility to sustain families as the bedrock of their community, incarceration causes cascading consequences that are widespread, wretched, and wrought by the moral failings of U.S. society.

MORAL FAILINGS OF A CRIMINAL LINE

At the heart of the United States' obsession with punishment is a vile and deleterious criminal line. This criminal line signifies ways in which perceptions, laws, policies, and regulations work together to identify criminalized Black bodies regarded as unworthy of moral concern and separate them from the imagined white and putatively innocent bodies regarded as morally worthy. This is to suggest that, within a fragmented social imagination, punitive devices collude with oppressive systems of power to separate maligned Black bodies as guilty, impure, deviant, and criminal from the occupied dominance of unscathed whiteness. The criminal line is evinced by disparaging identity politics, discriminatory ideologies, and punitive disparities that disadvantage and demoralize the dispossessed. Notwithstanding, when Black women do not comply with dominant customs, they cross a criminal line that exacts punishment for deviating from acceptable norms.

French philosopher Michel Foucault echoes the concept of a criminal line when he explains the ways in which carceral logic operates by punishing individuals who deviate from dominant social norms. He observed that apparatuses of power enforced mechanisms of surveillance, discipline, and punishment to control and subjugate docile bodies until habituated into normalized life. In a discussion about the penitentiary and carceral logic, Foucault states that individuals who are a "departure from the norm, the anomaly," are also "the social enemy [who] was transformed into a deviant, who brought with him the multiple danger of disorder, crime and madness."[10] Subsequently, punitive apparatuses function to regulate and police individuals who do not conform to a normative gaze. Crime, then, is more than a legal infraction when someone or an entity breaks the law, but penalty converges with the power to punish individuals who deviate from dominant standards. Seen this way, economies of power are vested in a legal process of normalization by using punishment for social control and to perpetuate a "carceral continuum," or the perpetuity of punitive systems that mutate across varied milieus, notwithstanding the church, a critique to which I will later return.

The reality of the criminal line and ensuing consequences for Black women is demonstrated by the infamous comparison between the legal cases of George Zimmerman and Marissa Alexander. In 2012, George Zimmerman, a half-white and half-Peruvian male, harassed, stalked, and fatally shot an unarmed Black teenage boy named Trayvon Martin, who was on his way home from purchasing Skittles and iced tea at his local mart. Two years prior, in 2010, Marissa Alexander, a Black woman and mother, brandished her weapon and fired a warning shot near her abusive partner because she feared for her life and wanted to protect her children. Both Alexander and Zimmerman invoked the stand-your-ground law before the same prosecutor, in the same state, and around the same time.[11] Despite these similarities, however, their outcomes were drastically different.

On August 1, 2010, in Jacksonville Florida, Marissa Daniel Alexander, a thirty-one-year-old Black married woman and mother of a toddler and eleven-year-old twins, made national headlines for firing a warning shot at or near her husband, Pico Gray, and her two stepchildren.[12] Alexander was not living in the marital home up to two months prior to the incident and had also given birth just ten days before.[13] On the evening of July 31, 2010, Alexander drove to her marital residence and parked in the garage. Alexander spent the night there and at some point showed pictures to her husband of her giving their newborn baby a bath at the hospital. Alexander went to the restroom and her husband proceeded to look at her text messages on her cellphone. Mr. Gray observed texts exchanged between Alexander and her ex-husband, which resulted in a dispute. As a result of a chase throughout the home, Alexander retrieved her gun from the glove box in her vehicle in the garage and fired a shot at her husband — narrowly missing his head. Subsequently, the husband and children left the residence and called 911. Alexander remained in the home and was eventually arrested on the same day.

Many people viewed Alexander's actions as courageous and life-saving. Others condemned Alexander for standing up to her abuser and jeopardizing the safety of her children. Along with public scrutiny, Alexander's Stand-Your-Ground[14] defense was unsuccessful, her motion of immunity was denied, and she was sentenced harshly. To be certain, according to dominant societal perceptions, Alexander was constructed as deviant, undeserving, and blameworthy before she was ever charged or convicted.

Negative societal perceptions of Black mothers produce punitive disparities that reinforce the criminal line. Alexander, married twice, bore three children by different men and was arguably involved in extramarital affairs because of communication with an ex-partner that led to her estranged husband's rage. Also, she often appeared irate during screaming matches and altercations. In contrast, Zimmerman was headlined as "once a Catholic altar boy—with a surname that could have been Jewish."[15] Despite Zimmerman's encounter with the law, violent history, and questionable character, he did not experience the same public and legal scrutiny as did Alexander. These differences in societal perception arguably impacted disparate legal outcomes.

As a result of Florida's 10-20-Life law and the problem of mandatory minimums, Alexander was originally sentenced to twenty years but faced sixty years during retrial.[16] On January 27, 2015, she ultimately served a capped sentenced of three years time served because of accepting a plea bargain. Racialized and gendered stereotypes worked together with the criminal line and resulted in the unequal application of laws within a larger double system of justice. In the end, Alexander, who killed no one, was punished more egregiously than Zimmerman, who benefited from white-privilege and was acquitted after killing an unarmed Black teenager.

Social constructionist policy experts Ann Schneider and Helen Ingram examine the ways in which societal perceptions reveal power dynamics that deceptively control policy outcomes, doing so according to social constructions of target populations.[17] Schneider and Ingram argue that "much of the public policy in the United States is produced in policy-making systems dominated by divisive social constructions that stigmatize some potential target populations and extol the virtues of others."[18] Schneider and Ingram explain: "These policy designs serve to reinforce the stereotypes of 'deserving' and 'undeserving people' so that policies afford privilege to some and stigmatize and disenfranchise others."[19] Thus, double standards in the legal system reinforce a criminal line by the ways in which discriminatory perceptions correspond to laws and policies that distribute benefits and burdens, or rewards and punishment, based on who is socially constructed as worthy or unworthy of moral concern. In the case of Alexander, she was effectively punished for deviating from the norms of "good" and moral desert (worth) that are reserved for putatively white innocent bodies.

It is important to note that the criminal line is new nomenclature but not a novel phenomenon. Womanist, religious, and legal scholars have captured the moral crisis and theological contradictions of mass punishment. In *Stand Your Ground*, Kelly Brown Douglas explores the death of Trayvon Martin and the ways in which U.S. exceptionalism works with anti-Black racism within the legal system to justify white impunity by constructing a priori the Black body as guilty.[20] In *Racial Purity and Dangerous Bodies*, Rima Vesely-Flad, compelled by the killing of Mike Brown, argues for the ways in which racialized boundaries construct Black bodies as moral pollutants and dangerous, to preserve white purity through policing and punishment.[21] In her book chapter "The Issue of Race and Lynching," Angela D. Sims connects lynching to the prison industrial complex.[22] In *Power in the Blood?*, Joann Terrell examines the suffering of Black women in public spheres and instantiates the prison industrial complex in connection to atonement theories that create an ethos of sacrifice and perpetuate Black nihilism through state violence.[23] In *The New Jim Crow*, legal scholar Michelle Alexander demystifies the war on drugs that is undergirded by an illusory color-blind society by paralleling racial segregation in the Jim Crow South to the ways in which racial codification in the contemporary criminal system uses drug sentencing to punish Black men more harshly than their white counterparts.[24] However, these thinkers, though concerned peripherally or primarily with the criminal system, do not center Black women's experience with criminality in a sustained conversation.

Indeed, there are womanist and Black feminist theologians and religious ethicists who are thinking about Black women and the prison system. For example, Keri Day, in *Unfinished Business*, dedicates a chapter to the impact of poverty and economic policies that disadvantage Black women.[25] Also, in *Disruptive Ethics,* Traci West exposits Mary and the Magnificat in parallel to poor Black mothers whose negative constructions influence punitive philosophies such as welfare reform.[26] In *Katie's Canon*, Katie Geneva Cannon draws attention to the ways in which society's standards of law and order and dominant ethical values perpetuate criminality against Black people.[27] Although these texts come closer to centering Black women and the carceral system, I contradistinctively use a womanist theo-ethical approach to public policy and criminal justice advocacy as a womanist-inspired methodology that goes further by problematizing a criminal line and creating a methodology for Black churches to use liberative theologies, ethical reappraisals, and public policies in accordance with abolitionist ideals to advocate for Black mothers and to dismantle the carceral state.

KATIE CANNON'S VIRTUE ETHICS AND
LIVING AN ETHICS UNDER OPPRESSION

Nearly one hundred years ago, William Edward Burghardt (W. E. B.) Du Bois, in *The Souls of Black Folk*, declared that the defining twentieth-century problem is the color line. However, I have shown that an urgent problem in the twenty-first century is the problem of a criminal line that limits and forecloses poor Black mothers who struggle to survive against unjust social conditions. In this section, I draw from Cannon's virtue ethics to show the ways in which leading beyond the criminal line requires alternative appraisals of Black mothers' moral agency in carceral contexts.

According to Cannon, the moral struggles of "common people" exemplify an "ethics of life under oppression" that is at odds with the established values of dominant society. In *Black Womanist Ethics*, Cannon explains that womanist virtue ethics should "(a) help Black women, and others who care, to understand and to appreciate the richness of their own moral struggle through the life of the common people and the oral tradition; [and] (b) further understandings of some of the differences between ethics of life under oppression and established moral approaches which take for granted freedom and a wide range of choices."[28] Thus, as a pioneering Christian womanist social ethicist, Cannon elucidates the double standard that emerges from Black women's moral struggle between an "ethics of life under oppression" and the established values of dominant society, according to white male privilege that delimits Black women's freedom and wide range of choice.

Cannon grounds her theory in a historical analysis that closely examines Black women in the Antebellum South who resisted the moral standards of their oppressive conditions. Cannon posits, "Black women and men, as early as the 1600s, refused to obey the moral precepts held up to them by white Christian slaveholders. They resented the white man's message of docility, which acted to render them defenseless in the face of white violence. Living under a system of cheating, lying, and stealing, enslaved Blacks learned to consider their vices as virtues in their dealing with whites."[29] Here, Cannon's observation of Black women's lawbreaking to defy the oppressive conditions of slavery is especially useful to establish ways in which Black women have historically done whatever is necessary to secure their liberation.[30] Cannon's observation is critical for laying a foundation of a radical reappraisal. This is to say, contrary to the punitive values of a criminal line, Cannon shows that living an ethics under oppression (cheating, lying, stealing, and breaking the law to overcome injustices) requires a valuation by an alternative ethical system that is different from the "white man's message of docility." Rather, by Cannon's transvaluation of moral values, what dominant society constitutes as vice is understood as a virtue by Black women and men who refuse to obey the moral precepts of dominant society if it means the acceptance and perpetuation of their oppression.

Ergo, I use Cannon's system of reappraisals to find moral worth in the agency of poor Black mothers who break laws to survive and secure quality of life for themselves and their families. Although the criminal line uses individual blame to construct Black bodies as guilty and morally unworthy, a womanist way of leading validates poor Black mothers' agency and practices to circumvent carceral crises amid interlocking systems of oppression. Contrary to punitive responses that condemn poor Black mothers, leading beyond the criminal line centers mothers who live an ethics under oppression and rely on an alternative value system to provide for themselves and their families when their backs are against a wall of no retreat.

Hence, womanist virtue ethics is critical for a model of leadership that (1) contextualizes the experiences of poor Black women living against oppressions, (2) provides rationale for the epistemic privileging of Black women's practical wisdom, and (3) reappraises Black women's moral decision-making according to alternative ethical systems that challenge white middle-class dominant values. These signposts also illuminate a pathway to construct a womanist theo-ethical approach to public policy and transformative justice advocacy that churches can use to lead a faith-based abolitionist movement promoting communal thriving based on Black mothers' struggle with survival and the carceral state.

WOMANIST THEO-ETHICAL APPROACH TO PUBLIC POLICY AND CRIMINAL JUSTICE ADVOCACY

As a three-pronged approach, a womanist theo-ethical approach to public policy and criminal justice advocacy consists of (1) a liberation theology of courageous change that redresses retributive church teachings and practices rooted in harmful interpretations of sacrifice, sin, and respectability politics; (2) four alternative community-based virtues: compassion, care, creativity, and courage, which are mined from the reappraised survival practices of Black mothers who contravene laws to provide for themselves and their families; and (3) a 2×2 quadrant for churches to evaluate their teachings and practices by moving from the condemnation and complicit left quadrants to the courage and change right quadrants, which is possible when churches catalyze public policies and transformative justice strategies that are impactful and disconnected from punitive responses. The culmination of this process should result in an ideal church, which I call the Abolitionist's Sanctuary.

First, a liberation theology of courageous change responds to harmful teachings of sin and sacrifice by emphasizing Jesus' life, ministry, and proximity to women in carceral crises. Jesus begins his ministry in Luke 4:18, announcing his prophetic purpose to "set the captives free." Also, Jesus gives a mandate for Christian discipleship in Matthew 25 to visit the imprisoned. In addition, Jesus ends his life and ministry by hanging between two criminals and dying a criminal's death. By redirecting salvific qualities away from vicarious punishment and death on a cross, a liberation theology of courageous change emphasizes Jesus' proximity to individuals who are criminalized and a God who meets poor Black mothers, like the biblical character Hagar, in the carceral wilderness. Thus a liberation theology of courageous change emphasizes the moral gumption of poor Black mothers to make a way out of no way as instructive for churches to find emancipatory pathways to meet criminalized women in carceral wildernesses so that indigent Black mothers can meet their basic needs and self-actualize.

Second, I build on Cannon's set of ethical values with four virtues (care, creativity, compassion, and courage) that highlight a communal ethic and abolitionist commitments that churches can embrace to advocate for poor Black mothers. The care virtue emphasizes the unique values that Black mothers demonstrate in their role as caregivers and providers when contravening laws in order to provide for themselves and their families against unjust social conditions. It encourages the church to approach an ethic of care that prioritizes the welfare of Black mothers and their families as, not a privilege or luxury, but a basic right that is imperative for human flourishing. The creative virtue challenges the church to engage in resourceful resistance to reimagine teachings and practices in ways that point toward a more equitable and just world. This compassionate virtue proposes a reorientation from punishment to accountability to restore, repair, and strengthen individuals for communal flourishing. Finally, the consummate virtue moves from Cannon's unshouted to a shouted courage that should compel churches to amass political power with policies and transformative justice strategies to advocate for poor Black mothers and to dismantle the carceral state. These virtues are mined from agentic survival practices of poor Black mothers, including my own, who violate laws to survive and provide for their families.

Finally, I construct a 2×2 quadrant called "Four Churches," which is a typology to help churches locate their ecclesial teachings and practices by moving from the punitive "Complicit" and "Condemnation" to the desired "Courage" and "Change" quadrants. I propose public policies and transformative justice strategies that emerge from the lived realities of poor Black mothers' struggles to survive carceral wildernesses of criminalization, impoverished conditions, and systemic injustices. In the final analysis, I imagine an aspirational church called the "Abolitionist Sanctuary," which uses abolitionist ideals, liberatory teachings, and identifies three public policy areas (education, economy, and criminal justice) that aim to repair, restore, and strengthen individuals and communities.

In the final analysis, I hope for a womanist theo-ethical approach to public policy and transformative justice advocacy to provide a resource for churches to advocate for Black mothers and abolish the carceral extremism of the state. However, a corollary outcome is the mining of poor Black mothers' moral decision-making powers to break the law as axiomatic directives for leadership that upholds the values of womanist virtue ethics. By this, I am suggesting that Cannon's virtue ethics, and by extension a womanist theo-ethical approach to transformative justice advocacy, exemplifies the ways in which Black women's moral discernment can disrupt dominant centers of power to advance the liberation and wholeness of the most vulnerable. Hence, a womanist way of leading shows compassion for the self-directed practices of individuals who would otherwise face punishment for deviating from the norm. Leading beyond the criminal line generates hope that poor Black mothers, along with their families and communities, can benefit from moral worthiness and social thriving without punitive reproach.

CONCLUSION

In conclusion, leading the womanist way, beyond the twenty-first century's urgent problem of the criminal line, centers poor Black mothers' unlawful agency for survival practices as instructive for pushing the boundaries of dominant social standards that uphold racial, gender, and economic inequities and reinforce the carceral state. Cannon's paradigmatic ethical inversion frames a style of leadership that should beckon the church to use liberatory religious values, public policies, and transformative justice strategies to assign positive reappraisals that advocate for impoverished Black mothers, despite society's obsession with constructing Black women as immoral, deviant, and criminal. Without question, an exemplary model of leading a womanist way emerges from poor Black mothers who navigate the death valleys of the prison system and yet traverse the wilderness with their faith in God intact and an unfettered belief in their self-directed practices to secure life-generating possibilities in a more just and equitable society, beyond prisons and punitive apparatuses. Affirmatively, though Black women were never meant to survive, *we are destined to thrive.*

PART FOUR

Embodied Ethics

10

"Pumping Up Air"

Toward a Womanist Epistemology of Black Choreography

EBONI MARSHALL TURMAN

In the article "Remembering What We Never Knew," Katie G. Cannon begins her discussion of embodied epistemology and pedagogy by asserting performance as a primary site of inquiry for womanist ethics. Invoking Black women's intimacy with Black church traditions in the U.S., Cannon recalls her own mid-1970s experience of hearing the Reverend Dr. Joseph Roberts, then pastor of the historic Ebenezer Baptist Church in Atlanta, Georgia, tell a story about "a renowned organist musician" who gave a majestic "performance in one of the great music halls of North America"; this story would serve as the impetus for her own consideration of womanist ethics at the interstices of Black bodies, Black performance, and Black women's ways of knowing.[1] The story goes that, "in the days of the pump organ," a Black man found himself pumping up air for a renowned white organist who refused to acknowledge the significance of his role in the (literally) breathtaking performance. When the Black man "who had been working behind the organ even harder than the [white organist] had been working out front" noted during intermission, "We're doing a wonderful job tonight," the organist was enraged: "What do you mean 'we'? *We* had nothing to do with it" (italics mine). When the organist touched the keys to begin the second half of the concert, no sound poured forth. In a frenzy, he kept hitting the keys, but there was no music. Then he remembered the Black man who sat beneath the pipe organ, pumping up the air that carried the melody and harmony of the music into the world. He paused to acknowledge publicly the importance and significance of his co-performer. Both men then "finished the concert with even greater power and presence" than before.[2]

The title of Cannon's essay announces its central argument: the epistemic erasure of the bodies, labor, and contributions of marginalized people and communities is characteristic of a distinct and convenient anti-Black project of invisibility that compels the womanist moral project of re-memory.[3] The story of the organ performance reveals the bizarre politics of memory in relation to those "invisible" women and men often socially located beneath the feet of the arbiters of public presence and power, those who are routinely called to use their bodies to "pump up air" for others in order to vivify otherwise dead situations.[4] Cannon more specifically contends that this Black experience of being made invisible or being outright expunged from public memory despite one's body having consistently performed and been put on the line as a present and active participant in the advancement of church, academy, and society is the overlooked but familiar reality of Black women's lives.

In light of the renewed pursuit of Black epistemic erasure at the behest of a bizarre white evangelical condemnation of critical race theory, I consider the textures of Cannon's Black womanist epistemological conjecture and its contemporary relevance for the study of women and religion. Through a secondary interrogation of embodied performance, I endeavor to see the bodies that are literally pumping up air as a heretofore discounted aspect of Black womanist epistemology. The foregrounded concepts of Cannon's epistemological triangle then guide an abbreviated choreographic analysis of "the swag surf," a Black social dance done to a song of the same name. "Swag Surfin'" is an unofficial anthem of the Women's National Basketball Association (WNBA) and has been described by millennials as "a spiritual experience . . . that builds community;" the "dance of our generation" that performatively embodies our "new Black national anthem" in ways that remember things that Black Generation Y never knew but confront every day as the grandchildren and great-grandchildren of the twentieth-century iteration of the Black Freedom Movement.[5] I conclude with a brief hermeneutical excursus on Black theological aesthetics and a preliminary consideration of Black choreography as womanist epistemology that has critical implications for the ethical task of tridimensional justice-making in the world.

Cannon proposes cognitive dissonance, human archaeology, and experiential wisdom as three critical epistemological considerations that drive womanist theological ethics. Foregrounding this conceptual triangle helps us to remember what we never knew and also begins the work of confronting and uncovering the disciplinary moral dilemma that haunts the study of religion and that is rooted in race, gender, and class bias.[6]

Cognitive dissonance is the first epistemological concept of womanist ethics. Cognitive dissonance is the conscious internal conflict that results when one becomes aware, for example, of the conspicuous invisibility of those who live at the intersection of race, gender, class, and sexual subordinations in dominant narratives and contexts. It is the intellectual discomfort that develops from experiential incongruity, provoking questions and responses that center the lives and experiences of persons who are made invisible in the white male-dominated public realm. It asks questions like these: "Where are Black women in this story?" "Where are the children?" "Where are the poor and disenfranchised in this narrative?" "Why have their voices, perspectives, and realities been subdued?" Cognitive dissonance compels critical interrogation of *why* whiteness and cisgender, heterosexual, middle-class maleness is centered in religious and theological inquiry. It evokes and affirms minoritized communities as essential to the study of religion rather than continuing to obscure them.[7]

Cannon's *human archaeology* then builds on the expository work of cognitive dissonance by beginning "a deep examination of relationships, developments, and experiences that seek to reveal the authentic core of reality."[8] The awareness of whose stories are *not* being remembered secondarily compels womanist ethics toward interdisciplinary engagement. Such engagement, in turn, combs the established boundaries of knowledge production to excavate different truths. Partnering with theology, ethics, Bible, history, literature, and the social sciences, it uncovers *what really happened* beyond the reports of religious and theological "heteropatriarchs" who "have worked out, . . . worked on, and . . . inscribed their death-dealing ideologies, theologies, and systems of value . . . on the flesh of Black people."[9] This engagement with human archaeology in womanist ethics "digs up" Black bodies that have been buried alive by the insidious silencing and abductive activities of white supremacy and male superiority. It offers space for disappeared persons literally to come out from under the feet, knees, and death grips of white men, speaking for themselves as those who pump up creative, life-giving air. Like the Black man from Cannon's story, we can hear these Black and poor and quare (queer) womenfolk saying of themselves, "We're doing a wonderful job," in contrast to the stories that the arbiters of power tell about them.[10]

Based on demographic evidence alone, theological and religious studies departments are disciplinary contexts that explicitly disavow the intellectual authority and scholarship of certain kinds of bodies that are marked[11] by minoritized and intersecting race, gender, class, and sexual indicators. By contrast, and given this stark reality, Cannon provocatively claims that Black women's bodies are *primary* sources of religious knowledge. She asserts that the "flesh houses memories" and identifies *remembering the unseen bodies* as an act of [re]incarnation. Accordingly, re-memory brings buried Black flesh back to life and reads the dormant memories housed within Black women's bodies as authoritative theological and ethical texts.[12] Cannon's epistemological project explicitly indicts religious studies for its active participation in obfuscating Black realities not only through its refusal to acknowledge the import of Black life, soul, and death for religious and theological inquiry and revelation, but also because of its explicit move to erase, render invisible, and/or caricature the specificity of Black women's experience and God-talk.

Cannon's charge directly leads to the third and final source of womanist epistemology: *experiential wisdom*, which points beyond normative textuality to the ways of knowing that emerge from the wells of Black women's realities. In other words, she contends against the ways that Black women have been imagined and spoken for in church, academy, and society. In radical contradistinction to the ways that the white mind has historically warped Black women's limited visibility and has rendered Black ways of being and doing as helplessly pathological, womanist epistemology asserts that Black women's lives have a distinct wisdom. Drawing a connection between Black women's biotexts, ancient African wisdom traditions, and the wisdom traditions of the Hebrew Bible, Cannon asserts that Black women's *experiential wisdom* is theologically supported by the fact that not all wisdom literature "was . . . invented by [so-called] biblical sources,"[13] but from the basic observations and "real-lived experiences" of independent folk movements that parallel the *everydayness* of Black women. Womanist epistemology, therefore, pushes back against the "theological-philosophical systems" that define "wisdom as an artificial form of dogmatic introspections" reserved "for the [white] male elite" only.[14] Instead, it claims that Black women's wisdom cannot be captured or known according to such narrow, falsely normative logics. No! Black women's wisdom is an embodied event that exceeds the boundaries of white speech and legibility insofar as it emerges from the garrets[15] of Black women's kitchen tables, beauty shops, front porches, creative play, sartorial effects, and other ordinary incidents that occur in those subaltern sacred spaces that are almost always imperceptible to the white Christian hegemonic gaze. Amid such banal realities of everyday life, Black women's bodies articulate truth claims about God and God's world that simultaneously reveal the deepest secrets of their yearning and suffering, as well as the mysteries of their abiding joy that are, respectively, too terrible and too captivating to relate otherwise.

To be sure, Cannon crafted her womanist epistemology in the late 1990s to underscore how white, Euro-dominated study of religion has rendered Black women's ways of knowing inconsequential, and to demonstrate the kinds of moral responses Black women have made to counter their disciplinary eclipse. Yet the content of her overarching claim of Black erasure remains acutely relevant in contemporary contexts where the arbiters of power pursue the erasure of the lived realities of Black people in the U.S. (in Cannon's terms, the experiences of those "pumping up the air"), or at least where they consistently challenge the reliability of Black experiences of explicit and structural anti-Blackness in the church, academy, and public square, as if Black people's stories and their wisdom are not true. Beyond the testimony of firsthand survivors, anti-Black racism and its death-dealing effects are largely disbelieved even when video recordings (seemingly, the most objective evidence of all) of Black social extermination in the public square are readily accessible. For example, in the shadow of George Floyd Jr.'s brutal lynching by Minneapolis police on May 25, 2020, that has publicly clarified the relentless ubiquity of anti-Black occupation, critical race theory has emerged as a primary target of white religious and political leaders who continue to render invisible the everyday realities of Black life amid white supremacist social structures and its other material colonial legacies. *Critical race theory* (CRT), a term coined by legal scholar Kimberlé Crenshaw in 1989, denotes the scholarly practice of acknowledging and interrogating the social construction of race and institutionalized racism in society. Rooted in the critical legal studies movement of the 1970s, 1980s, and 1990s, CRT explores how the structural legacies of "slavery, segregation, and the imposition of second-class citizenship on Black Americans and other people of color" continues "to permeate the social fabric" of the U.S. Any public acknowledgment of and accountability to this reality is intended to compel legal and societal transformation that is aligned with the claims of "liberty and justice for all" humankind and the inherent equality of all under God.[16]

White theological ire, however, has recently charged those who engage CRT with stoking racial divisiveness in church, academy, and society. The very inclusion of Black people who research Black contexts, produce Black thought, love other Black people, and actively engage in Black discursive grammars is construed as a racial affront to the command of white canonical traditions. CRT and its proponents in religious studies, typically Black scholars and other scholars of color who emphasize the significance of un/interrogated coloredness[17]—these have been targeted by conservative religious whites who have consistently and erroneously characterized them not only as anti-intellectual, vacuous, and overly sentient, but also as enemies of the church.

In November 2020, a mere six months after Floyd's murder, presidents of at least six Southern Baptist seminaries released a joint statement that publicly renounced religious, pedagogical, and political engagement of race in the theological academy. These religious leaders and those whom they represent insist that any intellectual engagement with the specificities of Black life and experience in the U.S. is not only "incompatible with the Baptist Faith & Message," but effectively inconsonant with Christianity[18] and indeed an offense to the gospel of Jesus Christ. Accordingly, they claim that Black life and Christian faith are mutually exclusive realities and that Black lives do not matter in the church or the academy—especially it would seem in white evangelical contexts historically emphasizing so-called pro-life hermeneutics that presumably hold the sacrality of all life as their own moral heartbeat, while effectively aborting the flesh-and-blood realities of persons of African descent not only from their theological centers but also from their curricular and institutional structures. Of course, such a scathing theological rejection of those who are "pumping up air" is not primarily about CRT. Because of their racism, most white religious scholars and theologians do not know what CRT is: their theologies largely center white, colonial, and orientalist sources, norms, methods, mission, and traditions, rendering Black life, witness, and testimony theologically irrelevant and inconsequential to the field of religious studies.

While it may appear obvious to some that the strident anti-Blackness of white evangelicalism ought to be publicly repudiated, the demographic and curricular facts even of white *liberal* theological institutions likewise reveal, albeit more covertly, that an anti-Black theological standpoint is the institutional rule, not the exception. This is precisely why Cannon's womanist epistemological intervention must be revisited. Echoing the theoretical concerns of critical race studies, her womanist epistemology makes visible the Black experiences of race discrimination and subordination by attending to the everydayness of Black life in the U.S. It claims that Black life presents an epistemological vector that advances the moral guidance and imagination needed to dismantle structural bias and construct a more just world for the racially minoritized. Amid the aforementioned efforts to render Black people and scholarship preemptively invisible in the religious and theological academy, Cannon's womanist epistemology impeaches structural anti-Blackness in the church and academy. It challenges the guild to recognize the bodies that are "pumping up air"; to embark on biotextual excavation that uncovers the nuanced consequences of the biopolitics of settler colonialism and its concomitant logics of genocide, slavery, and rape; and to acknowledge that moral wisdom and virtue can indeed be gleaned from the Black bodies buried, or at least concealed, under the feet, knees, and by the chokeholds of white men.

The most remarkable aspect of Cannon's epistemology, however, is her hypostatic aesthetic intervention that emphasizes the underlying reality of the unity of the embodied person, performance, and Black performativity for the tasks of constructive womanist theological ethics. Womanist epistemology thus begins with Black bodies. Following Andrew Parker and Eve Kosofsky Sedgwick's emphasis on mundane ordinariness as performative, as well as Saidiya Hartman's engagement of the everydayness of Black performance as resistance to terror, slavery, and other white supremacist performances of power, womanist epistemology reveals that knowledge, belief, and understanding is not subject to the illusion of disembodied Kantian rationality. Rather, it is ensconced in and recovered from the body that performs ordinarily—especially those bodies that the hegemony of racist-sexist-capitalist-heterosexist social and moral hierarchies have silenced or disappeared.[19] With historian of religions Charles S. Long, Black womanist epistemology acknowledges the erasure of those who have "undergone the creativity of the West," contending that the ensuing silence of the dispossessed is absolutely not "the absence of creativity." Instead, the bodies that "pump up air" are *posed* in ways that coerce imagination, composition, and orchestration beyond the normative legibility of sound and speech, doing so through their practices of living and thinking in and through the disorder of white power. Whether they are scrutinized in the cipher on Harlem's West 125th Street, also known as Martin Luther King Jr. Boulevard; overlooked while hustling on the uptown A train (subway); dissected for "walking while Black" down Park Avenue (or even across the university quad, for that matter); or even perched at the treasured Metropolitan Opera with "fire shut up" in their bones—in these practices of survival, Black people are performing *poiēsis* (creation), R. A. Judy's transgressive everydayness in the body. Even in white worlds where they cannot breathe, Black people are pumping up air or "making something out of nothing." Accordingly, Long concludes that the irony of Black silence and erasure is that Black bodies are, in fact, still speaking.[20] As a conscious constellation of embodied gesture, word, and/or nontextual vernaculars that evoke pertinent meanings of selfhood, such Black performativity compels consideration of how the body speaks when there is no sound and also of the substance of such embodied wisdom. Womanist epistemology thus begins with Black bodies. It does so to attend to the creative silences of the dispossessed. In so doing, it unearths and exposes new ways of knowing, thinking, and doing in religious studies.

THERE WAS NO MUSIC

Contending for the creative silence of Black bodies as the epistemic center of Black life, I am drawn back to my teenage years of working with legendary dancer and choreographer Fredrick Earl Mosley, formerly of the Alvin Ailey American Dance Theater Foundation and the founder and current artistic director of Diversity of Dance, Inc. In preparation for our winter in-studio performance, Mosley began to choreograph his new work on us young dancers, a regular occurrence in our world, where dancers were constantly engaging a variety of artists and were charged to perfect new choreography in a matter of hours, sometimes minutes. I had trained with Mosley for three years, mastering his unique variations of Lester Horton technique. Thus I was familiar with his style, his dynamics, and his choreographic vocabulary, and also was excited about the opportunity to learn to translate new repertory on his cue.

What made this experience completely different from any of my prior interactions with Mosley, and with any other choreographer, was the method that he used to set the choreography. With mere days before curtain opening and for the first time in my life, I encountered the choreographic charge to master movement without music; that is, to capture, rehearse, and perform an entire ballet while using my body to interpret silence. The day before the opening performance, Mosley further confounded his dancers by setting music to the movement while insisting that the dance remain disconnected from the sonic aurality of the arrangement and be propelled only by our embodied interpretation prior to the introduction of sound. In other words, his method not only emphasized but depended on our Black bodies and the creative agency of silence that is typically the material reality of minoritized groups. Recall the material dimensions of the Black body as instrument in the embodied performativity of slave religion enfleshed, for example, in the Easter rock and in the ring shout, long before there ever was an organ, a piano, or a hymnal to support the sacred practices of Black religion in the U.S. Recall the ingenuity of Black movement memorialized in the Black dance legend of the Queen Mother of Timbuktu and her twin sons, one known as "the drummer," the other as "the dancer." In the slavocratic context in which Blacks were forbidden to engage their indigenous forms of instrumentation, the twin powers of the drummer and the dancer were said to dwell in the feet of Black bodies. The drummer was thought to be instrumentalized in the heel and the dancer in the ball of the foot. The manipulation of the foot, then, opened up the possibility of an embodied musicality that, though silenced by the racist-sexist logics of capitalist acquisition, could narrate the flesh-and-blood realities of Black life in the body, beyond the bluster of white and white male vocality.

My repertory experience with Mosley experientially uncovers the truth of an articulating body, a truth continuous with Black experiences of navigating the silence that is coerced by Western creativity on the body (and on CRT). Amid such acts of epistemological violence, determining that the heel of one's foot is coterminous with the now criminalized "African drum," and determining that the ball of one's foot is the embodied variation of harmony that dances syncopation alongside the similarly illegitimatized drum—both clarify the aesthetic meaning of "making something out of nothing." Here finally the Black body underfoot "pumping up air" becomes a primary agent in the articulation of its own aesthetic prowess, *despite* white power's efforts to silence it.

Ethical consideration of a womanist epistemology of Black choreography compels the question: How *do* Black bodies continue to perform despite the evil of white racism in church, academy, and society? How *do* Black bodies articulate Black life and Black flourishing amid the silencing maneuvers of Western creativity that are conterminous with white Christianity? A womanist epistemology of Black choreography is not interested in how Black bodies can help white folks become aware of their sin. Black folks have already pumped up enough air for them. It is interested in how the Black body heals itself and embraces Black joy, hope, and increase.

TOWARD A BLACK WOMANIST EPISTEMOLOGY OF BLACK CHOREOGRAPHY

A Black womanist epistemology of Black choreography echoes Cannon's assertions of the theo-ethical significance of the aesthetic in Black religious life. It is continuous with the broad tradition of African American theological and ethical reflection that privileges the body as text. A womanist epistemology of Black choreography claims that God-talk is continuous with the Black body and, most critically, that *all Black bodies matter to God*. An epistemology of Black choreography takes its cue from Cannon as it engages performance art and performativity as its primary site of epistemological inquiry.[21] Such a centering of Black performance and performativity in womanist ethics insists on the primacy of the Black body and its aesthetic gestures, more specifically, its "pumping up air," for making normative claims about Black lives, Black flourishing, and Black futurity.

We see an example of the critical, prophetic, and gestural work of Black choreography in the "swag surf," the Black social dance that first emerged in 2009 with the release of the Fast Life Yungstaz (F.L.Y.) debut single "Swag Surfin'," which remains a favorite social dance among Black crowds. Although there are several variations of the movement, it regularly occurs in large gatherings of Black youth who, standing close to one another, begin to move concurrently from left to right while maintaining an energetic bounce on bent legs. While bouncing from side to side, the dancers' arms are suspended in the air as they *pump* back and forth or side to side in a way that mirrors a surfer's arms trying to keep balance . . . except with swag, "stylish confidence," or what Robert Farris Thompson calls the "aesthetic of the cool."[22]

At first glance, it might seem that this social dance is solely a response to good music, an embodied expression of Black joy and bodily freedom. Yet the formation and movement that drive the bodied expression reveal theo-ethical truths of the "swag surf" being a "spiritual experience that builds community," our "new Black national anthem." The proximity of the dancing bodies evokes a communal sensibility—that "we," which has historically stabilized Black moral expression in the U.S. (i.e., "*We* shall overcome"; "*We* don't die, *we* multiply"; "What do *we* want? *We* want justice"; "When *we* all get to heaven, what a day of rejoicing that will be!"). The synchronous swaying mobilized by the illusion of "surfin'" arms not only instantiates the communal sensibility at the heart of Black social dance, but also an intracommunal interdependency that requires flexibility to lean, rock, hustle, and flow with the community's current, even while appreciating individual dance variations coming from bodily distinctions. Finally, the syncopated down beats that cue the communal motions evince an embodied insurgency that *demands* breath, visibility, and mobility—the fundaments of life for all Black bodies. The "swag surf" is an embodied performance of cognitive dissonance by literally centering bodies that are regularly rendered negligible. The crowd's sway serves as its own biotextual excavation of narratives of communal interdependency that have "landed many a-thousand" across the long arc of the Black freedom struggle; and the insurgency, that bodied force of arms surfing through struggle with swag, is indicative of the resistance, survival, balance, and Black joy that has defiantly and consistently emerged as the moral content, the embodied wisdom compelling Black bodies to "keep on moving" even while under the feet of white supremacist evil that threatens Black erasure at every turn.[23]

To assert the epistemological potential of Black choreography or Black bodily movement as a *locus theologicus* makes it a resource for womanist ethics that can neutralize the primacy of Black suffering. It does so by repositioning Black bodily agency outside the bounds of reactivity and within an inconceivable Black interiority. Dance scholar Brenda Dixon-Gottschild, who authored the first definitive monograph on Black traditions in American dance, reminds us, "Black dance has to do with the spirit; it comes from the heart; it is something inside of you." It becomes legible through the enfleshed medium of the body, even as choreographically it emerges from the illegibility of creative silence amid racist impulses and acts.[24]

Notwithstanding such *kata sarka* realities,[25] Black dance does not require the look of *an other* for verification. One must only feel. A womanist epistemology of Black choreography rejects theological and ethical perspectives, and also ecclesial practices that abhor the body.

Centering Black choreography denounces religious antipathy toward Black bodies and its caricature of them as corruptible and demonic enemies of the church. It resists the ways that Christian body aversion has historically condemned Black women and femmes to the lowest, irrational, and emotional registers of creation. Instead, it trusts and feels.

Finally, thinking through Black choreography as womanist epistemology broadens the scope of a long-standing conversation in Black theologies, African American ethics, and especially Black womanist ethics beyond the visual, aural, and literary canon. It builds on Townes's "everydayness" by encouraging engagement with the ordinary experiences of Black bodies that "pump up air" in performance halls and on street corners. Moreover, it does not merely designate Black bodies as the image of God; it also acknowledges Black embodied wisdom as evidence of God's ethical presence in Black bodies. God is indeed with us. Such a consideration of womanist epistemology through Black choreography gestures toward the theo-ethical wisdom of "pumping up air," or Black swaggin' and surfin' amid violent social registers. This embodied wisdom is ethically contiguous with the movement and hope of "God made flesh," who insurgently sways with us in the world, in a divine dance-in-community that is profoundly Black womanist and beautiful.

11

Knowledge from the Marrow of Our Bones—A Talk

EMILIE M. TOWNES

I introduced my colleague, Daniel Patte, to the Black Martinican writer Patrick Chamoiseau's powerful novel *Texaco*.[1] Chamoiseau writes his novels in a powerful blend of French and creole; not enough of them have been translated into English. I suspect that this is because it is hard to capture his free-form use of the French language in English since his highly complex and fluid mixture of creole and French bends sentences and creates stunning word pictures that linger in the imagination. Daniel was so taken with Chamoiseau in English that he began reading his untranslated work and discovered his novel *Un dimanche au cachot: Roman* (*A Sunday in the Dungeon: Novel*). Daniel translated a passage that he thought captured the novel and that I would find compelling. In his contextualization, Daniel explains:

> These "notes" are Chamoiseau's effort of summarizing what he wants/ needs to describe in the next 150 pages of his novel—his storytelling to a traumatized girl (who has been repeatedly raped, and who has been brought to a youth center organized on what was a plantation) who instinctively took refuge in a "cachot" in which slaves were locked up until death as a punishment (and a lesson for other slaves). To help the young girl, Chamoiseau tells her the story of a slave who ended up in this cachot. These "notes" interrupt the novel. Which resumes on the next page . . . and becomes a haunting presentation of the experience of being slave(s). But these "notes" summarize what Chamoiseau tries (and does so powerfully) in the rest of the novel.

Here is Daniel's translation:

NOTES

They are hundreds who are surviving like this, without being hit, without wounds, who even escape the whip, just half-invisible in this inexistence, submitted to a slow, daily, invisible body-blow, fed by false directives, body-blow that very often does not draw blood, apparently not hurtful—and yet this is what makes out of this repeated body-blow the worst of cruelty.

I spoke with the master. He is a god since he has absolute power of life and death upon hundreds of creatures. He does not merely have this power, but he uses it almost without being aware that he is doing it. . . . He has become inhuman, the more so because he believes that having this power is legitimate, without boundaries, without limitations. It is a right that he appropriated for himself; it is a certitude that he built for himself . . .

Ever fearful to be inhuman.

The human is outrageous, and it is in this outrageousness that the inhuman is located.

Ever fearful, in order to live this outrageousness without risk.

And I saw those who suffer under his yoke. Even without whip, without torture, they have to live with the awareness that, any day, any time, without rhyme or reason, even because of a most insignificant thing, their immutable and even irremediable vocation is to be sacrificed. . . . To live like this is extreme barbary.

We have to admit it: horror does not need any blood, any spectacular torture or carnage. The most extreme horror can also be a daily affair, emotionless, motionless, in which the human can no longer imagine him/herself as human.[2]

RIDICULOUS

rather than outrageous, the word *ridiculous* came to mind as i sat with Daniel's translation

i have long believed that discrimination and hatred are ridiculous not because they make no sense

but because we often try to make them sensible, rational

  some angle of vision that passes for reality, or for what is true

so that we can ignore the worlds and peoples around us that contradict what we have decided are less than

inferior

the object of extreme disdain

  or violent tiki torches

  or gas chambers

  or lynching trees

  or armed border crossings

  or banking concept classrooms

ridiculous

  meaning shocking

  meaning outrageous

  meaning indecent (in the south and south midland according to the dictionary of american regional english)[3]

these meanings are so much more precise than the standard text about ridiculous

  where it is deserving or inviting derision or mockery; absurd

    causing or worthy of ridicule or derision, preposterous, laughable

    foolish or unreasonable and deserving to be laughed at

as a southern girl, now a southern woman; seeing and living the ridiculous as shocking or outrageous or indecent resonates

    in a deep moan, southern way that says something about how we explore the questions that capture our reason and imagination in the scholarship we do

    and then decide whether or not to let it in or throw it out like bad breath or a rotten fish in the midst of the storm of creation gone into arcane whams and shudders to survive and thrive in these troubling times of post-truth

a rather duplicitous notion that obscures the fact that most of us grew up calling this lying

i ask that you think with me in the three-frame activity of the shocking, the outrageous, and the indecent in our noble quest for knowledge from the marrow of our bones

for we are never very far from the note-taker's reminder of the ridiculous; his outrageous:

We have to admit it: horror does not need any blood, any spectacular torture or carnage. The most extreme horror can also be a daily affair, emotionless, motionless, in which the human can no longer imagine him/herself as human.[4]

SHOCKING

. . . or not imagining others as human

i grew up in a world where black folk were smart, dumb, wise, foolish, holy, profane, healthy, sickly, old, young, storytellers, jokesters, punsters, and willing to be a good audience for those who practiced the fine art of communicating an idea or bending a sentence

i learned early that the power and influence of a well-thought-out idea was indispensable when one had to negotiate the southern terrain of race and gender and class

> for the dangers and realities of senseless violence were everpresent in mundane ways that might erupt without warning

> and you found yourself having to negotiate with your mind and mouth your survival and that of others

> this gives one a kind of knowledge that comes from the deep marrow of one's bones

> that casts an introspective and critical eye on abstractions and when blended with them can open up scholarship in expansive ways

yes, in that little predominately black, transclass neighborhood of tobacco factory workers, nurses, policemen, grade-school teachers, secretaries, college professors, day laborers, insurance executives, lawyers, doctors, and even a house of ill repute (that the women in it called home) it was that neighborhood that bred organic inquisitiveness

where i had the first inklings of what acquiring and perfecting survival skills and then later blending them with scholarship can and must do

rather than remain cosseted in the hands of those who see scholarship as a possession rather than as a gift in a stumbling democracy such as ours

this organic inquisitiveness leads me to wonder how we will engage teaching religion in societies that have often been trained to see the religious as trite, conservative, mean, narrow, violent, and vindictive

and the lives of women, darker-skinned folk, folk that resist a cis-het norm, and others are herded into an essentialist swamp that circumscribes our thought with modifiers such as "black" or "queer" or "southern" to keep us off of the intellectual playing field of big ideas and scholarly discourses or away from church leader-ship because we represent micro-thoughts, micro-methodologies, micro-analysis, "interesting" ideas, and unholy calling

it is a wearying form of shocking that what passes for markers for excellence in our classrooms, our scholarship, and our research

for they are still too white and too christian and too middle class and too straight and too unreflective about who is not at the table

be it as colleagues or students or administrators or church councils

with all the decentering and speaking from the margins that has been going on for decades now that seeks to change our world and worldviews and usher in diversities of opinions and strategies and lifestyles

it seems that we've made some strategic dents in this thick armor, but not enough

perhaps this reflects a strategic error—we have not effectively resisted the power moves that privilege certain voices

voices, though different from the pale androcentric model, who are darker-skinned, multi-gendered, different ethnici-ties, a range of ages, and more

so these new voices, though different in shape, size, tenor, and look; have not yet brought a new model that would structurally change the society we live in it is reformist at best when what we must seek is transformation

and we should all check our methodological nerve and consider how we can keep our scholarship from devolving into an endgame of abstract urbanity that fails to have a public face in a society that needs to hear our scholarship in ways that can help us, as citizens or residents in a republic like the u.s. understand the rich plethora of religiosity that this world has

and the different voices that express it, have memories about it, may be able to provide new insights about our flawed humanity that yearns for better

and not content itself with stereotypes, demonarchy, war games, and plum foolishness when it comes to understanding the worlds we may inhabit and those of others

OUTRAGEOUS

this stuff matters because it builds toward a more just future and a more rigorous and adept body of scholarship that is forged in a diverse and robust daily exercise of excellence and not protecting one's scholarly derriere

theological worlds are vast and contain multitudes:

and we must open the doors of programs and religious houses so that a widening variety of interlocutors and resources have their say

we may decide they are relevant or not, but to foreclose the conversation is bad pedagogy, suspect scholarship, and cowardly discipleship

and it signals to all students and believers that intellectual inquiry is not truly free

and exploring the vastness of God's creation has yield signs and stop signs when peering into the mysteries of creation

so, we put on scholarly blinders that are employed when seeking admittance into the guild or we slide into a sneering elitism about who can possibly be called to the tables of deep thoughts we should not encourage our students to become talking myna birds of nonsense that does not land in full-bodied ways for people to use to think through their beliefs and then translate them into actions

> to not become like those who think being anti-multilingual or cultural is a sign of patriotism and pride rather than jingoism and spittle

> those folks, like folks who can only talk to each other, live lives in arrogant disdain and dismal ignorance

> and they/we are dangerous because they/we champion the notion that being magnificently ignorant of other cultures and worlds and worldviews is actually being smart or well-read or spiritual or presidential

so, if we are scholars, we must nurture passion and precision in our teaching and realize that we should not train students to be the dip sticks for intellectual hubris

> or the plumb line for narcissistic theological dread

we must cultivate students who refuse to perform a classist, heteronormative, racist, sexist drag show

> and resist accepting minstrelsy as rigorous scholarship and/or faith

the cultivation i am advocating is built on an integrative move that represents the complexity of our is-ness, ought-ness, and could be-ness in a complex sociocultural and political creation[5]

> where we draw on the knowledge that we carry from our own journeys

>> our respective life experiences

>> the marrow of our bones that marks us as human and urges us to the humane

> for many of us in this room

>> and throughout the whole of the academy

>> have been told to live in split, if not fractured, bodies and minds

>> to deny what interests us

to treat our ideas as suspect or folklorish or both if not
worse

and sometimes we have been told this is rigorous intellectual and spiritual exchange

we must combat encouraging the formation of this kind of
scholarship, this kind of self-annihilation and demonic shake
dance as a marker of excellence or profound thoughts or the
Holy Spirit

we must recognize that some folks think darker-skinned people are a sea of wanton colored pathologies in suits and ties
and dresses with pumps and pearls

and these folks threaten to not sit next to us in a scholarly
pew that is little more than a postmodern auction block

we should never let this outrage prevent any of us from continuing to look for spaces—faithfully, methodologically, and
theologically—to understand that there is no hiding place for
exploring the worlds of the religious

and plumbing the depths of the moral discourse found in
them

i believe that those of us who are teachers must cultivate students who are clear that whatever else they may be doing in
their lives, they are a body of fierce signification who realize
that it is a good thing to be among those folk who do not seem
to fit into the idealized and pristine visions of the status quo

we must be building a new, fresh, and healthy academy that
values crafting a community of scholars and teachers and
learners

who get excited when we translate our work from library
to classroom to study to community to home to religious
bodies and back and beyond

we are doing the work our souls and intellects must have to
stop a fantastic hegemonic imagination that circumscribes
learning into a narrow and constricting casing

placed within an evil matrix of racism, sexism, classism,
trans-ism, militarism, ageism, and more

and then has the nerve to say this is orthodox when it really
is a robust fear of change and the new in the ways we think
and how we ask questions and offer answers

knowledge from the marrow of our bones should not produce scholarship of death and destruction that is so terrified of the complexity of existence that it shapes answers before even hearing the questions

> it crafts reading lists that look like the high side of misery

> it sanctions curricula that believe it's a good thing to segregate the mind, body, and spirit

> it rolls over and plays dead when faced with disasters—natural and human-made

> it tries to respond to life and living but spends too much time primping in front of funhouse mirrors of theorems and dicta

we do not need more people who behave as if the world is a huge object lesson and a playground for us to test our ideas

> with no consequences and as if doing so is either value free or value neutral

INDECENT

somehow, we are moving toward a stance that a poorly educated public can sustain a vibrant democracy

> nothing can be further from the truth

for a vibrant democracy is built on the foundation of an informed and educated public

> part of that education must involve the nature of things religious and how they affect our daily lives

> the more capacious our understanding of religious worldviews, the better we understand the ways in which folks domestically and globally are responding to the world around them

>> their values

>> their cultures

and this is an important entry point for moral discourses that *can* disrupt traditional canons of theological thought

folks, we spend a good bit of time, energy, and money mastering many or some of these canons with precision and nuance as
interlocutors

> who may or may not approach our work with a different pair of
> lenses that prompt different questions and use different resources
> that may be from <u>conscious</u> social locations such as class or cul-
> tures or gender or race or sexualities

> and this has helped nudge our society into blending newer forms
> of inquiry into our annual meetings while holding the tradition
> in our grasp, but without allowing tradition to beget holified
> intellectual inertia

today's world does not need moral thought that is a threshing floor
for arrogant or aloof scholarship and totally divorced from experience

> that treat all of us as supporting players or as "interesting" side chap-
> ters in the debates within our disciplines or in our religious bodies

we cannot underestimate the value of these things in a globalizing
society like the US

> where we have tended to be uneducated about other peoples and
> cultures

> and we have not done as good a job as we should, internally, as
> we are often mere stereotypes to each other as citizens of this
> republic

we are a part of the formation of citizens

> and a key piece of the foundation for this—after developing rig-
> orous pedagogy, excellent colleagues, addressing the challenge of
> contingency, intellectual resources that help stretch their talents,
> curricula that are designed to address the concerns people must
> address in the 21st century, and student funding

>> is that we must do so with eyes, minds, and hearts finely tuned
>> to building a more inclusive future

>>> by crafting and maintaining an atmosphere of learning,
>>> scholarship, and collegiality

this may be more pressing for folks of color (or any of our kin) who
may be the only one or one of a few who look like them, have similar
sets of shared experiences, share similar cultural codings, and may be
questioning the absence of moral thought that reflects the religious

worlds in which they were raised and may continue to provide them
sustenance

> but i suspect that each of us can see some aspect of ourselves in
> this lacuna

and let me hasten to add that it is important to learn the traditional,
if not accepted, canon of our discipline because you cannot innovate
or transform what you do not know

> but we must not be shackled by intellectual hauteur that dis-
> dains or mocks new modes of inquiry or new methodological
> musings or different resources

you see, i believe that cultivating vibrant communities of knowledge
production means that we encourage one another to step out on
"the rim bones of nothingness"

> and bring new worlds into being while insisting that those old
> worlds that shaped so many of us, but have left many of us out
> of the common understanding of "the intellectual" or "the aca-
> demic" or "doing the real work," should make room for us at the
> welcome table of vibrant discourses as well

we must hold ourselves accountable for creating an intellectual
atmosphere that puts the spunk and spark back into moral engagement by reminding us that learning comes from a variety of sources

> and for every time the academy fails to pay attention to this or
> devalues this or considers this trite or inconsequential

the academy loses more of its credibility and ability to speak meaningfully in the lives of others and to have anything more to contribute
than foolishness all gussied up with big words and incomprehensible
concepts and, in some cases, a whoop that you stole from someone
else's revival sermon

DECENTERING DEHUMANIZATION

knowledge from the marrow of our bones that is shaped *and shapes*

> the shocking

> the outrageous

> the indecent

engages in deep and passionate commitment to engage in moral discourse by speaking out of a fierce determination to help others and ourselves imagine that black folk, queer folk, trans folk, poor folk, all folk who have been sidelined into the category of "the other" *are* human

> in fact, we are *very* human, and we are intent, many of us, on building societies that do not think that arguing for just relationships for all is a pipe dream, fantasy, or illusion

i do not think that the engaged isness i am arguing for can maintain the note taker's distance in reporting the horror of dehumanization to the body, mind, and soul

> or the carnage we inflict when we shuffle creativity into a swamp of unreasoning monologues that sound deep but are just as vapid as scary comb-overs and mindless tweets

>> but deadly because they are the foot soldiers for the power of privilege and hegemony to shape our vision, control our minds, stifle our conversations, steal our resolve, snatch our beliefs

damn it, most of us are brilliantly fine humans so rather than waste breath that i will need when i'm dying, trying to prove to people who think otherwise,

> i choose to focus my womanist eye in my remaining time, on what it would mean to decenter dehumanization

> it is crucial to remember that critical, engaged teaching, learning, and scholarship does not grow like topsy, it must develop the thick skin of ornery insistence that we have something to say and something to say

> and no, we are not perfect, but we sure ain't institutional gangstas stirring up the hot mess of a spiritually inept intellectual game of thrones

colleagues, it's hard work to decenter dehumanization because it is like a demonic watusi that finds its vibe from the drumbeat of a fantastic hegemonic imagination

so, one way that i try to decenter dehumanization is by practicing the fine art of colored orneriness

colored orneriness is a lived experience of belief and scholarship and teaching that is embodied in black people—in the very marrow of our bones

  and it is found in the concrete contexts in which we live out our beliefs and refuse to live lives of deep despair and hopelessness

  it is ornery because it stubbornly refuses the stereotypes foisted on black folk[6]—lazy, low IQ, welfare queens, drug dealers, overly violent, hypersexed, and more

  and it is outright mulish in its demand that black people be seen not only as human but also humane

although stubborn in its assertion of the humanity of black folks, colored orneriness is grounded in the struggle for love and justice

and it takes on antagonistic either/or thinking as unhealthy in many places in our faith journeys

  and urges us to live in the both/and of a deep sometimes biblical/sometimes sociopolitical witness

it is an unwavering ripening into wholeness that brings others along with us

we live our lives combating the outright ridiculous notion that some of us are not fully human

  that some forms of religiosity are more profound or more challenging or more helpful or more spiritual or more akin to what humans should do when making meaning

  that some folks are only intriguing holiday toys that are left, unwrapped, in the corner while the real business of theological mumbling is carried out in long, low, leisurely moans of witlessness

so, i am *not* talking about an ornery that is easily annoyed or angered

  not the ornery of having an irritable disposition (although some situations may call for it)

  or the ornery of being cantankerous (despite how much I like the sound of the word when engaged in verbal play)

the ornery i am talking about is when folk are difficult to deal with or control and *colored* orneriness has been a survival mechanism since black enslaved people were kidnapped in the name of progress and brought to the New World, which was really a very old world for the native peoples living here for centuries

> enslaved black people who were maimed and annihilated in the middle passage and worked like beasts of burden in the peculiar institution
>
> and *still* produced black genius
>
> and the inheritors of these folk are sitting right here, right now and beyond these doors
>
> *and we have allies*

difficult to deal with

> because we constantly contest and dispute a fiendish status quo that finds its solace and structure in the dehumanization of people based on class or ethnicity or gender or race or sexuality/sexual orientation or . . . just because and more

difficult to deal with

> because sheer orneriness is sometimes the only thing that can keep dreams alive, give us a creative edge, help us craft effective strategies for just-making social change, gives us the strength and the courage to keep walking into our classrooms or committee meetings or sanctuary doors and helps us keep our humor and sway with our swag
>
> > so that we have the good sense to celebrate even the smallest victories before we get back to work
> >
> > and the balance of spirit to know that defeat is an opportunity to learn and grow and craft a better strategy or insight in the future
> >
> > > and not to do it that way again—at least not immediately if the timing is all wrong

i am arguing that we do our first works over rather than live and practice a scholarship or witness that specializes in being the doo-wop pom-pom squad for the cultural production of evil and the ridiculous

> we must do the work our souls and intellects must have to stop a fantastic hegemonic imagination that has us performing impossible physical and intellectual contortions that not even cirque du soleil can do

when we lean into the knowledge that comes from the marrow of our bones, we are choosing a colored orneriness that has an attitude as it crafts moral thought, strategies, and actions that are not terrified of

the curve of our hips

the arch of our backs

the slow swing in our walks

the glide of our fingers

the fire in our eyes

the coil of our hair

the deep moans and shouts of our ecstasies

the bottomless welling cries of our sorrows

the slow bend of our smiles

the precision of our minds

the sass of our talk

perfectly and imperfectly

we are *not* chamoiseau's disinterested notetaker and we imagine the human and the humane every day

and then work to make it so

allowing our minds, our hearts, our isness to shimmer with theological fabulous

for our job is not to build the dungeon

but to allow the richness of insights and experiences beyond what we know and don't know to fill our scholarship with deeper meaning

to beget more piercing insights from our students and colleagues because we live into the lively banter of scholarship that frees and emboldens

as it offers more questions than answers

as we seek to be more relevant and strategic in the work that we do so, we create spaces that form a community of scholars and teachers and learners and administrators and clergy and layfolk and more who are moving into a more vibrant

more life bringing and giving

more welcoming

more humane

more alive with possibilities that cherish and use the deep knowledge we have that the Holy is not done with any of us yet so we must live our lives with justice and hope

and as the old black women who raised me used to say about such things:

ummmph . . . ummmph . . . ummmph

12

A Can(n)on of Embodied Ethics

M. SHAWN COPELAND

My folk have always been a race for theory—
though more in the form of the hieroglyph written figure,
which is both sensual and abstract, both beautiful and communicative.
                                                            —Barbara Christian

The mind of the man and the mind of the woman is the same,
but this business of living makes women use their minds in ways
that men don' even have to think about. . . .
It is life that makes all these differences, not nature.
                                                            —Ruth Shays

This chapter engages the theo-ethical praxis of the Reverend Dr. Katie Geneva Cannon. To quote Emilie Townes, "Cannon was and remains one of the most incisive, creative, and rigorous minds we have in contemporary Christian ethics."[1] She dared us to "think with our hearts and feel with our brains."[2] Cannon's critical cognitive praxis resisted, debunked, unmasked, disentangled, and analyzed the brutal and seductive oppressions of gender, sexuality, class, and race. She took, sharpened, and deftly wielded Zora Neale Hurston's oyster knife in order to carve a distinctive method that interrogated experience, generated theory, and developed a field of study; and that opened new pathways for teaching, mentoring, and empowering dozens of students and colleagues—taking us all with her to freedom. The *first* part of this chapter offers a definition of the notion of *canon* from the perspective of the Western intellectual tradition, sketching its function and the *cannon* that often accompanies it. The *second* part considers the entrance of Katie Geneva Cannon onto the terrain of the Western theo-ethical canon and her proposal of canon from womanist perspective. The *third* part contrasts Western practices of canon formation and transmission with the *praxis* of womanist canon formation and transmission.

CANON AND CANNONS

Canon: The ancient Greek word *kanōn* denotes "measuring rod," "standard," "rule." The early Greeks evaluated and ranked their cultural creations with the term *canon* in order to single out products that reflected qualities marking them as outstanding in comparison with others of their kind or category and, thus, were deemed essential. At the great library of Alexandria, Egypt, scholars assembled there coined the term *hoi enkrithentes* in order to denote works that were to be "included" or "admitted" to the library because these works were considered significant and essential.

The so-called Western canon comprises that body of literature or philosophy or music or theology or works of art emerging from Western-formed reflexive or high culture; this body of work is highly prized as classic, as authoritative. At the same time, it is worth noting that not *all* the books or products or authors incorporated into the Western canon originate from within the geographic boundaries of the West. Consider the Bible. In its Christian appropriation, the Bible has exerted decisive influence in shaping Western culture and inspiring many works of Western art, literature, music, and thought.[3] Yet the Bible is not Western, neither geographically nor culturally, neither conceptually nor literarily. Perhaps the Bible is best understood as the critically edited and redacted assemblage of reflected-on and recorded religious, historical, cultural, social, and existential experiences of ancient Hebrew Semitic peoples living in and around the eastern Mediterranean.

Construction of a scholarly canon entails the slow, meticulous, and persistent accumulation of works through research, interpretation, historical assessment, comparison and evaluation, judgment, and decision (i.e., clarification of what sustains a culture and contestation of what undermines a culture).[4] Through this critical cognitive process of evaluation and judgment, texts or music or artifacts are identified as exemplifying cultural excellence or beauty. These texts or music or artifacts represent the *epitome* of beauty or goodness or truth in their respective category and therefore constitute the standard by which all others of that category are to be measured.

In the case of written texts, those deemed canonical are considered significant or essential, even authoritative. These texts generate traditions of thinking and reading, of interpretation and criticism; these traditions, in turn, establish, regulate, and institutionalize courses of study, curricula, discrete disciplines and subdisciplines through which transmission of the canon is structured, reproduced, and made permanent. In too many instances, *the* canon valorizes and absolutizes *one* tradition (culture) to the detriment or even degradation of other traditions (or cultures).

A canon sometimes coaches or coaxes, sometimes pulls, but always intends to form human minds, to train and discipline those minds to appropriate a tradition, an *episteme*, a culture or way of living. But, should coaxing fail, a *cannon* may be turned against human persons in order to subjugate mind through violence against the body.

Cannons: A cannon is a type of gun classified as artillery that launches a projectile using propellant. Cannons are aimed to maim, to kill, to destroy; and canons may be equally injurious and destructive. In his novel *Ambiguous Adventure*, Cheikh Hamidou Kane describes the impact of *both* cannon *and* canon in a small African village:

> On the Black Continent, it began to be understood that [the new-comers'] true power lay not in the cannons of the first morning, but rather in what followed the cannons.
>
> Thus, behind the gunboats, the clear gaze of the Most Royal Lady of the Diallobé had seen the new school.
>
> The new school shares at the same time the characteristics of cannon and of magnet. From the cannon it draws its efficacy as an arm of combat. Better than the cannon, it makes conquest permanent. The cannon compels the body, the school [the canon] bewitches the soul.[5]

Kane clarifies colonial methods of conquest: The dazzling arrival; the fateful demand: friendship or war—and, if war, cannons fire. "The result was the same, nevertheless, everywhere. Those who had shown fight and those who had surrendered, those who had come to terms and those who had been obstinate—they all found themselves, when the day came, checked by census, divided up, classified, labeled, conscripted, administered."[6]

The colonists destroyed order, only to construct a different (dis)order; they demolished, only to build something quite different. Kenyan writer Ngũgĩ wa Thiong'o remarks: "The [cannon] was the means of the physical subjugation. [The canon] was the means of the spiritual subjugation."[7]

In *our* times, the manifold mutating forms of white racist supremacy surface in multiple geopolitical locales in the effort to control and to manipulate the lives and possibilities of us all—whether we are red or brown or black or yellow or white. Gun and taser, plunger and choke-hold, assault and battery, home invasion and street corner aggression brandished by men and women sworn to enforce the law—these have replaced the heavy metal cannons once deployed by colonial imperialists; but these implements and attitudes of domination populate our cities and neighborhoods and towns. At the same time, insidious (mis)education and (mis)information, sly propaganda and cunning half-truths, lies and stupid lies—*all* seek to subjugate body, mind, and spirit. But: enter Katie Geneva Cannon.

KATIE GENEVA CANNON

Alice Walker published the now well-known definition of the term *womanist* in 1983.[8] Once she discovered that definition, Katie Geneva Cannon declared, "Womanism became the *new* gatekeeper in [her] land of counterpain."[9] Cannon knew that land as a school-age girl whose "soul struggled whether to go to school or stay home and be healed from the injuries the world inflicted unknowingly."[10] At such times, her grandmother, Mrs. Rosa Cornelia White Lytle, offered comfort and healing treatment for wholeness—(re)knitting mind and body and soul. For Cannon, the doctoral student with a completed dissertation preparing to embark on an academic career, Walker's "all-encompassing definition was philosophically medicinal."[11] Womanism was a *pharmakon*—a remedy and cure, a means of healing and being healed, a means of producing.

Soon, Dr. Cannon fired off two essays: "Moral Wisdom in the Black Women's Literary Tradition" and "Resources for a Constructive Ethic: The Life and Work of Zora Neale Hurston."[12] In these early pieces, she excavates the Black women's literary tradition and identifies it as a crucial resource for moral insight and wisdom in constructing womanist ethics. Cannon singles out Zora Neale Hurston for her exemplary grasp in "reporting the positive sense of self that exists among poor marginal Blacks, 'the Negro farthest down.'"[13] Because the Black woman's literary tradition is reliable, womanists can count on it as an accurate account of the Black lifeworld that documents and exemplifies how it is that within that lifeworld Black people flourish.

In 1985, Professor Cannon fired again with "The Emergence of Black Feminist Consciousness." As the first Black female ethicist or theologian to use the term *womanist* in print, Cannon argues that Black women's "feminist consciousness cannot be understood and explained adequately apart from the historical context in which Black women have found themselves as moral agents."[14] For ways to live as an authentic moral agent, she proposes neither relativist nor absolutist approaches to ethics. The former approach confesses *no* criteria whatsoever; the latter approach recognizes *only the putatively universal criteria* that bind without exception. Cannon's formulation of womanist ethics is not "prescriptive" but "suggestive" of an approach available to all "who care, to understand and to appreciate the richness of their own moral struggle through the life of the common people and the oral tradition."[15] Moreover, this formulation accords serious attention to the historical and cultural situatedness of the moral agent and dismisses neither guides nor guidance. Not only is the Black woman's literary tradition accessible to a wide-range of readers; that tradition also *both* reflects on and expresses cautions and caveats of Black historical experience and judgment *and* celebrates, commends, and commemorates Black cultural products. That tradition suggests supple, subtle, and sage guidance for the doings of Black women (and men) within the Black lifeworld and beyond. Finally, for Cannon, Zora Neale Hurston stands as an exemplar of how (*and* how not) to negotiate the dynamics of power at work in culture, politics, economics, gender, sex, sexuality, and social class within a racist and racialized ordering of society. Hurston's ability to manage these negotiations in her own life gave rise to what Cannon calls "invisible dignity." Her literary talent enabled her to create Black female characters who negotiated dysfunctional social imaginaries with "quiet grace" and "unshouted courage." Hurston's creative appropriation of the Black lifeworld rendered its empowering collective wisdom accessible and galvanizing. She unearthed what Cannon called an "underground treasury of ethics."[16]

Steadfast, careful, loving, and critical in attending to biological, psychological, cultural and familial, religious and communal, aesthetic and artistic, political and economic experience; questioning and probing those patterns of experience; and reflecting on those experiences within the Black lifeworld—all these led Professor Cannon to the task of canon construction. She was determined to go about this differently. The chief function of a canon in womanist perspective, she argued,

is not merely to replace one set of elitist, hegemonic texts that have traditionally ignored, dismissed, or flat-out misunderstood the existential realities of women of the African Diaspora with another set of Afrocentric texts that had gotten short shrift and [were] pushed to the margins of the learned societies. Rather, our objective is to use Walker's four-part definition as a critical, methodological framework for challenging inherited traditions for their collusion with androcentric patriarchy as well as a catalyst in overcoming oppressive situations through revolutionary acts of rebellion. My overall goal . . . is to recast the very terms and terrain of religious scholarship.[17]

As a groundbreaking womanist intellectual, Katie Geneva Cannon brought about a paradigm shift in the study of religious ethics. She was a trailblazer for that cadre of Black women scholars whom Stacy Floyd-Thomas describes as "revolutionaries, . . . armed with pen and paper, not simply to dismantle the master's house, but [also] to do the more important work of building a house of their own."[18]

CANONICAL PRACTICE AND CANNONICAL PRAXIS

Practice refers to repetitive action aimed toward improvement or, better, virtuosity. The fruit of practice is habit. The Greek word *praxis* refers to activity engaged in by *free people* and, thus, insinuates the role of slavery in Athenian life.[19] On Aristotle's account, *praxis* denoted three types of human activity: *theoria* (thinking), *poiēsis* (making), and *praxis* (doing); further, he distinguished the knowledge derived from *praxis* as ethics, economics, and politics. Philosophies and theologies of liberation deploy the notion of *praxis* in accord with the definition of Brazilian educator Paolo Freire: *praxis* is reflection and action aimed to transform oppressive structures.[20]

What are canonical practices—*in the West*? The permanence or change, regularization and standardization, and transmission of a canon depends on and requires the formation or production (reproduction) of the academic mind (the professor). In other words, the academic mind must be trained and disciplined to service of a canon; in this process of inculcation, the academic mind acquires what French sociologist Pierre Bourdieu refers to as *habitus*. Habitus denotes "a system of shared social dispositions and cognitive structures which generates perceptions, appreciations and action."[21] In *Homo academicus*, Bourdieu exposes the stultifying, absolutist tendencies of institutionalized canonical practices by adverting to practices, dispositions, and structures of the university—an academic *habitus*.[22] These practices, actions, and behaviors include the following: submission to cognitive and behavioral conditioning, reinforcement of that conditioning through dispensation of academic capital or punitive measures, "resistance to innovation and to intellectual creativity, and aversion to new ideas and to a free critical spirit."[23] Research, researcher, academic knowledge or product, academic discourse or rhetoric—these are constructed along premises and principles that function to secure a canon.

Written texts achieve canonical status due to their significance or, in the case of ancient writings, verifiable accuracy, authenticity, and provenance. Texts so evaluated and judged attract attention, bestow authority, and insinuate power. Arbitrary power *over* a canon usurps its integrity, deflects its intention, dilutes its potential; arbitrary power mutates into coercion and force. The exercise of such power overcomes and subverts knowledge to conceal competing or conflicting opinions or positions, to reinscribe convention, to (mis)direct understanding, to disregard questions—to dismiss the questioner, to belittle the "noncanonical other."[24]

Katie Geneva Cannon was acutely aware of the practices and tactics of Western canon formation and transmission. Neither Western Christianity nor its theo-ethical canon (not to mention the discipline of ethics) had much, if anything, to say about Black women's role or predicament in church and society. Indeed, as Cannon pointed out, "This omission . . . provides continuing ideological support for [socioeconomic] conditions and public policies oppressive to Black women."[25] In "Hitting a Straight Lick with a Crooked Stick," she argues: "From behind the veil of race and sex neutrality, the Black female scholar understands that the metaphysical and ethical issues are mutually connected. The accepted canonical methods of moral reasoning contain deeply hidden biases that make it exceedingly difficult to turn them to the service of the best interest of Black women."[26]

Cannon concludes this paragraph with sharply pointed irony: "Universality does not include Black female experience."[27] She experienced—bodily, existentially, and intellectually—what it meant for a Black woman scholar to be tagged as "noncanonical other."[28] Cannon perceptively reflected on the meaning and implications of this injurious experience: "As the noncanonical other, [Black] women rightly recognize how family life, cultural expression, political organization, social and economic roles shape the Black community. . . . Under extremely harsh conditions, Black women buttress themselves against the dominant coercive apparatuses of society. Using a series of resistance modes, they weave together many disparate strands of survival skills, styles, and traditions in order to create a new synthesis which, in turn, serves as a catalyst for deepening the wisdom-source which is genuinely their own."[29]

Cannon advocated serious and critical opposition to the stultifying, absolutist practices, positions, and postures of the academic establishment. At the same time, she urged womanists to build on that establishment, putting it succinctly: "The liberation ethicist works both within and outside the guild."[30] In order to dismantle inaccurate conceptions of race, gender, class, sex, and sexuality, womanist analysis must contest the ideology that passes as theo-ethics and subverts the aesthetic-moral taxonomy of the West that scales and constructs blackness as a deficient and negative signifier. Such ideology and taxonomy maps and stigmatizes the minds and bodies of Black women and men as dangerous, diseased, deviant—ontologically inferior. This ideology and taxonomy is the spawn of what Townes names "the fantastic hegemonic imagination [which] traffics in peoples' lives that are caricatured or pillaged so that the imagination that creates the fantastic can control the world in its own image."[31] For thirty-five years Professor Cannon devoted her time, talent, and energy to challenging that hegemonic imagination through two significant practices of canon contestation and formation: theorizing and teaching. Cannonical praxis is *emancipatory* praxis.

Theorizing: In her 1987 essay "The Race for Theory," Black literary critic Barbara Christian engaged the multiple meanings of *race*. "My folk," Christian writes, "have always been a race for theory—though more in the form of the hieroglyph written figure which is both sensual and abstract, both beautiful and communicative."[32] Black folk have always been a race committed to knowledge, to book learning, to theory, "but in forms quite different from the Western form of abstract logic."[33] Christian argues that critics of all "races" are "racing," that is, competing to conceive, devise, and promote "prescriptive, exclusive, elitish" theories by which to interpret and evaluate literary works.[34] But, she contends, too often these theories are distant, disconnected, and detached not only from creativity, but importantly, from the lives of ordinary people, people of color in particular. For womanist religious thinkers—ethicists, exegetes, historians, and theologians—attending, questioning, researching, understanding, judging, deciding, and writing do not present an occasion for discourse simply among other scholars and critics; rather, theorizing is necessary nourishment for our people and provides one way by which "they come to understand their lives better."[35]

From childhood her irrepressible curiosity and fascination with words, and through to her doctoral studies in Bible *and* in ethics, Professor Cannon understood the potential of authentic theory and theorizing as spiritually, intellectually, and existentially nourishing for Black people. As a panel discussant in a session organized by the Womanist Approaches to Religion and Society Group at the 1991 annual meeting of the American Academy of Religion (AAR), Cannon recalled an incident that occurred a decade earlier. At that time, she was a tutor for the introductory course in Christian ethics taught by Beverly Harrison at Union Theological Seminary (NY). Students asked Cannon to "define the special nature of liberation ethics"—and she did. Cannon reported that she wrote the following questions and answers on the chalkboard:

> What is liberation ethics? *Liberation ethics is debunking, unmasking, and disentangling the ideologies, theologies, and systems of value operative in a particular society.*
>
> How is it done? *By analyzing the established power relationships that determine cultural, political, and economic presuppositions and by evaluating the legitimizing myths that sanction the enforcement of such values.*
>
> Why is it worth doing? *In order that we may become responsible decision-makers who envision structural and systemic alternatives that embrace the well-being of all.*[36]

From this exercise, a *Cannon law* may be generated: *Empower students with supple, subtle, sagacious action-oriented principles* that challenge, strengthen, and support their independence as thinkers, learners, doers—as origins of value in authentic agape. The classroom must be a living laboratory of learning.

In responding to those Union graduate students, Cannon called on methodological and pedagogical lessons she learned in homiletic studies with Dr. Isaac Rufus Clark Sr. "Definition," Clark taught his students, "is a one-sentence statement embracing the essential comprehensive meaning of an issue in a nutshell, the overall sense of the *what*, *how*, and *why*."[37] Elaboration (specificity of the issue) and exemplification (emphasis of the practical value of an issue as relevant to life) follow.

Cannon took Clark's instruction to another level. In her writing, teaching, and public lecturing, she demonstrated that *good* theory—*no matter how difficult*—never concealed or befuddled. Good theory—*no matter how simple-sounding*—never was simplistic. Rather, good (i.e., authentic, comprehensive, generative) theory was the product of careful, critical, reflective abstraction from human experience and was to be expressed in forms and styles that furthered understanding and resonated with living human subjects, who neither were objects nor were to be objectified. As Barbara Christian puts: "Our theorizing is often in narrative forms, in the stories we create, in riddles and proverbs, in the play with language, since dynamic rather than fixed ideas seem more to our liking. How else have we managed to survive with such spiritedness the assault on our bodies, our social institutions, countries, our very humanity?"[38]

Hence, another *Cannon Law*: *Theory/theorizing is not something in which merely to dabble, not something to mess around or to trifle with: theory/theorizing is serious.*

Serious theorizing, moreover, demonstrates what it means for a womanist to be traditionally capable. In the essays mentioned earlier, Professor Cannon drew a map that charted a path through "ossifying quagmires . . . to convey the pragmatic strategic work of [womanist] collective resistance."[39] In the later essay "Structured Academic Amnesia," she restates and spells out the womanist work so necessary in order to redress "the inequalities of power and the arbitrariness of violence": *power analyses, biotextual specificity*, and *embodied mediated knowledge*.[40]

In the context of the structured amnesia of the academy, womanists *must critically and thoroughly analyze the multiple refracting dynamics of power* operative in the wider cultural and societal orders. Womanists must "know how to debunk seamless histories, . . . unmask the deadly onslaught of stultifying intellectual mystification, . . . and continue to disentangle the ordinary absence of women of color in whole bodies of literature."[41] In the context of the structured amnesia of the academy, womanists must tell our stories: "Sometimes the gist of the creative ideas in the mining of our *biotexts*," Cannon asserts, "comes from negotiating difficult personal experiences. At other times," she continues, "it is the echoing of communal realities against the deadly onslaught of stultifying intellectual mystification that grab us as participant-observers in our family and community."[42] For Cannon, womanist scholarship requires deep, sustained, critical reflection on one's individual or personal story as situated within the context of Black collective historical, cultural, religious, political, and economic experience. Cannon was a *virtuoso* at telling her story, contextualizing that story within the wider story of the Black lifeworld, and mining and analyzing that story for "interpretive possibilities for creative change in our contemporary social locations."[43] Finally, womanist theorizing can never "idealize the detached, disembodied, mathematically calculated professional persona of armchair academicians, working from the neck up."[44] Still, another *Cannon Law: Theorizing ethics and acting/living (thinking, speaking, behaving) ethically are embodied moral tasks.*

Teaching: "Teaching is my ministry," Professor Cannon repeatedly insisted: "I love teaching to empower, to equip, to set people free."[45] Because the independence of the student was her goal, Cannon considered courses as "heuristic," opportunities for problem-solving, for lifelong learning. She taught so that students could "use cognitive, self-educating exploratory processes to discern mechanisms of exploitation and identity patterns [to which we all] must be alerted in order for justice to occur."[46]

Professor Cannon explicitly reflected on pedagogy in "Metalogues and Dialogues: Teaching the Womanist Idea." The term *metalogue* derives from the Greek prefix *meta*, connoting "about/after/beyond," and the Greek *logos*, referring to discourse or study, speech or reason. *Metalogues* refer to theoretical considerations about discourse or words or reason, "discourse about discourse," or "reasoning about reasoning." *Metalogue* denotes critical interrogations that "problematize the 'obvious' to create alternative ways of conceptualizing the 'natural.' In other words, African American women scholars create new modes of inquiry for dealing critically with the tradition, structure, and praxis of our fields."[47]

Cannon carefully crafted graduate courses in Christian social ethics—each course a *metalogue*—three courses in one, three concentric circles of discourse. She compared womanist liberation ethics to the vision of the prophet Ezekiel: "wheels in the middle of wheels, way up in the middle of the air." The Western theo-ethical intellectual tradition forms *one wheel*; the specificity of African American Christian culture, experience, history, and perspectives constitute a *second wheel*; and the "experiential dimensions of texts and interpretations" of women of the African diaspora comprise the content of a *third wheel*.[48]

As metalogues (or *meta-rules*), these courses critically grappled with, uncovered, and clarified the "methodocracy,"[49] misogyny, bad faith, anti-Black racism, and economic elitism that is insinuated in

Eurocentric canonical knowledge. At the same time, these courses excavated and analyzed, sifted and critiqued, generated and sustained compound-complex knowledge retrieved from slave narratives, folklore and stories, spirituals, culture (literature, recital, talk, the performances of everyday life), and prayer. This metalogic understanding reveals internal consistency (or noncontradiction); validity (or authority); creativity (or improvisation); completeness (or truth); soundness (or authenticity); aesthetics (or grace, beauty, and elegance). This knowledge equips womanist thinkers, exegetes, ethicists, scholars, and theologians with comparative and authoritative content, distinctive patterns for analysis, deduction, and reasoning—new logics that enable them (and their students) to act and deal creatively and critically with the violent injustice of cognitive, moral, social, sexual, and racial bias.

The term *dialogue* comes from the Greek *dialogos*, which, in commonsense usage, connotes conversation; in its verbal form, *dialogos* means "to converse" with someone. Plato "reformulated" the verbal meaning of *dialogos* and, gradually, it was associated with a specialized type of "intellectual investigation, namely, dialectical inquiry," or dialectics.[50] I read Professor Cannon's notion of *dialogue* as dialectics with an oyster knife—debunking, unmasking, and disentangling Western canonized meanings that have been structured and deformed by the dominative exercise of white racist supremacist power through assumptions, premises, methods, judgments, and conclusions of Eurocentric kyriarchal, misogynist, sociocultural-economic elites. Practices of debunking, unmasking, and disentangling enable womanists to "stay open-minded as heterogeneous theoreticians."[51] Womanists venture into scholarship unafraid to test, to verify, to renovate, and then to deploy constructive ideas, critical theories, and authenticated truths *wherever these may be discovered*. "The origin of the idea," Professor Cannon wrote, "dictates the claims of accountability."[52] Womanist analysis situates its accountability, its authoritative control of meaning and value in the cognitive, moral, and religious authenticity of what has been the despised identity and reality of Black women. Thus, womanists must be prepared to engage in "the ethical labor of wrestling with questions . . . of appropriation and reciprocity [for the sake] of future [womanist] scholarship."[53] And, another *Cannon law*: *Womanists reject criteria that implicitly presume an absolute incompatibility between womanist critical scholarship and liberationist or white feminist or other relevant sources that further the freedom and flourishing of Black people.*

"The mind of the man and the mind of the woman is the same,"

Ruth Shays declared, "but this business of living makes women use their minds in ways that men don't even have to think about. . . . It is life that makes all these differences, not nature."[54] To venture into the horizon constituted by the identity and reality of Black women means grappling strenuously with the history, religion, and culture that have shaped our situated-ness in the West: our encounters with other peoples of color and with whites; our reduction to capital, labor, and collateral—medium of exchange, objects of property, refuse; our embrace of life and love as daughters, sisters, spouses, lovers, mothers, mothers-in-law, cousins, aunts, grandmothers, great-grandmothers, friends—our embodied engagement with the business of living.

CONCLUSION

Katie Geneva Cannon possessed a lucid, luminous, and beautiful mind: she was a profound and dazzling thinker, a brilliant exegete of texts and contexts, a stunning wordsmith who hammered out crucial concepts in constituting complex theories on the anvil of her cultural inheritance. Like Audre Lorde, Cannon knew "to whom [she] owe[d] the power behind [her] voice, what strength [she had] become." She knew "to whom [she] owe[d] the symbols of [her] survival." Katie Cannon knew "to whom she owe[d]"[55] the person, woman, scholar, writer, teacher, theoretician, preacher, organizer, and friend she became / she was / she *is*—one who thought with her heart, felt with her brain, and brought forth testimonies of faith that history might otherwise have forgotten.

.

Contributors

M. Shawn Copeland is professor of systematic theology emerita at Boston College and has made groundbreaking contributions to the fields of theological anthropology and political theology as well as African and African American intellectual history and religious experience. Her book *Enfleshing Freedom: Body, Race, and Being* has been called a modern theological classic.

Nikky Finney was born by the sea in South Carolina and raised during the Civil Rights, Black Power, and Black Arts movements. She is the author of *On Wings Made of Gauze*; *Rice*; *The World Is Round*; and *Head Off & Split*, which won the National Book Award for Poetry in 2011. Her new collection of poems, *Love Child's Hotbed of Occasional Poetry*, was released in 2020 by TriQuarterly Books, an imprint of Northwestern University Press.

Stacey M. Floyd-Thomas is Dr. Cannon's first graduate student and serves as a board member of the Katie Geneva Cannon Center for Womanist Leadership. She is currently the E. Rhodes and Leona B. Carpenter Chair and associate professor of ethics and society at Vanderbilt University Divinity School. She has published numerous articles and eight books that highlight her research and award-winning teaching methods, employing womanist ethics at intersections of critical pedagogy, critical race theory, interfaith dialogue, liberation theology, and postcolonial studies. She has served as the executive director of the Black Religious Scholars Group, Inc.; the Society of Christian Ethics; and as past president of the Society of Race, Ethnicity and Religion.

Faith B. Harris is codirector of Virginia Interfaith Power & Light. As an environmental justice advocate, her work and writing centers on womanist approaches to mobilizing religious responses to climate change, as exemplified in her essay "A Womanist and Interfaith Response to Climate Change," in *Religion, Sustainability, and Place: Moral Geographies of the Anthropocene*.

Alison P. Gise Johnson is associate professor of philosophy at

Claflin University in Orangeburg, South Carolina. She is coauthor of *Exodus Women*, volume 1, *Securing the Sacred*.

Melanie C. Jones is a womanist ethicist, millennial preacher, and intellectual activist embodying radical love and revolutionary justice in the church, classroom, and global community. Melanie is the inaugural director of the Katie Geneva Cannon Center for Womanist Leadership and teaches theology and ethics at Union Presbyterian Seminary in Richmond, Virgina. A third-generation ordained Baptist preacher, sought-after lecturer, and global leader serving professional societies and international boards, Melanie is an emerging millennial voice with noted academic and popular publications as well as features on television, radio, and news outlets.

Vanessa Monroe, JD, is pastor of Bethel Church United Church of Christ in Houston, Texas. She is coauthor of *Exodus Women*, volume 1, *Securing the Sacred*, and creator of multiple resources for nurturing the spirituality of Black women and girls.

Paula Owens Parker is program associate of The Katie Geneva Cannon Center for Womanist Leadership at Union Presbyterian Seminary in Richmond, Virginia. She is the senior program developer of Roots Matter, LLC, and author of *Roots Matter: Healing History, Honoring Heritage, and Renewing Hope*.

Nikia Smith Robert uses mixed methods in the humanities and social sciences to conduct transdisciplinary research in womanist theological ethics, public policy, legal philosophy, and critical carceral studies. Reverend Dr. Robert is the founder and executive director of Abolitionist Sanctuary. She can be reached at www.nikiasrobert.com and @nikiasrobert.

Angela D. Sims is president of Colgate Rochester Crozer Divinity School in Rochester, New York. She is the author of *Lynched: The Power of Memory in a Culture of Terror*.

Emilie M. Townes is dean of Vanderbilt University Divinity School and university distinguished professor of womanist ethics and society and gender and sexuality studies. She is the author of *Womanist Ethics and the Cultural Production of Evil*, has served as president of the American Academy of Religion and the Society for the Study of Black Religion, and is in the presidential line of the Society of Christian Ethics and will be president from 2024–2025.

Eboni Marshall Turman is associate professor of theology and African American religion at Yale University Divinity School. She is the author of *Toward a Womanist Ethic of Incarnation: Black Bodies, the*

Black Church, and the Council of Chalcedon and is a first-career concert dancer and ordained National Baptist preacher whose research interests span the varieties of twentieth-century and twenty-first-century U.S. theological liberalisms, especially Black and womanist theological, socio-ethical, and theo-aesthetic traditions.

Renita J. Weems, PhD, is the first African American woman to earn a doctorate in Old Testament studies (Princeton Theological Seminary) and is an ordained elder in the African Methodist Episcopal Church. Weems is one of the founding scholarly voices in womanist biblical interpretation. She is a former professor at Vanderbilt University Divinity School and Spelman College.

Notes

Chapter 1: The Biblical Field's Loss Was Womanist Ethics' Gain

1. Katie Geneva Cannon, "The Emergence of Black Feminist Consciousness," in *Feminist Interpretation of the Bible*, ed. Letty M. Russell (Philadelphia: Westminster Press, 1985).

2. Novelist Alice Walker was the first to propose the use of the term *womanist* to distinguish Black women's realities and their commitments from those of white women in *In Search of Our Mother's Garden: Womanist Prose* (New York: Harcourt Brace Jovanovich, 1983).

3. Modern scholars often use the term *Hebrew Bible* to avoid the confessional terms Old Testament and Tanakh, and most Bible departments today refer to their departments and the field in similar terms: the Hebrew Bible. But in the 1970s the study of the first thirty-seven books of the Christian Bible was still being referred to as the Old Testament, the discipline as Old Testament studies, and those working in those books Old Testament scholars. Hence the use of "Old Testament department" in this essay when describing the culture of the field at that time.

4. Alice Walker, *Revolutionary Petunias and Other Poems* (San Diego: Harvest, 1971; New York: Harcourt Brace Jovanovich, 1973), 1.

5. I first learned about Katie's dream of becoming an Old Testament scholar by reading her interview in *I've Known Rivers*. Sarah Lightfoot, *I've Known Rivers: Lives of Loss and Liberation* (Reading, MA: Addison Wesley Pub., 1994).

6. Brittany C. Cooper, *Beyond Respectability: The Intellectual Thought of Race Women* (Champaign: University of Illinois Press, 2017), 11.

7. Philosopher-theologian Paul Tillich taught at Union Seminary (1933–55), as did theologian-ethicist Reinhold Niebuhr (1928–60). Jewish philosopher Abraham Heschel served as the Henry Emerson Fosdick Visiting Chair in the 1960s, as later did the premier Black liberation theologian James Cone (1970–2018). German pastor, theologian, and martyr Dietrich Bonhoeffer came to America in September 1930 to study at Union for a year.

8. Lightfoot, *I've Known Rivers*, 102.

9. Union was rife with conflict and student unrest in the 1960s and 1970s and even in the 1980s. Typical protests by students involved issues going on in the country (Black freedom movement, women's movement, Vietnam, Watergate, the Cold War, environment). But because of the special role religion played in

gender and race debates, those topics took on a peculiarly pernicious air at a place like UTS. Debates raged in the classroom, hallways, and refectory about race, the place of men, the role of women, white feminism, Black feminism, Black women's loyalty to their race and/or to gender issues, homosexuality and God, sexual harassment and domestic battery. In her 1983 Master of Divinity thesis, Anna Taylor, a graduating senior and journalist, pointed out that the political structure of the seminary contributed to the division among students, pitting groups against each other and eventually forcing Black women to split from the Black males and white women's caucuses to become an autonomous entity, committed to their own concerns and agenda for navigating with the administration. See Anna Taylor, "A History of the Black Women's Caucus of Union Theological Seminary" (Master of Divinity MDiv thesis, Union Theological Seminary, 1983).

10. Union Seminary had two Black women in PhD programs in the 1970s: womanist theologian Jacquelyn Grant in theology (1973–84) and Katie Geneva Cannon in Bible (1974–76) and then ethics (1977–83).

11. After her studies during the week, Katie would take the subway to East Harlem on Sundays to preach at Ascension Presbyterian Church, a small multicultural Presbyterian church known for its outreach ministries to its neighborhood. According to a current member of what now is Ascension Mt. Morris Presbyterian Church—Connie Williams Gant, a member back in the 1970s when Katie Geneva Cannon worked there—Katie served as supply pastor in 1975–77 and was beloved by the congregation for her warm, down-to-earth mannerisms and preaching and for her loud laugh, which brought back memories of home to parishioners who had migrated to New York from southern parts of the country.

12. Katie's adviser was the Old Testament scholar Professor George Landes, who eventually retired in 1995 after serving for thirty-nine years as professor of Hebrew and cognate languages at Union.

13. In 1980, four years after Katie's ordeal in the biblical studies department, Union hired Phyllis Trible as its first tenured Old Testament female professor. It took over a decade, however, for the biblical studies faculty to open its doors to more Black people. The school hired the Black New Testament scholar Vincent Wimbush in 1991 and graduated three Black students in New Testament in 1999, two of them Black women: Gay Byron and Anne Holmes Redding.

14. It is refreshing to read what younger BIPOC (Black, indigenous, and people of color) scholars in the field have to say about the issue of whiteness and biblical scholarship: Ekaputra Tupamahu, "The Stubborn Invisibility of Whiteness in Biblical Scholarship," https://politicaltheology.com/the-stubborn-invisibility-of-whiteness-in-biblical-scholarship/; Angela Parker, *If God Still Breathes, Why Can't I? Black Lives Matter & Biblical Authority* (Grand Rapids: Wm. B. Eerdmans Pub. Co., 2021).

15. See my essay "Better Than We Have Been Trained," in *Bitter the Chastening Rod: Africana Biblical Interpretation after Stony the Road We Trod in the Age of BLM, SayHerName, and MeToo*, ed. Mitzi Smith, Angela Parker, and Erika

Dunbar (Lanham, MD: Lexington Books; Minneapolis: Fortress Academic, 2022).

16. After earning a master's in religious education degree from Union Seminary (New York) in the 1950s, followed by a decade of campus chaplaincy work at University of California-Berkeley during the campus unrests of the 1960s, Harrison returned to Union in 1966 as an instructor and completed her PhD in ethics in 1975, a year before her conversation with Katie. Her experience in feminist and anti-racist activism in the 1960s inspired Harrison to become a generative force in Christian social ethics, serving as the originator of "feminist Christian ethics." Harrison obtained tenure at Union in 1980 and eventually retired from Union in 1999. See Melissa Snarr, "A New Discipline? Beverly Harrison and 'Malestream' Christian Ethics," *Journal of the Society of Christian Ethics* 25, no. 2 (2005): 79–94.

17. Professor and student decided in 1976 that Katie take a year off to regroup, during which time she would enroll in a few of Harrison's ethics courses and in a year apply for admission into the doctorate program in social ethics, with Harrison as her adviser.

18. Two fine examples of Katie Geneva Cannon's training in biblical criticism are "Womanist Interpretation and Preaching in the Black Church" (113–21) and "Slave Ideology and Biblical Interpretation" (38–46), both in *Katie's Canon: Womanism and the Soul of the Black Community* (New York: Continuum, 1995).

19. Stacey M. Floyd-Thomas, "Enfleshing Womanism, Mentoring, and the Soul of the Black Community," *Journal of Feminist Studies in Religion* 35 (2019): 104.

20. Zora Neale Hurston, *Their Eyes Were Watching God* (New York: Negro Universities Press, 1937), 16.

21. See Barbara Christian, "Remembering Audre Lorde," *The Women's Review of Books* 10 (1993): 5–6.

Chapter 2: Unearthing the Ethical Treasures of Cannon Formation

1. Katie Geneva Cannon, *Katie's Canon: Womanism and the Soul of the Black Community* (New York: Continuum, 1995), 24.

2. Jill Lepore, "When Black History Is Unearthed, Who Gets to Speak for the Dead?," in "American Chronicles," *New Yorker*, October 4, 2021, https://www.newyorker.com/magazine/2021/10/04/when-black-history-is-unearthed-who-gets-to-speak-for-the-dead.

3. See Michel Foucault, *The Archaeology of Knowledge* (New York: Routledge, 2002), for how he presents a methodological treatise that formulates an "archaeological" approach to the history of thought and knowledge production.

4. Foucault, *Archaeology of Knowledge*, 9.

5. Cannon, *Katie's Canon*, 17. To date, it remains one of my most cherished honors to be a part of Reagon's chorus alongside my classmates Edwin Aponte,

Miguel de la Torre, and Karen K. Seat, who affirmed that the compilation of our reserved readings of her essays and articles would become the work titled *Katie's Canon*.

6. Cannon, *Katie's Canon*, 122.

7. David P. Gushee, "Katie Cannon's Enduring Contribution to Christian Ethics," *Interpretation: A Journal of Bible and Theology* 74, no. 1 (2020): 27.

8. Katie Geneva Cannon, *Black Womanist Ethics* (Atlanta: Scholars Press, 1988), 2–3.

9. Cannon, *Katie's Canon*, 69.

10. Katie Geneva Cannon, "A Call Like Fire Shut Up in My Bones: An Interview with Katie Cannon," The Women in Ministry Initiative at Princeton Theological Seminary, March 2, 2018; https://www.ptsem.edu/news/katie-cannon-interview.

11. The American Academy of Religion honored Cannon with its 2011 Excellence in Teaching Award. In 2018, Cannon was posthumously honored at the Presbyterian Church (U.S.A.)'s General Assembly, receiving the Excellence in Theological Education Award: https://vimeo.com/276246157.

12. Renita Weems, panelist, "Making It Plain: Unmasking the Cultural Production of Evil in the Black Church and World at Large," Black Religious Scholars Group Consultation, Panel, October 29, 2010, Atlanta. At a panel honoring womanist ethicist Emilie Townes in 2010 at the American Academy of Religion, an audience member posed the question "Who can be a womanist?" Hebrew Bible and womanist scholar Renita Weems responded, "While only Black women can be womanist, anyone can benefit from it. And the way that I see it, if someone offers you a window into salvation, you take it."

13. bell hooks, *Yearning: Race, Gender, and Cultural Politics* (Boston: South End Press, 1990), 15.

14. Cannon, *Katie's Canon*, 140.

15. Hortense J. Spillers, "Mama's Baby, Papa's Maybe: An American Grammar Book," *Diacritics* 17, no. 2, "Culture and Countermemory: The 'American' Connection" (Summer 1987): 64.

16. Katie Geneva Cannon, "Structured Academic Amnesia: As If This True Womanist Story Never Happened," in Stacey M Floyd-Thomas, ed., *Deeper Shades of Purple: Womanism in Religion and Society* (New York: New York University Press, 2006), 19–28.

17. Cannon, *Katie's Canon*, 122.

18. Cannon, "Structured Academic Amnesia," 19.

19. Cannon, "Structured Academic Amnesia," 26.

20. Gloria T. Hull, Patricia Bell Scott, and Barbara Smith, eds., *All the Women Are White, All the Blacks Are Men, but Some of Us Are Brave: Black Women's Studies* (1982; repr., New York: The Feminist Press at the City University of New York, 2016).

21. Michelle Wallace, *Invisibility Blues: From Pop to Theory* (London: Verso, 1990), 7.

22. Cannon, "Structured Academic Amnesia," 19.

23. See Elizabeth D. Samet, *No Man's Land: Preparing for War and Peace in Post-9/11 America* (New York: Farrar, Straus & Giroux, 2014).

24. Delores S. Williams, *Sisters in the Wilderness: The Challenge of Womanist God-Talk* (Maryknoll, NY: Orbis Books, 1993), 108.

25. Siva Vaidhyanathan, "What Is at Stake with Nikole Hannah-Jones Being Denied Tenure?," *The Guardian*, May 23, 2021, https://www.theguardian.com /commentisfree/2021/may/23/nikole-hannah-jones-tenure-universities-new-york -times.

26. See Koritha Mitchell, *From Slave Cabins to the White House: Homemade Citizenship in African American Culture* (Urbana: University of Illinois Press, 2021).

27. Katie G. Cannon, "Response," in Monica A. Coleman et al., "Roundtable Discussion: Must I Be Womanist? [With Response]," *Journal of Feminist Studies in Religion* 22, no. 1 (April 1, 2006): 97.

28. Cannon, "Response," 96.

29. This quote is from Audre Lorde's speech at Harvard University in 1982, "Learning from the 60s," http://www.Blackpast.org/1982-audre-lorde -learning-60s.

30. Audre Lorde, "The Master's Tools Will Never Dismantle the Master's House," in *Sister Outsider: Essays and Speeches* (Trumansburg, NY: Crossing Press, 1984), 112.

31. Stacey M. Floyd-Thomas, *Mining the Motherlode: Methods in Womanist Ethics* (Cleveland: Pilgrim Press, 2006), 21.

32. Cannon, "Structured Academic Amnesia," 20.

33. Ralph Ellison, "What America Would Be Like without Blacks," as quoted by Cornel West, in *Race Matters* (Boston: Beacon Press, 2001), 1.

34. Matthew 13:52, New Revised Standard Version.

35. Katie Geneva Cannon, "What Is a Sermon? Women and the Word," Boston University, Anna Howard Shaw Center, 1986, https://www.bu.edu /shaw/events/women-in-the-world-conference/past_women-in-the-world/women -in-the-world/what-is-a-sermon/.

Chapter 3: The House That Cannon Built and "The Hinges upon Which the Future Swings"

1. Katie Geneva Cannon, "Teaching Afrocentric Ethics: 'The Hinges upon Which the Future Swings,'" Daughters of the African Atlantic Fund, April 26, 2016, https://www.africanatlanticdaughters.com/2016/04/26/the-hinges-upon-which -the-future-swings/.

2. Katie G. Cannon, "Response," in Monica A. Coleman et al., "Roundtable Discussion: Must I Be Womanist? [With Response]," *Journal of Feminist Studies in Religion* 22, no. 1 (April 1, 2006): 97.

3. Alice Walker, *In Search of Our Mothers' Gardens: Womanist Prose* (New York: Harcourt Brace Jovanovich, 1983), xi.

4. See Layli Phillips, ed., *The Womanist Reader* (New York: Routledge, 2006).

5. Katie Geneva Cannon, *Katie's Canon: Womanism and the Soul of the Black Community* (New York: Continuum, 1995), 47.

6. Cannon, *Katie's Canon*, 56.

7. Cannon, *Katie's Canon*, 56.

8. Monica A. Coleman et al., "Roundtable Discussion," 96.

9. Cannon, *Katie's Canon*, 138.

10. Cannon, *Katie's Canon*, 124.

11. Brian K. Blount, "Presidential Letter for The Katie Geneva Cannon Center for Womanist Leadership 2021 Spring Conference Digital Guide," April 8, 2021.

12. "A Call Like Fire Shut Up in My Bones: An Interview with Dr. Katie Cannon (1950–2018)," Princeton Theological Seminary, March 2, 2018, https://www.ptsem.edu/news/katie-cannon-interview.

13. Mary Hunt, "1,500 Attend Center for Womanist Leadership Inaugural Gathering," Union Presbyterian Seminary, June 1, 2018, https://www.upsem.edu/news/1500-attend-center-for-womanist-leadership-inaugural-gathering/.

14. Toni C. King and S. Alease Ferguson, eds., *Black Womanist Leadership: Tracing the Motherline* (Albany: State University of New York Press, 2011).

15. Robert Michael Franklin, *Moral Leadership: Integrity, Courage, Imagination* (Maryknoll, NY: Orbis Books, 2020), xxvii.

16. Franklin, *Moral Leadership*, 6.

17. Franklin, *Moral Leadership*, 7.

18. Franklin, *Moral Leadership*, 9.

19. Franklin, *Moral Leadership*, 9.

20. Cannon, *Katie's Canon*, 23.

21. Cannon, *Katie's Canon*, 23.

22. Walker, *Our Mothers' Gardens*, xi.

23. Toni C. King and S. Alease Ferguson, eds., *Black Womanist Leadership: Tracing the Motherline* (Albany: State University of New York Press, 2011), 11.

24. Cannon, "Teaching Afrocentric Ethics."

25. Delores S. Williams, "Rituals of Resistance in Womanist Worship," in *Women at Worship: Interpretations of North American Diversity*, ed. Marjorie Procter-Smith and Janet Roland Walton (Louisville, KY: Westminster/John Knox Press, 1993), 216.

26. Cannon, "Teaching Afrocentric Ethics."

Chapter 4: Redeeming Black Survival

1. Katie Geneva Cannon, *Katie's Canon: Womanism and the Soul of the Black Community* (New York: Continuum, 1995), 148–49.

2. *Forced Serial Displacement* is a term coined by Mindy Thompson to describe the transgenerational effects of housing and banking policies systemically controlling/limiting living choices of African Americans through redlining, divestment, and shrinkage of Black communities through removal. This process will be discussed more fully in following sections.

3. For extensive discussion of the interrelatedness of social and political strati-fication endemic to capitalism, see Oliver C. Cox, *Cast, Class, and Race: A Study in Social Dynamics* (New York: Monthly Review Press, 1959).

4. Alice Walker, the second part of the definition of *womanism* as articulated in *In Search of Our Mothers' Gardens: Womanist Prose* (New York: Harcourt Brace & Co., 1983), xi-xii.

5. Barbara Bailey, "Feminization of Poverty across Pan-African Societies: The Church's Response—Alleviate or Emancipatory?," in *Poverty and Religion: Pan-African Perspectives*, ed. Peter J. Paris (Durham, NC: Duke University Press, 2009), 39–65.

6. *Sacrificial zones* describes, beyond race, the threat that systems of values held by ethnic groups represent to American imperialism. The term was coined by Chris Hedges and Joe Sacco, in *Days of Destruction, Days of Revolt* (New York: Nation Books, 2012).

7. Cannon, *Katie's Canon*, 49. See also Isabel Wilkerson, *Caste: The Origins of Our Discontent* (New York: Random House, 2020).

8. Kelly Brown Douglas, in *Sexuality and the Black Church: A Womanist Perspective* (Maryknoll, NY: Orbis Books, 1999), 13–16, discusses the meaning of whiteness with particular attention given to George Frederickson's analysis of Black inferiority in discourse related to the presumed philosophical authority of white supremacy. He takes this as a foundation for a worldview suggesting that Black inferiority is the product of nature, therefore explaining as reality the "perpetual slavishness and subordination" of Black people. See also Elisabeth Schüssler Fiorenza, *In Memory of Her* (New York: Crossroad, 2002), discussing hierarchical relationships of kyriarchal societies.

9. See Cannon, *Katie's Canon*, 153.

10. Sustainability of Black survival occurred through grafting the tenets of survival to the robust theological perspective of the Black faith organizations or churches substantive enough to see economic, social, mental, educational, and communal resources in addition to worship as central to the faith(s); this was con-scientious enough to filter out oppressive biblical and theological sourcing from the larger community. See Ralph Warnock, *Divided Mind of the Black Church* (New York: New York University Press, 2013).

11. President Lyndon B. Johnson, 1964 State of the Union Address, https://www.presidency.ucsb.edu/documents/annual-message-the-congress-the-state-the-union-25; and https://history.house.gov/Media?mediaID=1503240456.

12. Robert J. Desiderio and Raymond G. Sanchez, *The Community Development Corporation*, 10 B.C.L. Rev. 217 (1969), http://lawdigitalcommons.bc.edu/bclr/vol10/iss2/2. The original 1964 framework was robust enough to resource community development corporations (CDC), underwritten using public and private funds, and owned by community-based stockholders. The planned com-munities would have schools, housing, health facilities, and commerce.

13. Robert Collinson, Ingrid Gould Ellen, and Jens Ludwig, "Low-Income

Housing Policy" (Kreisman Working Papers Series in Housing Law and Policy No. 29, 2015).

14. For contemporary policies mirroring 1960s' practices, see Rahim Kurwa (2020), "The New *Man in the House* Rules: How the Regulation of Housing Vouchers Turns Personal Bonds into Eviction Liabilities," *Housing Policy Debate* 30, no. 6 (March 2020): 926–49, https://doi.org/10.1080/10511482.2020.1778056.

15. Rahim Kurwa, "The New *Man in the House* Rules."

16. Edwin Black, *War against the Weak: Eugenics and America's Campaign to Create a Master Race* (Washington, DC: Dialog Press, 2012), 12.

17. Cannon, *Katie's Canon*, 149.

18. Tax-increment financing is a method of diverting future property taxes as subsidy for redevelopment, typically in blighted areas, but not necessarily so.

19. See in-depth discussions on the impact of cultural productions in Emilie M. Townes, *Womanist Ethics and the Cultural Production of Evil*, Black Religion, Womanist Thought, Social Justice (New York: Palgrave Macmillan, 2006). See also Tom Burrell, *Brain Washed: Challenging the Myth of Black Inferiority* (Carlsbad, NM: Hay House, 2010).

20. Mindy Thompson Fullilove and Rodrick Wallace, "Serial Forced Displacement in American Cities, 1916–2010," *Journal of Urban Health: Bulletin of the New York Academy of Medicine* 88, no. 3 (2011): 381–89, doi:10.1007/s11524-011-9585-2.

21. Fullilove and Wallace, "Serial Forced Displacement," 381–89.

22. In data collected that is related to HOPE VI HUD funding and legislation in the years 1993 to 1999, only 11.4 percent of displaced public housing residents were slated to reoccupy units in their neighborhoods after redevelopment. Additionally, in some cities there ranges a loss of available affordable units from 40–90 percent. See "False HOPE: A Critical Assessment of the HOPE VI Public Housing Redevelopment Program," Oakland: National Housing Law Project, June 2002, https://www.nhlp.org/files/FalseHOPE.pdf.

23. Adam Smith, *Wealth of Nations* (New York: Classic House Books, 2009).

24. John Locke in chap. 5, "Of Property," in *The Second Treatise of Government* (1689, https://www.gutenberg.org/files/7370/7370-h/7370-h.htm). Here Locke makes a shift from Western interpretations of the doctrine of common dominion to private ownership.

25. Jae H. Cho, "Moral Implication of Acquisitive Instinct under the Separation of Ownership and Control," *Review of Social Economy* 35, no. 2 (1977): 143–48, https://www.tandfonline.com/doi/abs/10.1080/00346767700000016.

26. R. H. Tawney, *The Acquisitive Society* (New York: Harcourt Brace & Co., 1920), 7–8.

27. Described in the work of Edwin Nichols as philosophical aspects of cultural difference, in Bruce A. Jones and Edwin J. Nichols, *Cultural Competence*

in America's Schools: Leadership, Engagement and Understanding (Charlotte, NC: Information Age Pub., 2013).

28. Nichols contends that this mode of behavior and worldview are characteristic of peoples of European descent, due primarily to environmental factors limiting food production to three months of the year, often threatening the ability to survive and bringing the need to contend with nature and develop technologies in order to survive. He further suggests, just as Mindy Thompson-Fulilove, that this worldview is epigenetic, existing and replicating for thousands of years. See Jones and Nichols, *Cultural Competence*, 31–41. Further consideration needs to be given to analyze specificity among ethnic populations now largely grouped under the umbrella term *Europeans* and the impact that globalization has had on more ancient cultural expressions.

29. Brian Hall, *Values Shift: A Guide to Personal and Organizational Transformation* (1994; Eugene: Wipf & Stock, 2006). See also Delores Williams, *Sisters in the Wilderness: The Challenge of Womanist God-Talk* (Maryknoll, NY: Orbis Books, 2001).

30. The historical origins and use of the term *soul murder* is discussed and employed by Leonard Shengold in *Soul Murder: The Effects of Childhood Abuse and Deprivation* (New York: Fawcett Columbine, 1989).

31. Discussion of Shengold and soul murder appears in Nell Irvin Painter, *Soul Murder* (Waco, TX: Baylor University Press, 1993), 7–8.

32. Fullilove and Wallace, "Serial Forced Displacement," 384.

33. Marimba Ani, *Yorugu: An African-Centered Critique of European Cultural Thought and Behavior* (Trenton, NJ: Africa World Press, 1994), 316.

34. Harry Belafonte, "Is America a Burning House? We Need a Voice of Moral Courage to Offer a Vision for the Twenty-First Century," *Essence* 27 (November 1996): 218; "Harry Belafonte Reflects on Working toward Peace," https://www .scu.edu/mcae/architects-of-peace/Belafonte/essay.html.

35. Resmaa Menakem theorizes that much of the violence perpetuated against Black people is a response to European (white-on-white body) trauma unanalyzed or metabolized. Resmaa Menakem, *My Grandmother's Hands: Racialized Trauma and the Pathway to Mending Our Hearts and Bodies* (London: Penguin Books, 2017).

36. Jerome Ross, in *A History of Israel and Judah: A Compilation* (Pittsburgh: Dorrance Pub., 2003), reads the ancient Israelite experience as that of a relationship-centered people trying to survive.

37. Rosetta Ross, in *Witnessing and Testifying: Black Women, Religion, and Civil Rights* (Minneapolis: Fortress Press, 2003), discusses education and mobilizing strategies of civil rights activists Ella Josephine Baker and Fannie Lou Hamer that exemplify sovereignty-based survival.

Chapter 5: Excavating Darkness

1. From "Black Mother Woman," first published by Audre Lorde in *From a Land Where Other People Live* (Detroit: Broadside Press, 1973).

2. Audre Lorde, "Poetry Is Not a Luxury," in *Sister Outsider: Essays and Speeches* (Trumansburg, NY: Crossing Press, 1984), 36.

3. This phrase is used by Katie Geneva Cannon to define the outcomes of womanist pedagogical praxis, in *Remembering What We Never Knew: The Epistemology of Womanist Theology* (Richmond, VA: Center for Womanist Leadership Pub., 2018), 13. The connotation of the expression is also found in the work of Toni Morrison in suggesting that a "before" existed prior to a beginning, especially in relationship to the origins of racialized othering. See Toni Morrison, *Playing in the Dark: Whiteness and Literary Imagination* (Cambridge, MA: Harvard University Press, 1992); and Morrison, *The Origin of Others* (Cambridge, MA: Harvard University Press, 2017).

4. *Human archaeologists* is a term created by Sara Lawrence-Lightfoot in *I've Known Rivers: Lives of Loss and Liberation* (Reading, MA: Addison-Wesley Pub. Co., 1994) as a method for unearthing stories.

5. Here "othering" is defined as morally tutored debilitating conditions informed by the intersection of legislation, religious authority, and moral philosophy, expressed overtly through multilayered systemic race, sex, and class oppression that scars the human heart.

6. Kenneth Leech defines the term *soul friend* in *Soul Friend: Spiritual Direction in the Modern World* (1977; Harrisburg, PA: Morehouse Pub., 2001).

7. Howard Thurman, *Deep Is the Hunger: Meditations for Apostles of Sensitiveness* (New York: Harper, 1951), 15. See also Barbara Holmes discussion of Thurman in *Joy Unspeakable: Contemplative Practices of the Black Church* (Minneapolis: Fortress Press, 2017), 4.

8. bell hooks quotes Jack Kornfield in *All about Love: New Visions* (New York: Harper Collins Pub., 2000), xiii.

9. The *dance of redemption* as defined by Katie Cannon is designed as womanist pedagogy of liberation in her chapter "Metalogues and Dialogues," in Katie Geneva Cannon, *Katie's Canon: Womanism and Soul of the Black Community* (New York: Continuum, 1995), 136–43.

10. The term *conscientization narrative* also relates to the term *sacred soliloquies*, discussed in Alison P. Gise Johnson and Vanessa D. Monroe, *Exodus Women, Volume One: Securing the Sacred; Usable Truths, Secret Pledges, and Clarion Calls in the Story of Shiphrah and Puah, the Midwives* (independently published, 2019).

11. Here "soul" is defined in parallel with the work of Na'im Akbar as encompassing full integration of the body, mind, core of a person; this core is viewed as a site hosting ancestors, as outlined in Paul Pearsall, *The Heart's Code: Tapping the Wisdom and Power of Our Heart's Energy* (New York: Broadway Books, 1999) and is parallel to the definition of "community" by Peter J. Paris in *The Spirituality of African Peoples: The Search for a Common Moral Discourse* (Minneapolis: Fortress Press, 1995). See also Audre Lorde, "Poetry Is Not a Luxury," in *Sister Outsider*, 36.

12. Paris, *Spirituality of African Peoples*, 51.

13. Details of the life of Jochebed are found in Exod. 2:1–10a; 6:20.

14. This presentation is by Alison Gise Johnson and Vanessa Monroe, 2021, to be in *Exodus Women, Volume Two* (2022), from a manuscript in preparation.

15. The Qur'an 28.7.

16. While being interviewed, Nell Painter recounts how she came to the project of writing a biography about Sojourner Truth. Karen J. Winkler, "A New Biography Examines the Life of Sojourner Truth," *The Chronicle of Higher Education*, September 13, 1996, https://www.chronicle.com/article/a-new-biography-examines-the-life-of-sojourner-truth/.

17. Barbara Holmes, *Joy Unspeakable*, 22.

18. Delores S. Williams, "Womanist Theology: Black Women's Voices," *Christianity and Crisis*, March 2, 1987; *Religion Online*, https://www.religion-online.org/article/womanist-theology-black-womens-voices/.

Chapter 6: Rooted Woman or Root Woman

1. Willie James Jennings, "Redeeming the Creature: Race, Place and the Hope of the Church," quoted and adapted from 17:03–17:41, from the video lecture on "The Land Speaks: Rethinking Both the Private and Possession," in the Sprunt Lectures, Union Presbyterian Seminary, May 2018, https://www.youtube.com/watch?v=uAsKuK_XAmk.

2. Charles H. Long, STVU [Samuel DeWitt Proctor School of Theology is the graduate theological school of Virginia Union University, Richmond, VA] Class Lectures, 2005 [e.g., Allen Seager, "Women and the Church in New France," History 204: The Social History of Canada (class lecture, Simon Fraser University, Burnaby, BC, January 13, 2011)].

3. M. Shawn Copeland, *Enfleshing Freedom: Body, Race, and Being* (Minneapolis: Fortress Press, 2010), 65–66.

4. Melissa Florer-Bixler, "The Kin-Dom of Christ," *Sojourners*, November 20, 2018, https://sojo.net/articles/kin-dom-christ.

5. Walter Brueggemann, *Sabbath as Resistance: Saying No to the Culture of Now* (Louisville, KY: Westminster John Knox Press, 2017), 1–19.

6. Brueggemann, *Sabbath as Resistance*, 56.

7. bell hooks, *Belonging: A Culture of Place* (New York: Routledge, 2019), 117.

8. Melanie L. Harris, *Ecowomanism: African American Women and Earth-Honoring Faiths* (Maryknoll, NY: Orbis Books, 2017), 5.

9. Isabel Wilkerson, *The Warmth of Other Suns: The Epic Story of America's Great Migration* (New York: Random House, 2010).

10. Harris, *Ecowomanism*, 28.

11. hooks, *Belonging*, 117.

12. Harris, *Ecowomanism*, 40.

13. hooks, *Belonging*, 117.

14. "Advocacy Basics," United Church of Christ, March 8, 2021, https://www.ucc.org/justice_advocacy_resources_advocacy-basics.

15. Wati Longchar, "Liberation Theology and Indigenous People," in *The Reemergence of Liberation Theologies: Models for the Twenty-First Century*, ed. Thia Cooper, New Approaches to Religion and Power (New York: Palgrave Macmillan, 2013), 111.

16. Longchar, "Liberation Theology and Indigenous People," 114.

17. Longchar, "Liberation Theology and Indigenous People," 115.

Chapter 7: Walking through the Valley

1. Ronald A. Heifetz, Marty Linsky, and Alexander Grashow, *The Practice of Adaptive Leadership: Tools and Tactics for Changing Your Organization and the World* (Cambridge, MA: Harvard Business Press, 2009), 13–40, chap. 2.

2. Katie Geneva Cannon, *The Womanist Theology Primer: Remembering What We Never Knew; The Epistemology of Womanist Theology* (2001; repr., Richmond, VA: Union Presbyterian Seminary Center for Womanist Leadership, 2018), 3.

3. Mary Margaret Schley, "The United Order of Tents and 73 Cannon Street: A Study of Identity and Place," unpublished thesis for master of science, historic preservation degree (Clemson [SC] University, 2013), 7, https://tigerprints.clemson.edu/cgi/viewcontent.cgi?referer=&httpsredir=1&article=2667&context=all_theses.

4. Some historians refer to this period in history, 1890–1930, as the "Black women's club movement."

5. Marcia Y. Riggs, *Awake, Arise, & Act: A Womanist Call for Black Liberation* (Cleveland: Pilgrim Press, 1994), 67–75.

6. Mary Church Terrell, "In Union There Is Strength," BlackPast, January 27, 2007, https://www.Blackpast.org/african-american-history/1897-mary-church-terrell-union-there-strength/.

7. James H. Cone, *A Black Theology of Liberation* (Philadelphia: J. B. Lippincott, 1970).

8. Mary Daly, *Beyond God the Father: Toward a Philosophy of Women's Liberation* (Boston: Beacon Press, 1973).

9. Terrell, "In Union There Is Strength."

10. "Dancing Redemption's Song, across Generations," *Journal of Feminist Studies in Religion* 34, issue 2 (Fall 2018): 78, https://www.fsrinc.org/web-articles/in-memory-of-cannon/.

11. Katie Geneva Cannon, "Teaching Afrocentric Ethics: 'The Hinges upon Which the Future Swings,'" Daughters of the African Atlantic Fund, 2016, https://www.africanatlanticdaughters.com/2016/04/26/the-hinges-upon-which-the-future-swings/.

12. Gayraud S. Wilmore, foreword to *Africa at the Crossroads*, by James H. Robinson (Philadelphia: Westminster Press, 1962).

13. Cannon, "Teaching Afrocentric Ethics."

14. Katie Geneva Cannon, *Katie's Canon: Womanism and the Soul of the Black Community*, (New York: Continuum, 1995), 24.

15. Celeste Kennel-Shank, "Katie Geneva Cannon, Groundbreaking Womanist Ethicist and Theologian, Dies at Age 68," *Christian Century*, August 9, 2018, https://www.christiancentury.org/article/people/katie-geneva-cannon -groundbreaking-womanist-ethicist-and-theologian-dies-age-68.

16. Katie Geneva Cannon, "Identity," YouTube video, March 19, 2014, https://www.youtube.com/results?search_query=Katie+Cannon+identity.

17. Katie Geneva Cannon, "Lifetime of Learning," Plenary Panel, American Academy of Religion, Annual Meeting, San Francisco, CA, November 21, 2011.

18. The Annual Honorary and Memorial Banquet Program Bulletin, St. John's AME Church, Norfolk, VA, April 15, 1991, "Strengthening the Black Family thru Christian Leadership," True Love Tent #37 of the J. R. Giddings and Jollifee Union. J. R. Giddings and Jollifee Union, named after two white abolitionists, was the original name incorporated in Norfolk, Virginia, on June 17, 1883. A charter amendment to change the name to the United Order of Tents was granted June 28, 1912.

19. Layli Phillips, ed., *The Womanist Reader: The First Quarter Century of Womanist Thought* (New York: Routledge, 2006), xx.

20. Schley, "United Order of Tents," 7.

Chapter 8: Even When One's Face Is on Fire

1. Sara Lawrence-Lightfoot, *I've Known Rivers: Lives of Loss and Liberation* (New York: Penguin Books,1995), 70.

2. Katie Geneva Cannon, *Black Womanist Ethics* (Atlanta: Scholars Press, 1988), 5.

3. Lawrence-Lightfoot, *I've Known Rivers*, 72.

4. See Colleen Flaherty, "Legislating against Critical Race Theory," Inside Higher Ed, June 9, 2021, https://www.insidehighered.com/news/2021/06/09 /legislating-against-critical-race-theory-curricular-implications-some-states; Nick Anderson and Susan Svrluga, "College Faculty Are Fighting Back against State Bills on Critical Race Theory," *Washington Post*, February 19, 2022, https:// www.washingtonpost.com/education/2022/02/19/colleges-critical-race-theory-bills/; Adam Friedman, "Tennessee Republican Leaders Renew Critical Race Theory Crusade, Target Universities," *Tennessean*, February 20, 2022, https://www .tennessean.com/story/news/politics/2022/02/21/critical-race-theory-tennessee -colleges-republicans-battle-renewed/6828898001/; Rashawn Ray and Alexandra Gibbons, "Why Are States Banning Critical Race Theory?," Brookings, November 2021, https://www.brookings.edu/blog/fixgov/2021/07/02/why-are -states-banning-critical-race-theory/.

5. See Janice Gassam Asare, "What People Misunderstand about Anti-Racism

Training," *Forbes*, January 4, 2022, https://www.forbes.com/sites/janicegassam /2022/01/04/what-people-misunderstand-about-anti-racism-training/?sh=182b 13b5243b; Laura Smith, Susan Kashubeck-West, Gregory Payton, and Eve Adams, "White Professors Teaching about Racism: Challenges and Rewards," *The Counseling Psychologist* 45, no. 5 (2017): 651–68.

6. Voting legislation is one example of an erosion of civil rights. See "Voting Laws Roundup: October 2021," Brennan Center for Justice, October 4, 2021, https://www.brennancenter.org/our-work/research-reports/voting-laws-roundup -october-2021; Grace Panetta, "What's in the Major Voting Rights Bill That Senate Republicans Voted to Block," Insider, January 20, 2022, https://www.businessinsider .com/freedom-to-vote-act-john-lewis-voting-rights-bill-explainer-2022-1. It is also important to note that two Senate Democrats also voted against the plan, which "would have massively reshaped the landscape of voting and election administration in the United States."

7. Alice Walker, *In Search of Our Mothers' Gardens: Womanist Prose* (New York: Harcourt Brace Jovanovich, 1983), 170.

8. AnneMarie Mingo's forthcoming ethnographic study of Black church women activists during the 1960s Civil Rights Movement will be a valued leadership resource.

9. Jason A. Gillmer, "On the Urgency of Intersectionality," *The Spokesman-Review* (Spokane, WA), March 30, 2019, https://www.spokesman.com/stories /2019/mar/30/jason-a-gillmer-on-the-urgency-of-intersectionalit/.

10. Gillmer, "Urgency of Intersectionality."

11. Gillmer, "Urgency of Intersectionality."

12. Gillmer, "Urgency of Intersectionality."

13. For instances of this practice, see Noel King, "A Brief History of How Racism Shaped Interstate Highways," NPR (National Public Radio), April 7, 2021, https://www.npr.org/2021/04/07/984784455/a-brief-history-of-how-racism -shaped-interstate-highways; Jr. Forasteros, "How Can Highways Be Racist?," *Sojourners*, November 24, 2021, https://sojo.net/articles/how-can-highways-be -racist; Ray Rogers, "What Can the Transcontinental Railroad Teach Us about Anti-Asian Racism?," *National Geographic*, May 17, 2021, https://www .nationalgeographic.com/travel/article/what-can-transcontinental-railroad-teach-us -about-anti-asian-racism-in-america; N. D. B. Connolly, "Timely Innovations: Planes, Trains and the 'Whites Only' Economy of a Pan-American City," *Urban History,* 36, no. 2 (2009): 243–61; Robert Bullard, Glenn Johnson, and Angel Torress, eds., *Highway Robbery: Transportation Racism and New Routes to Equity* (Boston: South End Press, 2004).

14. Laurel Hanna (contact), "Amid Great Change, the Ongoing Exploration of Theological Education between the Times," https://candler.emory.edu/news /releases/2020/12/theological-education-between-the-times.html.

15. Elizabeth Conde-Frazier, *Atando Cabos: Latinx Contributions to Theological Education* (Grand Rapids: William B. Eerdmans Pub. Co., 2021), 108.

16. Walker, *Our Mothers' Gardens*, 276.

17. Walker, *Our Mothers' Gardens*, 275.

18. Walker, *Our Mothers' Gardens*, 273.

19. Walker, *Our Mothers' Gardens*, 264.

20. Walker, *Our Mothers' Gardens*, 264.

Chapter 9: "Not Meant to Survive"

1. Audre Lorde, *The Black Unicorn: Poems*, reissue ed. (New York: W. W. Norton & Co., 1995), 31.

2. Melanie L. Harris, *Gifts of Virtue, Alice Walker, and Womanist Ethics*, Black Religion, Womanist Thought, Social Justice (New York: Palgrave Macmillan, 2010), 1.

3. American Civil Liberties Union, "Facts about the Over-Incarceration of Women in the United States," https://www.aclu.org/other/facts-about-over-incarceration-women-united-states.

4. American Civil Liberties Union, "Banking on Bondage: Private Prisons and Mass Incarceration," https://www.aclu.org/banking-bondage-private-prisons-and-mass-incarceration.

5. American Civil Liberties Union, "Facts about the Over-Incarceration of Women in the United States," https://www.aclu.org/other/facts-about-over-incarceration-women-united-states.

6. Elizabeth Swavola, Kristi Riley, and Ram Subramanian, "Overlooked: Women and Jails in an Era of Reform," New York: Vera Institute of Justice, 2016, https://www.vera.org/downloads/publications/overlooked-women-and-jails-report-updated.pdf.

7. Angela Y. Davis, *Are Prisons Obsolete?*, Open Media Book (New York: Seven Stories Press, 2003), 16.

8. Barbara Bloom and Stephanie Covington, "Addressing the Mental Health Needs of Women Offenders," in *Women's Mental Health Issues across the Criminal Justice System*, ed. Rosemary L. Gido and Lannette Dalley (Columbus, OH: Prentice Hall Pub. Co., 2008), 160–76, https://www.researchgate.net/publication/347943244_Addressing_the_Mental_Health_Needs_of_Women_Offenders, PDF, 8–9.

9. U.S. Department of Justice, "Attorney General Loretta E. Lynch Delivers Remarks at the White House Women and the Criminal Justice System Convening," March 30, 2016, https://www.justice.gov/opa/speech/attorney-general-loretta-e-lynch-delivers-remarks-white-house-women-and-criminal-justice.

10. Michel Foucault, *Discipline and Punish: The Birth of the Prison* (New York: Pantheon Books, 1977), 300.

11. According to Florida Statute 776.013(13), the Stand Your Ground Law states that a person who is not engaged in an unlawful act and who is attacked in any other place where he or she has a right to be has no duty to retreat and has the right to stand his or her ground and meet force with force, including deadly force

if he or she reasonably believes it is necessary to prevent death or great bodily harm to himself or herself or another or to prevent the commission of a forcible felony. See Marissa Alexander, Appellant, v. State of Florida, Appellee. No. 1D12–2469. Decided: September 26, 2013. "State of Florida v. Marissa Danielle Alexander, State's Motion in Opposition of Defendant's Motion for Immunity," https:// caselaw.findlaw.com/fl-district-court-of-appeal/1645234.html.

12. "Timeline," Free Marissa Now, https://www.freemarissanow.org/timeline .html.

13. "Marissa Alexander Alleged Victim Disposition," dokumen.tips, 92, https://dokumen.tips/documents/marissa-alexander-alleged-victim-disposition.html.

14. Florida's Stand-Your-Ground law frees state's residents of having to retreat before using lethal force in the case of a deadly imminent threat. This statute is related to the concept of Duty to Retreat, which states that a person facing an imminent threat must retreat before responding with deadly force in self-defense. Stand-Your-Ground revokes the Duty to Retreat by permitting individuals to use force in self-defense without having to retreat first. (cf. https://www.lexisnexis .com/legalnewsroom/criminal/b/criminal-law-blog/posts/nearly-half-of-states-have -quot-stand-your-ground-quot-laws-like-florida-39-s and https://criminal.findlaw .com/criminal-law-basics/stand-your-ground-laws.html).

15. Manuel Roig-Franzia, Tom Jackman, and Darryl Fears, "Who Is George Zimmerman?," *The Washington Post*," March 22, 2012, https://www .washingtonpost.com/lifestyle/style/who-is-george-zimmerman/2012/03/22/ gIQAkXdbUS_story.html.

16. Steven Hsieh, "Marissa Alexander Now Faces 60 Years in Prison for Firing a Warning Shot in Self Defense," March 3, 2014, https://www .thenation.com/article/archive/marissa-alexander-now-faces-60-years-prison-firing -warning-shot-self-defense/.

17. Womanist ethicist Emilie M. Townes draws from Schneider and Ingram's policy framework to excavate religious values that parallel a hegemonic social imagination targeting the poor for not embodying neoliberal capitalist ideals of individualism and prosperity. See Emilie Maureen Townes, *Womanist Ethics and the Cultural Production of Evil*, Black Religion, Womanist Thought, Social Justice (New York: Palgrave Macmillan, 2006).

18. Anne L. Schneider and Helen M. Ingram, *Policy Design for Democracy*, Studies in Government and Public Policy (Lawrence: University Press of Kansas, 1997), 102.

19. Schneider and Ingram, *Policy Design for Democracy*, 102.

20. Kelly Brown Douglas, *Stand Your Ground: Black Bodies and the Justice of God* (Maryknoll, NY: Orbis Books, 2015).

21. Rima Vesely-Flad, *Racial Purity and Dangerous Bodies: Moral Pollution, Black Lives, and the Struggle for Justice* (Minneapolis: Fortress Press, 2017).

22. Angela D. Sims, "The Issue of Race and Lynching," in *Womanist Theologi- cal Ethics: A Reader*, ed. Katie Geneva Cannon, Emilie M. Townes, and Angela

D. Sims, Library of Theological Ethics (Louisville, KY: Westminster John Knox Press, 2011).

23. JoAnne Marie Terrell, *Power in the Blood? The Cross in the African American Experience* (Eugene, OR: Wipf & Stock, 2005).

24. Michelle Alexander, *The New Jim Crow: Mass Incarceration in the Age of Colorblindness*, rev. ed. (New York: The New Press, 2012).

25. Keri Day, *Unfinished Business: Black Women, the Black Church, and the Struggle to Thrive in America* (Maryknoll, NY: Orbis Books, 2012).

26. Traci C. West, *Disruptive Christian Ethics: When Racism and Women's Lives Matter* (Louisville, KY: Westminster John Knox Press, 2006).

27. Katie Geneva Cannon, *Katie's Canon: Womanism and the Soul of the Black Community* (1995; New York: Continuum, 2002), 59.

28. Katie Geneva Cannon, *Black Womanist Ethics*, American Academy of Religion Academy Series 60 (Atlanta: Scholars Press, 1988), 5.

29. Cannon, *Black Womanist Ethics*, 76.

30. I realize the dangers of making a comparison between Black women's resistance to overcome the evils of slavery and Black women's lawbreaking to survive the perils of the carceral state. Though I view the prison industrial complex as an extension of slavery and discriminating laws undergirding the carceral state and functioning as a new Jim Crow, the risks that slaves took to gain freedom against the depraved institution of slavery and to resist the dehumanizing subjugation as chattel and nonbeing is different from the extralegal survival strategies Black women use to overcome unjust social conditions to provide for their families. I cautiously make the parallel between slavery and imprisonment not to trivialize the slave experience but to contextualize Black women's agency, which is rooted in a history of subverting white-middle-class values to prevail over social injustices.

Chapter 10: "Pumping Up Air"

1. Katie Geneva Cannon, "Remembering What We Never Knew," in *The Journal of Woman and Religion* 16 (1998): 168.

2. Cannon, "Remembering What We Never Knew," 169.

3. Cannon, "Remembering What We Never Knew," 171. For detailed treatment of anti-Black violence and memory in womanist ethics, see Angela D. Sims, *Lynched: The Power of Memory in a Culture of Terror* (Waco: Baylor University Press, 2017); see also Emilie M. Townes, *Womanist Ethics and the Cultural Production of Evil*, Black Religion, Womanist Thought, Social Justice (New York: Palgrave Macmillan, 2006), 11–27.

4. Cannon, "Remembering What We Never Knew," 169.

5. See Sylvia Obell, "'Swag Surfin' Is the Dance of Our Generation," BuzzFeed, February 28, 2016, https://www.buzzfeed.com/sylviaobell/im-on-hypnotic-exotic.

6. Cannon, "Remembering What We Never Knew," 169.

7. Cannon, "Remembering What We Never Knew," 169.

8. Cannon, "Remembering What We Never Knew," 170.

9. Cannon, "Remembering What We Never Knew," 170–71.

10. In his article "'Quare' Studies, or (Almost) Everything I Know about Queer Studies I Learned from My Grandmother," *Text and Performance Quarterly* 21, no. 1 (2001): 1–25, E. Patrick Johnson introduces the term *quare* as a rejoinder to being called "queer" for those whose sexual and gender identities intersect with racial subjectivity.

11. For further treatment of the significance of bodily "marks" in womanist theology, see M. Shawn Copeland, *Enfleshing Freedom: Body, Race, and Being* (Minneapolis: Fortress Press, 2009).

12. Cannon, "Remembering What We Never Knew," 172.

13. Cannon, "Remembering What We Never Knew," 172.

14. Cannon, "Remembering What We Never Knew," 173.

15. For further treatment of the significance of the garret in Black feminist theory, see Katherine McKittrick, *Demonic Grounds: Black Women and the Cartographies of Struggle* (Minneapolis: University of Minnesota Press, 2006), 37–64.

16. See Kimberlé Crenshaw et al., eds., *Critical Race Theory: The Key Writings That Formed the Movement* (New York: The New Press, 1996). See also Janel George, "A Lesson on Critical Race Theory," American Bar Association, January 11, 2021, https://www.americanbar.org/groups/crsj/publications/human_rights_magazine_home/civil-rights-reimagining-policing/a-lesson-on-critical-race-theory/.

17. For further treatment of "uninterrogated coloredness," see Townes, *Womanist Ethics*, 60.

18. See Wendell Griffin, "Why Are SBC Seminary Presidents Rejecting Critical Race Theory If They Teach about Jesus and the Prophets Who Denounced Injustice?," Baptist News Global, December 16, 2020, https://baptistnews.com/article/why-are-sbc-seminary-presidents-rejecting-critical-race-theory-if-they-teach-about-jesus-and-the-prophets-who-denounced-injustice/. See also Yonat Shimron, "Southern Baptist Seminary Presidents Nix Critical Race Theory," Religion News Service, December 1, 2020, https://religionnews.com/2020/12/01/southern-baptist-seminary-presidents-nix-critical-race-theory/.

19. See Andrew Parker and Eve Kosofsky Sedgwick, eds., *Performativity and Performance* (New York: Routledge, 1995), 1–17. See also Saidiya Hartman, *Scenes of Subjection: Terror, Slavery, and Self-Making in Nineteenth-Century America* (New York: Oxford University Press, 1997).

20. See R. A. Judy, *Sentient Flesh: Thinking in Disorder, Poiesis in Black* (Durham, NC: Duke University Press, 2020), 1–24. For further treatment of opaque theologies, see also Charles S. Long, *Significations: Signs, Symbols, and Images in the Interpretation of Religion* (Aurora, CO: The Davies Group, 1995), 199–213.

21. For further treatment of gender bias in Black art, see Uri McMillan, *Embodied Avatars: Genealogies of Black Feminist Art and Performance* (New York: New York University Press, 2016), 6.

22. See F.L.Y.—Fast Life Yungstaz, "Swag Surfin' Instructional Video," May 6, 2009, Instructional Dance Video, https://www.youtube.com/watch?v =nGj4RMHe2s4. See also Robert Farris Thompson, "An Aesthetic of the Cool," in *African Arts* 7, no. 1 (1973): 40–43, 64, 67, 89–91.

23. See Soul II Soul, *Keep on Movin' (Official Video)*, June 2, 2009, music video, https://www.youtube.com/watch?v=1iQl46-zIcM.

24. See Brenda Dixon-Gottschild, *The Black Dancing Body: A Geography from Coon to Cool* (New York: Palgrave MacMillan, 2005).

25. For further treatment of *kata sarka*, "according to the flesh" social realities, see Eboni Marshall Turman, *Toward a Womanist Ethic of Incarnation: Black Bodies, the Black Church, and the Council of Chalcedon* (New York: Palgrave MacMillan, 2013).

Chapter 11: Knowledge from the Marrow of Our Bones

1. Patrick Chamoiseau, *Texaco: A Novel* (New York: Vintage: 1998). Through his narrator—Marie-Sophie Laborieux, a daughter of slaves—he chronicles 150 years in the history of Martinique, starting with the birth of Marie-Sophie's beloved father, Esternome, on a sugar plantation sometime in the early 19th century. It ends with her founding Texaco, a shanty town built on the grounds of an old oil refinery on the outskirts of Fort-de-France, the capital city of Martinique.

2. Patrick Chamoiseau, *Un Dimanche au Cachot: Roman* (Paris: Gallimard, 2007), 180–81.

3. See https://www.daredictionary.com.

4. Chamoiseau, *Un Dimanche au Cachot,* 180–81.

5. In other words, we must create ways in which we live into our bodies as we live into the larger creation and the societies in which we sit. We eschew the forms of rampant individualism that put us into extreme navel-gazing postures and thus beget deadly jingoism that despises any notion of the common good and any exploration of what the common good must look like.

6. Older stereotypes include the mammy, Mandingo, Sapphire, and Uncle Tom. See "Popular and Pervasive Stereotypes of African Americans," October 23, 2018, https://nmaahc.si.edu/blog-post/popular-and-pervasive-stereotypes -african-americans.

Chapter 12: A Can(n)on of Embodied Ethics

1. Emilie M. Townes, "Katie Geneva Cannon (1950–2018): Scholar, Teacher, and Minister," *Religious Studies News*, August 28, 2018, http://rsn.aarweb.org /articles/katie-geneva-cannon-1950–2018/.

2. Katie Geneva Cannon, "Thinking with Our Hearts / Feeling with Our Brains: Testimonies of Faith That History Might Otherwise Forget," Lecture, October 24, 2017, Princeton Theological Seminary, Princeton, New Jersey, https://www.youtube.com/watch?v=o8rOCHJFvH4.

3. John Riches, *The Bible: A Very Short Introduction* (Oxford: Oxford University Press, 2000), 134.

4. See Bernard Lonergan, *Method in Theology* (New York: Herder & Herder, 1972), 125–45.

5. Cheikh Hamidou Kane, *Ambiguous Adventure*, trans. Katherine Woods (1962; Brooklyn: Melville House, 2012), Kindle ed., 43.

6. Kane, *Ambiguous Adventure*, 43.

7. Ngũgĩ wa Thiong'o, *Decolonising the Mind: The Politics of Language in African Literature* (Oxford: James Curry; Nairobi: Heinemann, 1986), 9: "The bullet was the means of the physical subjugation. Language was the means of the spiritual subjugation."

8. Alice Walker, *In Search of Our Mothers' Gardens: Womanist Prose by Alice Walker* (San Diego: Harcourt Brace Jovanovich, 1983), xi.

9. Cannon, "Introduction," in *Katie's Canon: Womanism and the Soul of the Black Community* (1995; New York: Continuum, 2002), 23.

10. Cannon, "Introduction," 23.

11. Cannon, "Introduction," 23.

12. Cannon, "Moral Wisdom in the Black Women's Literary Tradition," in *Katie's Canon*, 57–68; Cannon, "Resources for a Constructive Ethic: The Life and Work of Zora Neale Hurston," in *Katie's Canon*, 77–90.

13. Zora Neale Hurston, *Dust Tracks on a Road* (Philadelphia: Lippincott, 1942), 177, cited in Cannon, *Katie's Canon*, 77.

14. Cannon, "The Emergence of Black Feminist Consciousness," in *Katie's Canon,* 47–56, at 47.

15. Cannon, "Moral Wisdom in the Black Women's Literary Tradition," in *Katie's Canon*, 57–68, at 60–61.

16. Katie Geneva Cannon, *Black Womanist Ethics* (Atlanta: Scholars Press, 1988), 17, 143. Cannon takes these three virtues or criteria—invisible dignity, quiet grace, and unshouted courage—from Mary Burgher, "Images of Self and Race in the Autobiographies of Black Women," in *Sturdy Black Bridges*, ed. Roseanne Bell et al. (New York: Anchor Books, 1979), 113.

17. Cannon, "Introduction," in *Katie's Canon*, 23.

18. Stacey Floyd-Thomas, ed., *Deeper Shades of Womanism in Religion and Society* (New York: New York University Press, 2006), 1–2.

19. For Aristotle, free persons are those [men] capable of orienting themselves and their actions toward the common good of their households and of the state (*Metaphysics* 12.10.3). The free man, the *politēs* or citizen, is one who has the capacity for active participation in political life and, thus, with and for the common good. Nor is the citizen simply identical with a person who inhabits the city-state: women, children, slaves, foreigners, *metics* (resident aliens, freed slaves) all inhabit the *polis* yet *without* participating as citizens. Slaves are deprived of the freedom to control their own lives; they have no share in the common good or the state. Perversely, Aristotle counts slavery as natural, although it was a social decision and practice.

20. Paolo Freire, *Pedagogy of the Oppressed* (New York: Continuum), 36.

21. Pierre Bourdieu, *Homo Academicus*, trans. Peter Collier (Stanford, CA: Stanford University Press, 1988), 91–95.

22. "The conditionings associated with a specific class of conditions of existence produce *habitus*, systems of durable and transposable dispositions, structured structures predisposed to function as structuring structures, that is, as principles that generate and organize practices and representations that can be objectively adapted to their outcomes without presupposing a conscious aiming at ends or an express mastery of the operations necessary in order to obtain them." Pierre Bourdieu, *The Logic of Practice*, trans. Richard Nice (Stanford, CA: Stanford University Press, 1990), 53.

23. Bourdieu, *Homo Academicus*, 95.

24. In a lecture at Princeton, "Thinking with Our Hearts / Feeling with Our Brains: Testimonies of Faith That History Might Otherwise Forget" (October 24, 2017), Katie Cannon relates her encounter with such hierarchy in the person of a "world-renowned white biblical scholar" who refuses "to *feel* with his brain." The professor will neither complete the reading of her paper nor grade her paper because her paper—for the seminar on the Passion Narratives—was *passionate*. See Katie Geneva Cannon, "Hitting a Straight Lick with a Crooked Stick: The Womanist Dilemma in the Development of a Black Liberation Ethic," in *Katie's Canon*, 124.

25. Cannon, "Hitting a Straight Lick," in *Katie's Canon*, 123.

26. Cannon, "Hitting a Straight Lick," in *Katie's Canon*, 123.

27. Cannon, "Hitting a Straight Lick," in *Katie's Canon*, 123.

28. Cannon, "Hitting a Straight Lick," in *Katie's Canon*, 123.

29. Cannon, "Hitting a Straight Lick," in *Katie's Canon*, 123.

30. Cannon, "Hitting a Straight Lick," in *Katie's Canon*, 124.

31. Emilie M. Townes, *Womanist Ethics and the Cultural Production of Evil*, Black Religion, Womanist Thought, Social Justice (New York: Palgrave Macmillan, 2006), 21.

32. Barbara Christian, "The Race for Theory," *Cultural Critique* 6 (Spring 1987): 51–63, at 52.

33. Christian, "The Race for Theory," 52.

34. Christian, "The Race for Theory," 58.

35. Christian, "The Race for Theory," 53. Christian may have in mind the phrase "race wo/man." This phrase commands venerable status in the history of African American struggle for life, liberty, and dignity. It denotes one who dedicated oneself with fearlessness, energy, dignity, and skill to the survival, flourishing, and advancement of Black people. Examples are legion, but certainly include the following: *Maria Stewart* (1803–80), teacher, journalist, abolitionist, lecturer, women's rights activist—first African American woman to give public lectures; *Anna Julia Cooper* (1858–1964), born into slavery in North Carolina, an educator, sociologist, author, and the fourth African American woman to earn a doctoral

degree—hers from the Sorbonne in 1924; *Mary McCleod Bethune* (1875–1955), educator, stateswoman, humanitarian, civil rights activist, founded Bethune-Cookman College (now University) and the National Council of Negro Women; *Ida B. Wells* (1862–1931), an investigative journalist who exposed lynching and was a civil rights activist, one of the founders of the NAACP; *Mary Church Terrell* (1863–1954), activist for civil rights and women's suffrage, charter member of the NAACP; *Dorothy Height* (1912–2010), educator, civil rights activist, women's rights activist, president of National Council of Negro Women, who expressed the "creed" of the "race woman [or man]": "I want to be remembered as someone who used herself and anything she could to work for justice and freedom. I want to be remembered as one who tried."

36. Cannon, "Metalogues and Dialogues: Teaching the Womanist Idea," in *Katie's Canon*, 136–43, at 138.

37. Katie Geneva Cannon paid tribute to Clark's influence in *Teaching Preaching: Isaac Rufus Clark and Black Sacred Rhetoric* (New York: Continuum., 2002), 111.

38. Christian, "The Race for Theory," 53.

39. Katie Geneva Cannon, "Structured Academic Amnesia: As If This True Womanist Story Never Happened," in Floyd-Thomas, *Deeper Shades of Womanism*, 19–28, at 23–24.

40. Cannon, "Structured Academic Amnesia," 24.

41. Cannon, "Structured Academic Amnesia," 25.

42. Cannon, "Structured Academic Amnesia," 25.

43. Cannon, "Structured Academic Amnesia," 25.

44. Cannon, "Structured Academic Amnesia," 25–26.

45. Presbyterian Foundation, Vimeo, "Rev. Dr. Katie Geneva Cannon was the first African-American woman ordained in the Presbyterian church in 1974. She went on to become one of the foremost scholars of the womanist movement. Since 2001, she has served as the Annie Scales Rogers Professor of Christian Ethics at Union Presbyterian Seminary in Richmond, Virginia. She received the Excellence in Theological Education award at General Assembly in St. Louis on June 21, 2018." From https://vimeo.com/276246157.

46. Cannon, "Metalogues and Dialogues," 139.

47. Cannon, "Metalogues and Dialogues," 137–38.

48. Cannon, "Metalogues and Dialogues," 138.

49. See Sheila Ruth, "Methodocracy, Misogyny, and Bad Faith: Sexism in the Philosophical Establishment," *Metaphilosophy* 10 (1979): 48–61.

50. Katarzyna Jazdewska, "From *Dialogos* to Dialogue: The Use of the Term from Plato to the Second Century," *Greek, Roman, and Byzantine Studies* 54 (2014): 17–36, at 23. "In Plato's works the word is associated with a particular type of conversation—an inquiry carried out by two interlocutors, shaped as an interchange of questions and answers. The connection of the term διάλογος with question-and-answer format, and therefore with dialectical argumentation, can therefore be observed" (34).

51. Katie Geneva Cannon, "Appropriation and Reciprocity in Doing Womanist Ethics," in *Katie's Canon*, 131.

52. Cannon, "Appropriation and Reciprocity," 135.

53. Cannon, "Appropriation and Reciprocity," 135.

54. Ruth Shays, quoted in *Drylongso: A Self-Portrait of Black America*, ed. John Langston Gwaltney (New York: Vintage Books, 1981), 33.

55. Audre Lorde, *Zami: A New Spelling of My Name* (Trumansburg, NY: Crossing Press, 1982), via Kindle, 3; Katie Geneva Cannon, "Surviving the Blight," in *Katie's Canon*, 33–37.

Index

academic communities, 18, 20–21, 126,
128, 156–57. *See also* Cannon,
Katie: life: academic career
acquisitive instinct, 50–51
adaptive leadership, 83–84
advocacy, 76
African American church, 77
African sacred traditions, 57–58, 63
Afrocentrism, 88
agency, 104
Alexander, Marissa, 112–13
Alexander, Michelle, 114
Ani, Marimba, 52
annunciation and celebration, 18
archaeology, and stories, 55–56
art, 38–39
asthma, 69
axiology, 50, 52–54, 64

Baker, Ella, 98
Baptist denominations, 128
Barber-Scotia College, 27
baskets, 58
"Bearing Witness to Womanism: What
Was, What Is, What Shall Be"
(conference), 32
beauty to burden (Ruffin), 73, 77
Bennet, Lerone, x
Bethune, Mary McLeod, 30
Bible
canon and, 152
collectivity and community in, 77–78
references
Genesis 1: 62, 70, 78, 79
Genesis 2: 70, 79
Exodus 20: 71
Leviticus 25: 71
Psalm 23: xv

Isaiah 6: 79
Amos 5: 79
Matthew 25: 117
Luke 4: 117
1 Corinthians 3: 39
biblical authority, xvi, xvi–xvii
biblical studies, 3–4, 6, 8, 9. *See also*
Cannon, Katie: life: academic
career
biomythography (Lorde), 24
Black, Edwin, 47–48
Black bodies
Cannon's archaeological method and, 125
as commodities, 68, 76
as criminal, 111
dance and, 132–33
erasure of, 124
performativity of, 131–32
religious knowledge (as sources of), 126
silence (creative) of, 130
See also bodies
Black choreography, 130–34
Black mothers, 107–11, 116, 117
Black Power movement, 5, 6
Black Theology of Liberation, A (Cone), 86
Black women
in biblical studies, 3–5
centering of, 36–37
enslaved (histories of), 84
humanity of, xvi
intersectionality and, 97
leadership and, 95
literary tradition of, 155
as mothers, 107–8
(negative) images of, 47
oppression (experiences of), 109
organizing of, 85–86
perceived as religious, 63

Printed in Great Britain
by Amazon

11000899R00130